# FINDING CANNON BALL'S TRAIL™

# FINDING CANNON BALL'S

BY DON EMDE

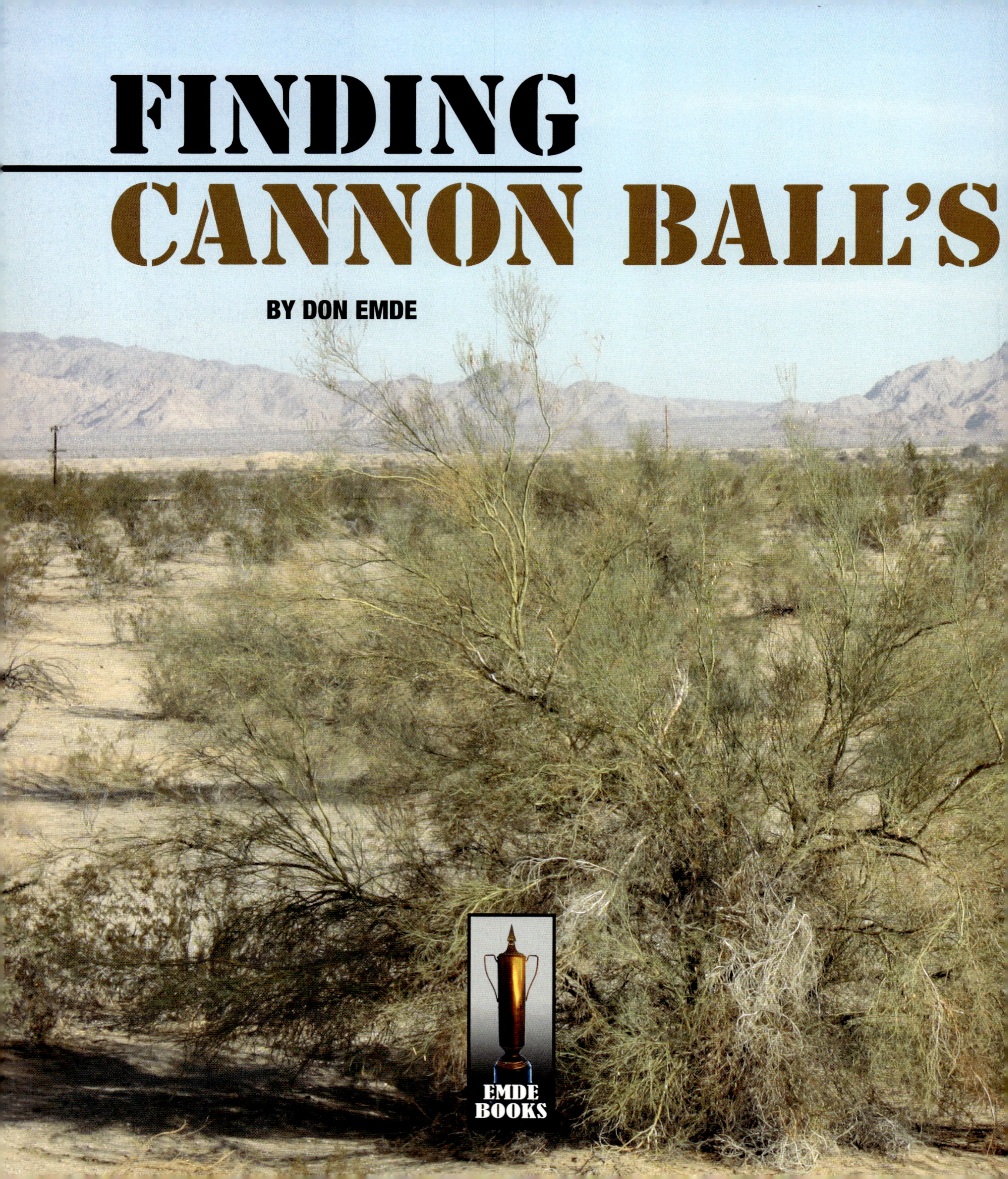

# TRAIL

# FINDING CANNON BALL'S TRAIL



First Edition

ISBN #: 978-0-9972720-0-0

Author: Don Emde
Art Director: Nancy Wegrowski
Editors: Tracy Emde / Jennifer Rose
Map Art: Bill Tipton
Photography: Joe Colombero, Don Emde, Barry Hathaway, Kinney Jones

Mapping / Transportation / Logistics: Joe Colombero

Historic Materials: Indiana Historical Society, Indianapolis Motor Speedway Archives, Motorcyclepedia Museum, Ohio Historical Society, San Diego History Center, Wheels of Time Museum, Yuma Crossing Heritage Area

Other historic photography, Chadeayne logbook, catalogs, postcards, magazine ads and other content from the Don Emde Collection

EMDE BOOKS

Emde Books is an imprint of Don Emde, Inc.
92 Argonaut, Suite 160, Aliso Viejo, CA 92656

Ph: 949-215-4780
Fax: 949-215-9042
Web: www.EmdeBooks.com

Printed in the United States of America

# TABLE OF CONTENTS

***Don Emde Collection***

**PROLOGUE:**

# IN HIS OWN WORDS

## By Erwin G. Baker

*"I was always inclined towards outdoor sports and athletics and had often trained for boxing and sparring, which brought me in contact with throwing the medicine ball, jumping rope and all the physical culture performances that go to train a man for endurance. I found when I purchased my first motorcycle that I had endurance and stamina that seemed to be far in advance of the ordinary motorcycle rider. I found it an easy matter to ride a great deal further and faster in a day without fatigue than the ordinary rider, which finally led me into road-racing and long-distance riding.*

*From time to time there had been men crossing the continent, driving automobiles or riding motorcycles, and I began to have a longing to accomplish such a feat; but before attempting such a thing I recognized that there was considerable training to be done on my part, not so much physically as in the handling of a motorcycle at terrific speed through sand and mud and over rough roads; in other words, to find the knack of doing this. I also realized that if I desired to make a mark in time that would be recognized by the entire world, that a trip of this kind was far distant from me at that time and I began to roam around the world on a motorcycle, always seeking highways and byways that were of the roughest and most difficult nature to master. So one day I made up my mind that I would go off on one good long 'roll.' No one can deny but that it was sure some 'roll.' However, 'rolling' across the continent from the Pacific to the Atlantic on a motorcycle is not quite as simple a performance as rolling off the proverbial log."*

**The text above appeared in the May 28, 1914 edition of *Motorcycle Illustrated.***

*Image: Indianapolis Motor Speedway Archive.*

# THE CANNON BALL PROJECT

## By Don Emde

In 2010 I heard about an organized motorcycle group ride called the "Motorcycle Cannonball," like the '70s film, "Cannonball Run," starring Burt Reynolds, but for pre-1916 motorcycles instead of ultra-fast sports cars. It would run that September from North Carolina to Los Angeles.

As someone who has studied motorcycle history all my life, I knew that Reynold's movie played off the life and times of Erwin G. "Cannon Ball" Baker, a legendary motorcycle and automotive enthusiast who spent practically his entire life breaking American coast-to-coast and other speed records. In 1914, Baker had set a new transcontinental record on an Indian motorcycle, riding from San Diego, CA to New York City in 11½ days.

It didn't take long until I began hearing the details of the route of the 2010 ride to Los Angeles and wondered where Baker had actually ridden in 1914, and how long it had taken him to go coast to coast? Then I remembered that some years before I had acquired an original sales booklet that the Indian Motocycle Company had published in 1914 with Baker's written account of his record setting ride.

I pulled out the booklet and read through to see the cities that he mentioned in his route all the way from San Diego to New York City. I also noted that Baker achieved his 1914 ride in 11½ days compared to 17 days for the 2010 "Cannonball." No disrespect to the plans of the modern ride, as the fragile old motorcycles that have been sitting almost 100 years shouldn't be expected to run at full chat for 3,000+ miles as in Baker's day. Additionally Erwin Baker was a professional motorcycle long-distance rider, while the modern Cannonball ride would be ridden by motorcycle collectors and enthusiasts generally not conditioned for the sustained long hours that Baker required to achieve his result.

Once I had confirmed the basic facts of the 1914 ride, I gave the fragile old booklet a slower read and noted some fun comments that Baker had made about certain experiences he had. Like using an old Indian technique (the people, not the motorcycle) of placing a small rock under his tongue to help fight off the urge for water as he crossed the desert in 119-degree heat. Or telling about running out of gas five miles short of a fuel stop and having to push the bike the rest of the way in deep sand.

It hit me then that Baker was a very different breed of cat with a story that needed to be told. But just reprinting his written journal wouldn't really be enough. I decided I wanted to devote some serious time to this and figure

San Diego

COAST
TO
COAST

3378.9 Miles
276 Hours
May 3-14, 1914

Baker's Bumper "Alfalfa" Crop
Raised in 11 1-2 Days

New York

By

E. G. "Cannon Ball" Baker

Riding a STRICTLY STOCK Model

Indian Motocycle

**The booklet published by the Indian Motocycle Company in 1914 detailing E.G. Baker's full day-by-day account of his transcontinental ride from San Diego to New York City. It's likely that if I had never acquired a copy of this booklet, this project and book would have never happened.**

**After almost a year of online searches and collecting old maps and printed materials, it was time for Joe Colombero (right) and I to hit the road and see if we could connect the dots on the many different roads that Baker had noted in the Indian Motocycle booklet. This photo was taken on Arizona Highway 60 north of Globe, AZ.**

**KTM North America provided the two KTMs that Joe and I used for this portion of the project. We outfitted the two machines slightly differently.**

**The one on the right is the bike that Joe rode. It was outfitted with only a few extras from stock, such as the Saddlemen soft luggage and adventure seat, Garmin GPS, and a few other add-ons.**

**On the left is the Dakar Replica 990 Adventure that I rode and it was outfitted with a more top-of-the-line setup. Seen here are the KTM hard bags and tank bag, Saddleman soft tail bag and adventure seat, Touratech skid plate, Garmin GPS and other accessories.**

exactly where he had ridden, and if those routes could still be ridden today?

When I decided to really get into this, the first thing I did was study his accounts in the Indian booklet and used Google Search to locate online places he mentioned. My research started where he started, San Diego, and I went east from there. It turned out that California and Arizona had the most "unknowns," as much of what Baker rode in the west has remained unimproved.

One connection I had with my project to retrace Baker's 1914 transcontinental ride was that it began in my hometown of San Diego. From there he traveled east through California's Imperial County, also familiar territory to my family. Before moving to San Diego, my great-grandparent's families both lived in the El Centro community of Imperial County from the late-1800s into the 1900s.

Eventually I was able to start connecting the dots, and it actually got easier to track as the ride moved east. Once he made it to Albuquerque, New Mexico he got onto the historic Santa Fe Trail and followed that through Kansas where he eventually intercepted the National Road (primarily what is today U.S. Highway 40) and went east from there.

There came a point where the many hours of internet searches began to yield less and less new information. My next step was to begin contacting some history libraries along his route. The first one was the San Diego History Library in Balboa Park. I showed up there one day and told one of the staff members what I was working on and what my needs were. Basically I was looking for road maps from 1914 as well as photography of the roads and towns in that year. I had good success in San Diego with a few copies of maps that showed what the main route was then to get from downtown San Diego to Yuma, Arizona. They also had some photos of the road out to the desert and I made arrangements to use them in my project.

Over the next 12 months or so, I had some business travel that allowed me to make similar stops at history libraries in Kansas City, Missouri; Indianapolis, Indiana; and Columbus, Ohio. I had similar results at these three libraries as well and they were used in this book.

Another key step in the project that needed to happen as I was doing my research was that I needed to get on a motorcycle and go out and see if this route I was piecing together on paper could actually still be ridden? While I own a few bikes, I didn't have anything that was really suitable to ride the old dirt roads of the California and Arizona deserts, and also do the job on the long stretches of roads that have long since been converted to highways since Baker passed through.

I have a magazine publishing business in the modern motorcycle industry with contacts at many of the major motorcycle manufacturers. So I decided to inquire if I could borrow a couple of adventure bikes to ride, one for myself and one for my friend Joe Colombero, who had agreed to assist me with the project. Joe is an experienced motorcycle rider and he also has written feature stories for my magazines, so he was a great choice to come along with me out on the road and trails.

The 1914 route of Erwin Baker called for one of today's adventure bikes, which are capable of off-roading and also long-distance touring with luggage onboard for an extended time period. I knew I needed a bike that would do a good job on the highway sections, but not knowing just how remote we would get in the dirt sections, I made a list of desired machines based pretty much on which of the large, multi-cylinder adventure bikes weighed the least. That turned out to be the 2011 KTM Adventure 990.

As it turned out I had a good contact at the KTM North America home office in Murrietta, CA. Jon-Erik Burleson has been president there since 2005 and I have known him and his dad, the legendary 8-time National Enduro champion and 8-time ISDE Gold Medalist Dick Burleson, for many years. The industry's biggest tradeshow at the time, the annual Dealer Expo, was held then each year in February, ironically, in Baker's hometown of Indianapolis. I set up a meeting there with Jon-Erik at the 2011 show and told him what I had going on. We talked about my needs and he agreed to the loan of two KTM 990 adventure bikes. The Cannon Ball Project was on!

Joe and I picked up the two KTM Adventure 990s in May. One was a standard 990 model in white, the other a blue and orange 30th Edition Dakar Replica model that came with a few more features. We decided that since the two bikes were already slightly different that we should accessorize them at different price levels. The white one Joe would ride just received minimal add-ons while the changes to the Dakar model I would ride were more extensive. Being journalists, Joe and I were thinking about stories about the bikes and wanted to show what could be done to the 990 by a person on a tight budget, and the other for someone who wanted to go all out. Other prime supporters of the project were Butler Maps, Continental Tires, DP Brakes, Moose Racing, Motion Pro, Motorcycle Industry Council, Parts Unlimited, Saddlemen Seats & Luggage, Touratech and Toyota Motor Sales, USA.

After the research and mapping work had been completed, we decided to take advantage in May of 2014 of the centennial of Baker's historic ride. Yamaha Motor Corporation USA stepped in as the Presenting Sponsor of a group celebration ride from San Diego to New York City beginning and ending exactly 100 years to the day that Baker did. That ride is covered beginning on page 112.

**Yamaha Super Tenere adventure bikes were provided as part of the Yamaha sponsorship deal and they were outfitted similar to the KTMs. This photo was shot in the parking lot at Cycle Visions' store in San Diego where the group checked in the day before the start of the Finding Cannon Ball's Trail Centennial Ride Presented by Yamaha. In the background is a Toyota Tundra provided by Toyota Motor Sales, USA as a sweep vehicle.**

# CHAPTER 1

# TRANSCONTINENTAL FEVER

Around 1900, the first mass-produced motorcycles and automobiles were beginning to hit the market in America. The introduction of two, three and four-wheel vehicles powered by steam, battery or gasoline, created a lot of curiosity and interest by the buying public. Hundreds of new motorized products came into the market. The press and public were mostly seeing these new-age transportation vehicles at shows at places such as New York's Madison Square Garden, and also at dealerships, in magazines, and spotting some passing by in the big cities.

The benefit these new inventions promised was the independence one had at the controls. You could now go anywhere at any time, which created the prospect of traveling and seeing the country. It was an exciting time, and anything seemed possible...until it rained!

**George Wyman heads towards New York City in July of 1903 on a 1.5 horsepower California motor bike. After an adventure of 52 days, he reached his destination on July 6th to complete the first-ever coast to coast journey on a motorized vehicle. The motor on his machine actually gave up the ghost in Albany, NY and Wyman pedaled it like a bicycle for the final 150 miles.** ***Photo courtesy of Ted Doering / Motorcyclepedia Museum.***

**Seen above is a press photo of a 1904 Yale motorcycle. Following George Wyman's transcontinental ride the previous year, the Yale company acquired the California company and marketed a Yale-California model in the years to come.**

When the motor vehicle industry was born, the condition of the roads became an immediate problem. According to Pete Davies, author of *American Road*, *"...as late as 1907, there was not a single mile of paved road in the United States."* A sudden rainstorm could turn a country road into a mud bog, often leaving riders and drivers stranded miles from home.

In addition to road conditions, another problem was the lack of information about what roads went where? People knew how to get places in their local areas, but most had never traveled long distances. Most of the settlers heading west back in the 1800s did so in large wagon trains led by guides who knew the way. Others took trains.

As the sales of motor vehicles exploded after 1900, there really was no highway system in place to support the new "independent" travelers all the way from one coast to the other. There were no highway numbers, few directional signs or road maps, no way to know where certain necessities could be found in unfamiliar areas, such as finding gasoline to keep the engine running. Overall, the idea of taking off to cross the whole country would have appealed only to the very adventurous.

In 1903, one thing that had not been done yet was a trip from coast to coast in an automobile or a motorcycle. With the goal in mind to become the first to accomplish a motorized transcontinental journey, George Wyman headed east on May 16, 1903 from San Francisco on a lightweight "motor-bicycle" called a "California" (later sold as a Yale-California). Destination: New York City. What Wyman didn't know when he departed was that he would soon have some competition behind him, albeit unintended. Only seven days later, Horatio Nelson

Jackson left San Francisco with Sewall Crocker in the passenger seat of a Winton automobile as a ride-along mechanic and backup driver. His trip came about as more of a bet, however, with friends that the journey could not be done in an automobile in less than three months.

Jackson, whose story became a book as well as a film documentary in 2003 by Ken Burns, took a different route out of San Francisco than Wyman, heading north to Oregon before turning east into Idaho and Wyoming. Wyman and his motorbike traveled by boat across the San Francisco Bay to Oakland and proceeded east thru the rugged Sierra Mountains and on to Salt Lake City. Both eventually made it to Chicago and followed similar routes from there to New York City.

Horatio Nelson Jackson completed his journey on July 26, 1903, becoming the first to cross the country in an *automobile*, doing so in a little over sixty-three days. But if along the way he had seen a single tire track on the roads, that would likely have been the track of George Wyman's motor-bicycle, who made it into New York nearly two weeks faster than Jackson, arriving on July 6th, a journey of fifty-two days.

The California that Wyman rode had a small 1.25-horsepower engine, which worked well, but it often fell victim to the strains of climbing and descending steep mountain roads as well as the added load on the motor from long stretches of road. On one day Wyman reported suffering five breakdowns. He had to make the repairs himself, and sometime replacement parts were needed. His crankshaft was one of the major failed parts en route and he sat waiting for five long days for a parts shipment to arrive with a new one.

*continued on page 18...*

**In 1905 William Chadeayne of the Thomas Auto-Bi company of Buffalo, NY lowered Wyman's coast-to-coast record to 49 days. Unlike Wyman who had gone west to east, Chadeayne went from east to west and is seen here at the conclusion of his ride in San Francisco. *Don Emde Collection.***

**In addition to being a competent rider, a person also had to be a good mechanic to be able to make it from coast to coast in the early 1900s. Chadeayne's Thomas Auto-Bi is seen here getting some attention on his 1905 record ride. *Don Emde Collection.***

**William Chadeayne takes a break in Wyoming. He often found he could make better time riding on or near the railroad tracks that followed his route west. *Don Emde Collection.***

# WILLIAM CHADEAYNE'S 1905 LOGBOOK

*Don Emde Collection*

Before the Cannon Ball Project had even begun, I was lucky to find a logbook for sale on eBay that has significant details about early day transcontinental travel. The package included the logbook with 68 pages of handwritten notes and a number of photos from William Chadeayne's record-setting trip on a Thomas Auto-Bi in 1905.

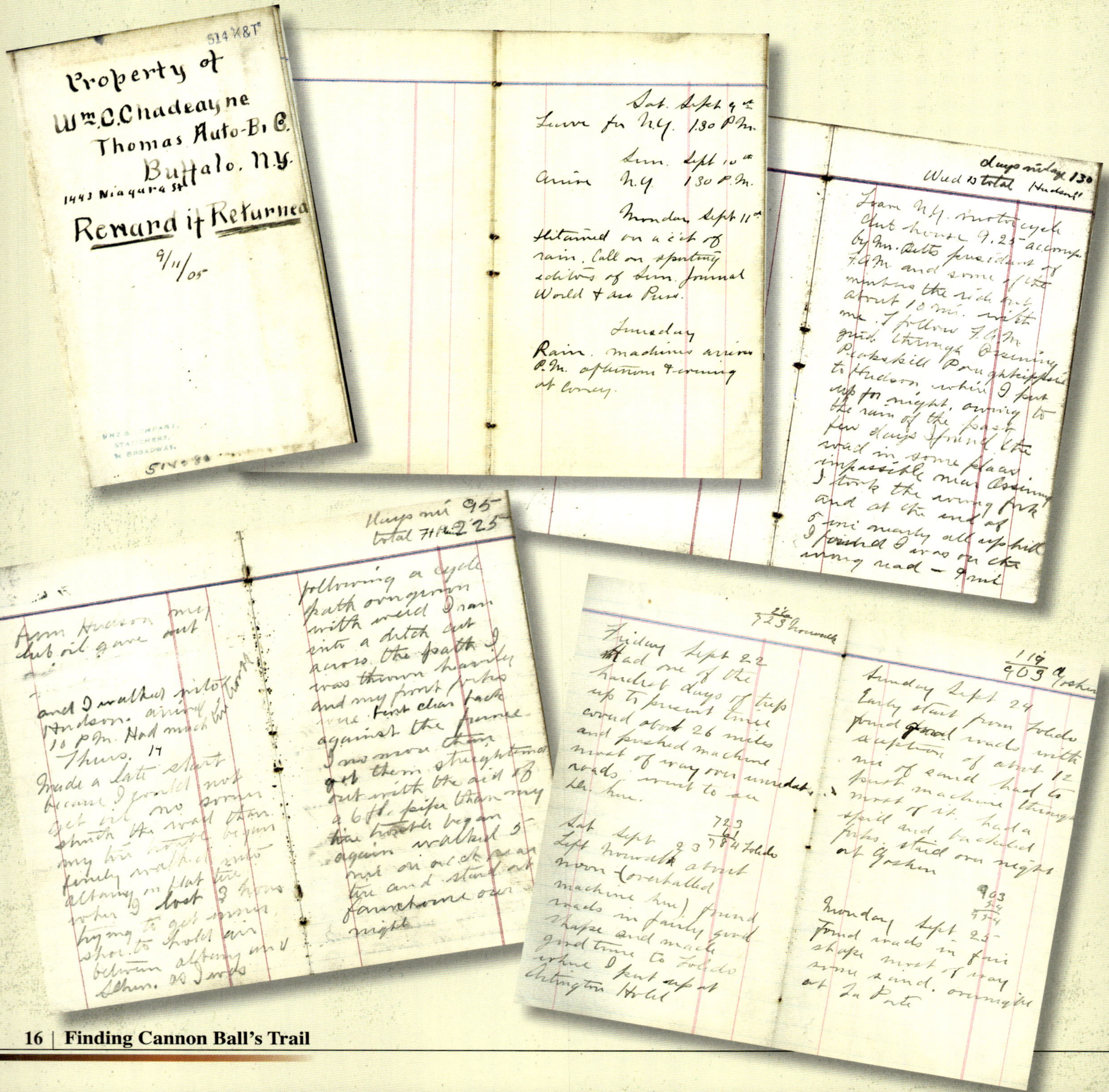
Property of
Wm. C. Chadeayne
Thomas Auto-Bi Co.
Buffalo, N.Y.
1443 Niagara St.
Reward if Returned
9/11/05

Sat. Sept 9th
Leave for N.Y. 1:30 P.M.
Sun. Sept 10th
Arrive N.Y. 1:30 P.M.
Monday Sept 11th
Detained on a/c of rain. Call on sporting editors of Sun, Journal, World & Ass. Press.
Tuesday
Rain. machine arrives P.M. afternoon & evening at Coney.

**SEPT 13th**

*Leave NY motorcycle clubhouse 9:25 accomp. by Mr. Betts, president of FAM and some of the members ride out about 10 miles with me. My hub oil gave out and I walked into Hudson. Arrived 10 PM. Had much tire trouble.*

**SEPT 14th**

*Made a late start because I could not get oil. No sooner my tire troubles began, walked into Albany on flat tire where I lost 3 hours trying to get tube to hold air. As I was following a cycle path overgrown with mulch I ran into a ditch across the path. I was thrown heavily and front forks were bent back against the fender. I got them straightened out with the aid of a 6 ft. pipe. My tire trouble began again. Walked 5 mi. stayed at farmhouse overnight.*

**SEPT 22nd**

*Had one of the hardest days of trip up to present time. Covered about 26 miles and pushed machine much of the way over unrideable roads*

**SEPT 30th**

*Left Princeton about 6 AM. Made good time to Geneseo where the roads became sandy and it took me 4 hours to cover 20 mi. to Rock Island. Crossed the Mississippi on Ferry and arrived at Davenport IA about 1 PM. Had lunch at Saratoga Hotel and repaired wheel just as I was about to start it been to rain and I decided to stay overnight.*

**OCT 1st**

*Could not get oil or gasoline until 9 AM. When well on my way to Guthrie the shafts to my spark control broke and I had to return to Davenport and make a new one. The result was a late start. Roads were rough, muddy and sandy. Pushed the machine for miles and had a bad day of it. Arrived at Iowa City where I put up at the Beckley Imperial and enjoyed one of the best meals I have had since Albany NY*

**OCT 4th**

*Left Des Moines about 10 or 11 AM. Found it very hilly but was in good shape. My motor developed a skip which I could not locate and I limped along for 86 mi. and got nearly to Atlantic when my motor refused to go. I spent the night in a straw stack.*

**OCT 8th**

*Left Omaha about 12 AM followed the route of the Union Pacific. My idler was bent and I went to a farmhouse to repair. I was bitten three times by a large dog before I could get away. A little later I found I lost the cap to my oil tank and the oil had slopped over everything. I soon ran out of oil and secured some mowing machine oil and managed to run on that until about dark. I got a puncture in rear tire. After repairing tire I continued over generally good roads (some sand) to Fremont where I arrived about 12 PM.*

**OCT 11th**

*After stopping for a few hours I continued my trip over hills and through sand through Kearney & Lexington to N. Platt. Have had full moons for the last 2 nights and find I can ride almost as well as I can by daylight. Arrive about 6 AM, go to Commercial Hotel and sleep about 6 hours then strike the road again. Here I entered a most interesting section of country and see for the first time large droves of cattle, cowboys, ranchers and prairie schooners. Pass the ranch of W.F. Cody and stop to take a picture.*

**OCT 13th**

*About 9 or 10 o'clock it started snowing. I had about 80 mi ahead of me. Was miles from any house, chilled to the bone and without sufficient clothing. Things looked dismal indeed. The prairie road soon filled with snow so it was unrideable I then went onto the railroad track and bumped over the ties for miles through the dark, ran into hole between ties that had run out array for switch and bent my fork, also smashed front rim, but the wheel would revolve so I managed to get along about 59 mi. The snow got so think and heavy that I could hardly manage machine.*

**OCT 19th**

*Clear & warmer. Made good start over the desert the road is in shape and the track good. Follow the R.R. for mi. and mi. occasions, taking the road which parallel the track. A lonesome trip - there are ranches in some places 20 or 30 mi. apart the towns are mostly sign posts with occasionally a section was inhabited. Arrived at Rawlins after dark.*

**OCT 22nd**

*Leave Green River and find fairly good roads. Climb for about 14 miles then began to descend following Weaver Canyon all down grade to Ogden 75 mi - have a series of small mishaps delaying me somewhat. About 30 mi from Ogden I have my worst spill. Going down grade at a rapid rate I strike snow and mud on a sharp turn of road. Can not hold turn and go over 20 or 30 foot embankment. When I come to, two men and a girl were trying to carry me up to road. No bones were broken and besides being badly bruised up I somehow am ok. But the machine. Both wheels badly buckled, rear stay and forks bent and other disasters. I take it to R.R. ride to first station and wait for moonlight after which I continue my trip to Ogden arriving about 5 AM.*

**OCT 28th**

*In room at Hotel Winnemucca until about 2 PM. Have unrideable trouble in starting my motor - the oil has frozen in cylinder and it take lots of swearing & flooding of gasoline to get it started. I sleep alongside the R.R. track til daylight when I find a broken battery wire. It is a steady climb now and I follow RR most of time.*

**OCT 29th**

*Asleep on a bench in a shed near a saloon. Don't know what time I awakened. But it was in time to get early start for Sacramento. Started out on road which ended in a cemetery. Disgusted I went back and took the more direct RR route.*

**OCT 30th**

*Leave Sacramento about 3 AM after making necessary repairs. About 13 mi from Stockton I run off ridge. Work on it til dark - no more than make it start before the handlebar on my left breaks and I am delayed another half hour - arriving in Stockton long after dark - go to sleep in a garage.*

*Make start for Frisco about 9 PM. The roads very dusty - a long ride for I can barely keep my eyes open - fall asleep while pumping air in my tire and don't awaken until daylight.*

**OCT 31st**

*Again make the start for Frisco and arrive in Oakland about 8 AM. Here I see for the first time the waters of the bay with Frisco in the distance can hardly realize that the end of the trip is close at hand. Late ferry for the city and complete the trip arriving 9:15 AM, Tuesday Oct 31, 1905.*
*3633 miles.*

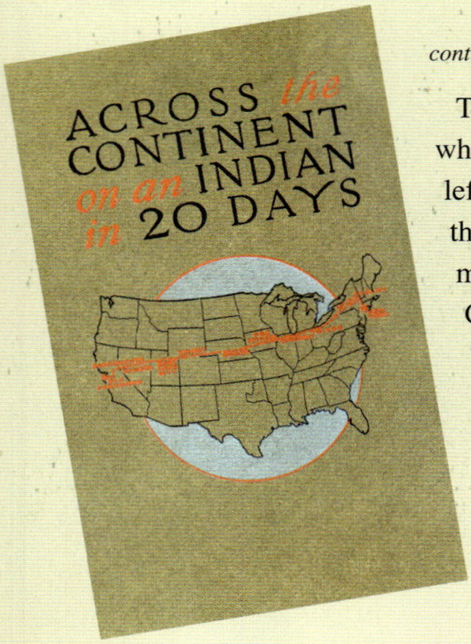


**This is a booklet published by the Indian Motocycle Company detailing the route and ride highlights of Volney Davis' 1911 record ride. *Don Emde Collection.***

*continued from page 15...*

The motor gave up the ghost completely when he reached Albany, New York. This left George with only one option: pedaling the machine like a bicycle for the final 150 miles. But he finally arrived in New York City to become the first-ever motorized "trans-continentalist."

The publicity of the cross-country accomplishments on both two- and four-wheels by Wyman and Jackson created great interest in the motorized-transportation world. The bar was now set by Wyman at fifty-two days for a cross country journey and many adventurous riders and drivers caught the fever of trying to lower the transcontinental record. Many tried, and many failed.

It was not until the fall of 1905 that Wyman's record finally fell. William C. Chadeayne, the Secretary-Treasurer of the Thomas Auto-Bi Company of Buffalo, New York and an avid motorcycle enthusiast, departed on an east-to-west ride on a single-cylinder Model 44 Auto-Bi to promote the reliability of his company's machines.

Like George Wyman, Chadeayne has his share of adventure along the way. His motorcycle was slightly more reliable that Wyman's, but he had some difficulties finding gasoline, and also lost time due to some crashes. One happened in Utah where he went over a thirty-foot cliff and was knocked unconscious. When he awoke two men and a girl were carrying him to a ranch house. There, Chadeayne repaired his machine and got going again. He overcame many mechanical problems along the way and after navigating through the rest of Utah and Nevada, he made his way through the Sierra Mountains and arrived in San Francisco 49 days after departing New York City to become the new coast to coast record holder.

Chadeayne's record was short-lived however. The following year, L.J. Mueller, a motorcycle dealer from Cleveland, dropped the record by 16 days to 31 days, 15 hours and 12 minutes, a record that stood for five years.

In 1910, Volney Davis, the captain of the San Francisco Motorcycle Club, began planning for a record attempt of his own. Already with one coast-to-coast ride to his credit, Davis had some understanding of what it would take to succeed. He decided that riding was the best way to prepare, so he took off from San Francisco on February 10th on a 5-horsepower Indian on what would be a 10,400-mile round-trip journey to New York City and back. This ride took him through 26 states and parts of Mexico and Canada. Davis was in no hurry this time, but he learned a lot about riding the muddy roads, and climbing hills, and basically keeping the motorcycle going down the road at a good, steady pace. He knew he would encounter all of that, and more, when he was on the clock on a record attempt.

Davis began his 3,700-mile coast-to-coast record attempt to New York City on June, 26, 1911, aboard a 7-horsepower Indian twin. He had a rather ominous beginning, which proved that even the best plan-

**By 1911, William Chadeayne's record had already been broken once when L.J. Mueller from Cleveland, OH lowered it to 31 days, 15 hours and 12 minutes. Volney Davis of San Francisco, CA (seen here) lowered it again to 20 days, 9 hours and 1 minute. *Don Emde Collection.***

ning doesn't always deliver intended results. He had planned to leave San Francisco exactly at midnight, but lost twenty minutes right at the start because there were no boats crossing the bay for Oakland until 12:20 a.m.

He had rough going through the Sierra Mountains, some of it due to steep hills, but there was also mud and snow in places. From Sacramento through Salt Lake City, Davis had numerous falls as he navigated rain, mud, rocks, sand and more. It took him almost a week just to get past Salt Lake City.

From there, his pace began to pick up and with the exception of some bad rain storms, and one serious crash, he made pretty good time as he moved through the mid-western states. In Iowa, he suffered a crash that knocked him unconscious for over an hour. One passing motorist who saw him laying in the road reported him to be dead, but luckily he was revived and back on his way having lost just a couple of hours.

He fell many more times, but Davis continued to ride as fast as he could and finally did arrive in New York City on July 16th to put his name in the record book with a coast-to-coast record of 20 days, 9 hours and 1 minute. He had smashed Mueller's record by 11¼ days!

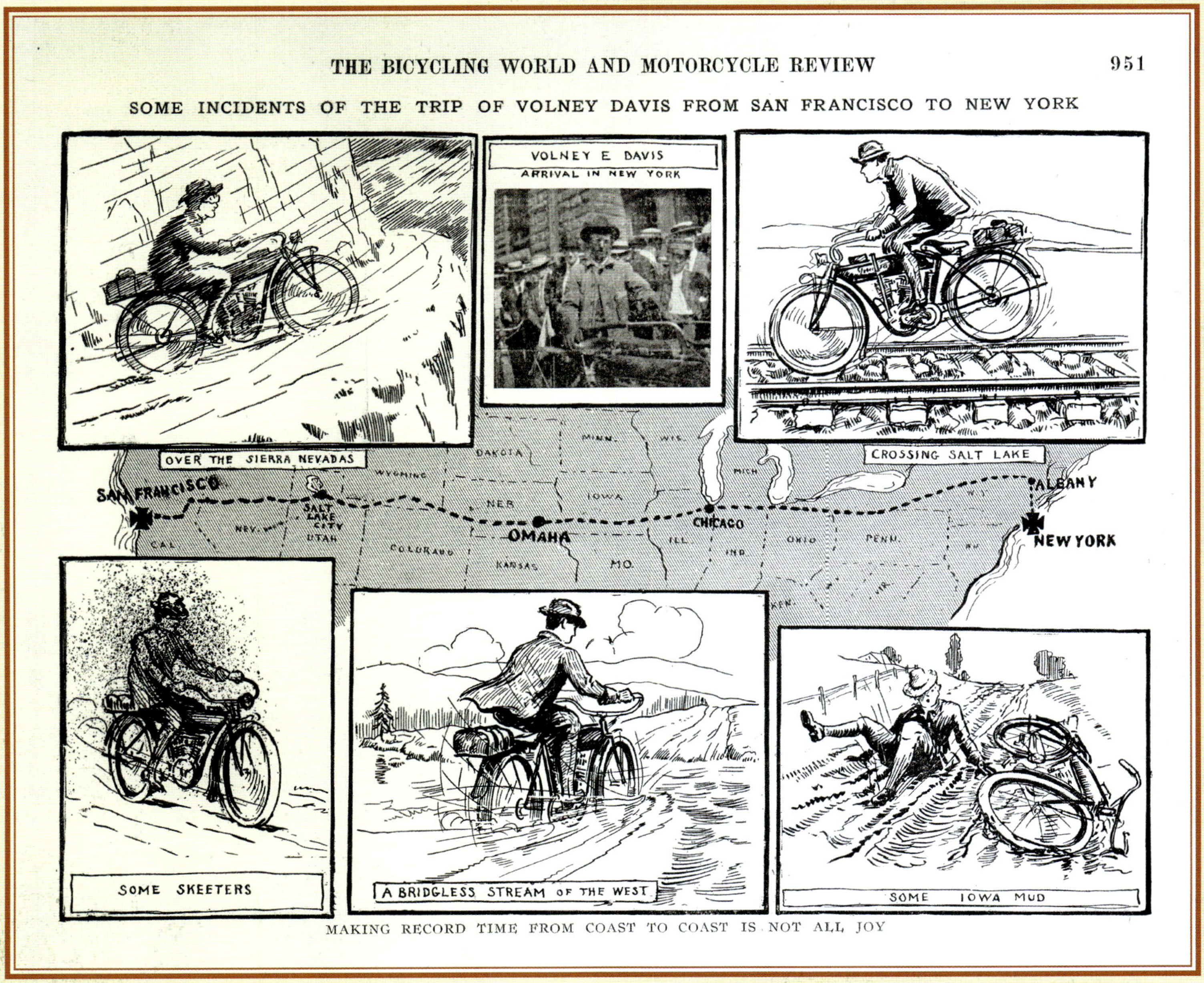


**This art came from an issue of The Bicycling World and Motorcycle Review magazine following the Volney Davis record setting ride of 1911. Some of his various challenges are shown.**

# CHAPTER 2

# THE EARLY YEARS OF ERWIN G. BAKER

The life story of Erwin George Baker really begins long before he was ever called "Cannon Ball." Before earning his nickname in 1914 he was known as Erwin, or to his friends, "E.G." or "Bake." He was born on March 12, 1882 in a four-room log cabin in Weisburg, Indiana...farming country.

His family lived on the Baker farm until Erwin was 12 years old. His father Henry was barely making ends meet as a farmer and moved the family to Indianapolis where conventional employment showed greater promise. Erwin had made it through the sixth grade, but with the move came the family's need for him to contribute financially and he got his first job at the Indianapolis Drop Forging Company. He worked for a few years as an apprentice machinist and earned $3.50 a week.

Baker grew to be a large man...at full height he stood six foot-two inches and weighed 225 pounds. He became interested in athletics at an early age and participated in boxing, wrestling and tumbling. He worked out in a gymnasium faithfully and gained a reputation as quite an athlete. Despite his large size, he also became interested in becoming an acrobat, a vocation normally done by lighter and more agile athletes. But he worked hard to learn the techniques and eventually quit his job to become part of a traveling vaudeville troupe called the *Fox Zouave Drill Team* that performed around the country.

By 1906, Baker had tired of the constant travel and returned to Indianapolis where he became a machinist. He reunited with his friends and at a social event met a local girl named Elenora Seitz. Their relationship grew and Erwin eventually proposed marriage. She agreed, but on the condition that the wedding would have to wait until he had sufficient income to support a married couple, and eventually a family.

About the same time he bought himself a single-cylinder Indian *"just to get around on,"* but he became a very active rider. In 1908 he joined a local motorcycle club and other members talked him into competing in a race on the 4th of July at the Crawfordsville Fairgrounds. He placed 2nd in the first race that day and later won the Main Event, an impressive racing debut to be sure.

Baker's immediate success hooked him for life. He continued to develop his motorcycle riding skills in local events around Indianapolis and did a lot of riding throughout the area in all types of weather. With snow in the winter and plenty of rain the rest of the year, the dirt roads in the Midwest were often quite muddy and difficult to navigate, but his physical strength got him through whatever situations arose.

Indianapolis was at the time America's fourth largest community of automobile production volume. As far back as 1906 a local automobile industry visionary named Carl Fisher began promoting the idea of a closed circuit racetrack that would be used primarily for testing by the many automakers who were based in the area. Racing was almost secondary in his plans, his biggest

**Before there was a 500-mile auto race or any bricks at the Indianapolis Motor Speedway, the inaugural motor racing event there was a day of motorcycle races in August of 1909. Loose gravel covered layers of thick "asphaltum" oil around the original track, which proved to be not conducive to high speed vehicles. While some of the nation's top motorcycle racers crashed out that day, unknown local rider Erwin G. Baker rode without incident to win the Ten-Mile Amateur race. Track owners saw the need for a better racing surface and the 2.5-mile circuit was covered in bricks in time for the first-ever Indianapolis 500 auto race in 1911. *Image: Indianapolis Motor Speedway Archives.***

concern was that development of new cars would be hampered if R&D was limited only to the local roads. There was a need for testing at higher speeds, as well as more severe conditions that could be setup on the test track, just as the automakers would do around the world in the years to come.

In December 1908 Fisher convinced three investors that his idea for a track was sound, and a 320-acre parcel of land was purchased in Indianapolis at Crawfordsville Pike and Georgetown Road. At the time, the Prest-O-Lite headlight factory that he owned was located across the street. Fisher made sure everything moved fast from that point forward and in early 1909 the big news was that grand opening events were scheduled that summer at his all-new Indianapolis Motor Speedway, including races for two- and four-wheelers. The first event of any type would be hot air balloon races on June 5, 1909, followed by a 2-day motorcycle meet on August 13-14 and then auto races on August 19th.

Rather than just use a dirt surface for the racecourse, Fisher came up with a concept of what later might be called an "asphalt" surface. It was made up of a concoction of gravel, limestone, tar and 220 gallons of asphaltum oil. It took 500 workers many months to apply layers of the mixture and pressing it with steam rollers.

As production of the race track and its facilities went forth, leading motorcycle manufacturers and their riders began making plans to participate in the inaugural races in August. One news report in July of 1909 listed top factory riders such as Stanley Kellogg, A.G. Chapple, Paul "Daredevil" Derkum and America's biggest professional star, Jake DeRosier all listed among the pre-entries. Little known local amateur rider Erwin G. Baker was also entered, but wasn't mentioned in the article.

Plans called for the first-ever motorcycle races at the Indianapolis Motor Speedway to be run on Friday, August 13th, but rain forced the schedule to be bumped one day. When the riders got on the racetrack on Saturday, in practice sessions they immediately noticed how abrasive the surface was and safety concerns were expressed.

Their concerns proved to be valid when Jake DeRosier crashed heavily in the Ten Mile Professional race after his front tire blew and was torn off the rim. Some initially feared that his injuries might be fatal, a shocking prospect for the greatest star of the sport at that time.

DeRosier's injuries were not as serious as first feared, but at the track that did not stop some riders from threatening to strike, which would bring the racing to an end that day. The F.A.M. official in charge of the event threatened a suspension for any racer who did not race. The riders grudgingly agreed to continue with the event.

Later in the day, the Ten Mile Amateur race had to be stopped when a leading Amateur rider, J.S. Tomey, suffered the same fate as DeRosier when he too had his front tire come off the rim. Like DeRosier, Tomey was done for the day and on the restart Baker jumped into the lead and rode to victory.

The injuries to DeRosier and Tomey left a bad impression on motorcycle fans of the 1909 races at the new Speedway. Baker was rightfully proud of his accomplishments, though, and had the diamond medal he won affixed to his watch chain and wore it the rest of his life.

Erwin Baker's victory at the first-ever motorsports race event at the Indianapolis Motor Speedway remains significant to this day. At the time it put him on the map in the motorcycle community around Indianapolis and helped land him a job for the United States Motorcycle Tires, a leading tire manufacturer at the time that was located in Indianapolis. He eventually was promoted to the position of Superintendent of motorcycle tire testing. That had to be a dream job for Baker as it called for riding motorcycles for long distances while putting tires to the test.

In the years to follow Baker continued to compete in motorcycle events in the Midwest every chance he got and he had great success in many different types of events. In 1911 his next significant addition to his racing resume came at a big 4th of July race. This one was held at another venue in the Indianapolis area, the Indiana State Fairgrounds on the same one-mile dirt track that is still used today for motorcycle racing.

**Before he was known as "Cannon Ball" or as a long distance endurance rider, Erwin G. Baker raced in dirt track events in and around his hometown of Indianapolis, Indiana.** ***Image: Indianapolis Motor Speedway Archives.***

**E.G. Baker (2nd from left) takes off at the start of the Ten-Mile Amateur event at the 1909 Grand Opening Races at the Indianapolis Motor Speedway. His race almost didn't happen. The loose gravel surface was unpopular as soon as riders started riding on it that day, but when America's leading motorcycle pro racer Jake DeRosier crashed and suffered serious injuries in the Ten-Mile Professional race, the call spread throughout the pits to cancel the rest of the events. Organizers were able to calm the concerns (albeit with threats of suspensions to riders refusing to race) and the schedule of events continued. The Ten-Mile Amateur race was red-flagged once due to a crash, but after the restart Baker took the lead and sped to the biggest victory of his still-young motorcycling competition career. *Image: Indianapolis Motor Speedway Archives.***

## POST SCRIPT: 1909 INDIANAPOLIS RACE

**Only a few days later the automobile races were held and the track conditions led to even greater carnage than at the motorcycle races. Two drivers, two mechanics and two spectators were killed the day of the car races.**

**Carl Fisher and his partners immediately decided to resurface the entire race course. 3.2 million bricks would line the track, soon to be known as "The Brickyard." The other major change was the decision that instead of many short distance races at an event, one long race should be held thereafter. May 30, 1911 saw the inaugural running of the famed Indianapolis 500.**

**Fisher went on to be a major supporter and planner of "Good Roads" across America. Despite the bad result of the early paved surface at the Indianapolis Motor Speedway, he would go on to head up the creation and building of the Lincoln Highway.**

With 40,000 spectators watching, Baker won 6 races over the two-day event, with the most notable being "The President's Race," a 5-mile match race against just one other rider with the President of the United States, Howard Taft, in attendance. The President congratulated Baker on his victory and shook his hand following the race. Talk about an instant celebrity. Anyone who had not heard of Erwin G. Baker before certainly knew who he was now.

Baker had become a skilled motorcycle rider in many different types of riding. Despite his successes at Indianapolis and other track races, he knew his large size and weight were a bit of a handicap for him against the smaller riders, who often looked like horse racing jockeys. He preferred the longer distance, endurance type events anyway which he really excelled at, both as a rider as well as having good endurance. He was also becoming a person of influence in the motorcycling community in Indianapolis, helping organize club activities and for a time was part of a group trying to build a large motordrome racetrack in the area.

Publicity from his success riding Indians caught the eye of the management at Indian Motocycle headquarters in Springfield, Massachusetts. Always on the lookout for riders who could help promote the brand in their local areas, Indian President and co-founder George Hendee, and Sales Manager and eventual President, Frank Weschler, reached out to Baker to come on board as an official sponsored rider for Indian. Thus began a relationship that would last for many years.

In 1912, Baker took off on his first major assignment for the company to promote the reliability of Indian motorcycles. It would be a three-month, 14,000-mile marathon ride, starting in Indianapolis southeast to Miami, then traveling by boat to Cuba where he rode west, then took another boat to Jamaica and another to Colon and after riding many miles through the jungles of Central America, took a steamer to San Diego.

This long distance adventure affected him in many ways. In addition to getting plenty of saddle time for fitness, he had a lot of logistics to work out to keep rolling through such remote areas, and he also had a lot of time to think whether he was up for the trans-continental record run that he was seriously contemplating. Another Indian rider, Volney Davis from San Francisco, had set the trans-continental record back in 1911 at 20 days, 9 hours and 1 minute.

Baker wrote about his Central America journey, saying: ***"On January 7, 1912, I groomed up my 1912 two-speed Indian and left Indianapolis and rode clear through to Miami, Fla., and from the Florida Keys I took passage on a streamer to Havana. I rode over the entire island of Cuba and from there I rode over the entire island of Jamaica. Then I took a steamer to Colon and crossed the Isthmus on my Indian, and then took a steamer up to San Diego, Cal. I spent three months riding through the tropics and over trails covered with vegetation, covering 14,000 miles on the Indian, and spending 20 days of the three months aboard steamships.***

***After completing this trip I rode in a great many endurance runs and road races throughout California and across the deserts of Arizona. This, with my physical training, placed me in a frame of mind where I considered that I was ready to make the transcontinental trip that would make them all 'sit up and take notice.'"***

Upon his return, Baker had little time off. There were numerous events and races going on in the Spring and Summer months in the Midwest. On the 4th of July Baker repeated his previous success at the Indiana State Fairgrounds with a victory in a 100-mile race there. He averaged 63.06 miles per hour.

As the riding season was winding down in the Midwest, Erwin and Elenora relocated temporarily to Phoenix, Arizona. From a base there, Erwin would be able to continue riding constantly and participate in numerous events, knowing snow would soon coat the streets of Indianapolis.

One event that he was looking forward to was the annual San Diego to Phoenix race. It was a 441-mile race that included over 300 miles of desert and some of the roughest riding conditions a motorcyclist of the early-1900s could imagine trying to ride.

The race was held in October, when the desert Southwest is still capable of dishing out 100+ degree temperatures. It would take the 19 entered riders three days of riding to get to Phoenix, with a stop each night. *Motorcycling Magazine* called it at the time "the most grueling motorcycle contest ever undertaken."

As treacherous as it was in places, the route of the San Diego to Phoenix race was actually the regular route at the time for all travelers going from one of those cities to the other. On Day 1 of the race, the competitors rode east from San Diego towards the desert on what is today California Highway 94. When they made it to the floor of the desert, the condition of the road worsened but was still passable. They made their first gas stops in Brawley, north of El Centro. Indian rider Paul "Dare Devil" Derkum from Los Angeles was the leader at that point with Erwin G. Baker in 2nd, but about 25 minutes behind. Baker had crashed his Indian on the dirt road through Devil's Canyon (today paved over and part of Interstate 8). He broke his speedometer in the crash, then suffered another crash a while later avoiding an automobile and damaged his handlebar controls.

After leaving Brawley, Mammoth Wash, one of the toughest sections of the entire race, lay ahead. A story in the November 24, 1913 edition of *Motorcycling Magazine* described Mammoth Wash as follows: *"Out of Brawley are eleven miles of good road, then five miles of silt as fine as flour and really not sand but powdered clay; after this comes rutty*

**Baker in 1910 getting a bite to eat while waiting for a ferry in Ohio. *Don Emde Collection.***

**Typical travel across the roads of America in 1910. Erwin Baker draws a crowd to talk about his motorcycle as they await the arrival of a ferry to cross a river in Ohio. *Don Emde Collection.***

**Now known to the motorcycling world as "E.G." Baker (or Bake to his friends), the October 11, 1913 edition of *Motor Cycling magazine* reported on another race victory.**

*desert road until the "High Line" irrigation canal, with its two troughs, which form the automobile bridge, marks the beginning of that much dreaded four miles of desert sink known as Mammoth Wash."*

At the east end of Mammoth Wash the route intersected Southern Pacific railroad track, which is still there and in use today. Riders at that point could choose to ride a deep sandy road 50+ miles south to Yuma that parallels the track, or it was also possible to get up on the center of the tracks and navigate south keeping an eye on the tracks for any oncoming trains. Despite the constant pounding on the wooden ties, many chose the tracks over the deep sand.

For riders with a 5-to-7 horsepower motorcycle with virtually no suspension front or back, the deep sand and ruts were extremely challenging and taxed the condition of the engine and frame to the max. In most cases riders had nothing more than a single gear with an "in-and-out" clutch pull lever like a tractor would have.

For Baker, Mammoth Wash would be the end for him in the 1913 San Diego to Phoenix race. He was already nursing his machine and body along following his two crashes earlier in the day. He encountered more troubles with his machine and abandoned the contest in the wash. He reportedly was able to board a train coming though heading to Yuma, which was the first night's stop, and the following day he again traveled by train to Phoenix to see the finish of the race. He was not alone... only 6 riders finished the race on their motorcycles.

**Baker (2nd from right) lined up with some fellow Indian riders for the start of the Eighth National Motorcycle Endurance Race in the early-1910s. *Image: Indianapolis Motor Speedway Archives.***

Paul Derkum went on to win the race on a 7-horsepower, V-twin Indian TT (Tourist Trophy) model with some modifications that he had learned to do from previous riding and races in the desert. His bike had special-made double capacity gas and oil tanks, double carburetor feed, double brake and clutch control and extra braces.

For Erwin Baker, it was surely humbling to be a non-finisher, but there were a lot of things that he learned that would serve him well in the future. Not only did he get a good look at Mammoth Wash, but also learned a thing or two from Derkum about setting his machine up for the rugged desert roads of Arizona and Southern California. The next time Baker came through the desert he was much better prepared.

While Baker now had the ocean-to-ocean record attempt in his head, before any more long distance riding would take place he needed to convince Elenora that he could now support her financially as they had agreed years before. He was now earning good money with his sponsorship deals with Indian and accessory manufacturers who he worked with. He convinced her it was time for the long-awaited wedding. After being engaged for seven years the two returned to their hometown of Indianapolis in December to be married.

Their stay in Indiana was short-lived and the newlyweds soon departed in a 40-horsepower Pathfinder automobile bound for Phoenix. Baker had a race in his plans down south in Savannah, and just before they reached Phoenix she dropped him off at a train station to catch a train bound for Georgia where an Indian race bike awaited him. Elenora then continued on to Phoenix in the car.

Baker competed in a 300-mile race at Savannah, which was one of the big-time events at the time. He ran 2nd on an Indian twin until the 214-mile mark when he dropped out with mechanical trouble, his second long distance event in a row where his motorcycle failed him. This surely was cause for some concern as he had in mind a ride coming up ten times the length of the Savannah race, but he never voiced any doubts.

1914 would turn out to be a very significant year in

the life of Erwin G. Baker. First, he learned early in the year that he was going to be a father. Also his wife suggested to Erwin that perhaps the time had come for him to go after that transcontinental record he had been thinking about.

He reflected on it later in the Indian sales booklet, which also appeared in the May 28, 1914 edition of *Motorcycle Illustrated Magazine*, ***"About the first of January, 1914, my wife got to joking about my dream of a transcontinental trip, so I made up my mind that I was not even going to permit my wife to kid me along and I then and there made up my mind to perform the "stunt" during the year of 1914. Then, I walked down the street and called on a friend of mine, Louis Brant, who was the Government weather clerk at Phoenix, Arizona, the town where I was then living. I asked him if he could not in some way help me out, preferably by the prediction of the weather for the next three months, so that he could sandwich me in between a couple of rainstorms and get me pretty well across the continent without muddy roads. This weather business I don't know much about myself, only from day to day, and I found that I had asked my friend a question that involved a serious problem, but he assured me that he would spend a little of his own time in aiding me.***

***For the next three months during his spare time he made researches for ten years back, as to just how the weather stood during the various months, and he decided the month of May was the most favorable time for me to leave the Pacific Coast, and predicted that if I started at a certain time he could get me across the Mississippi Valley before a storm would overtake me. Boys, this kind of fortune-telling is hard to believe, but I felt that I had to believe somebody and I knew figures would not lie, so I decided to make the start on the day the weather clerk arranged for me.***

***Then I went back and talked it over with my wife, as only she and myself and the weather clerk knew anything about my intentions. She finally became convinced that I had the nerve to do what I claimed I could do and what I started out to do, and she then helped me in the most loyal manner.***

***The first thing we did was to get a logbook from Westgard, the veteran pathfinder, showing the various trails across the continent, and which gave a brief description of conditions. We found in this logbook two routes, one of which had what we considered fairly good going, but the mileage was longer and I decided I was toughened up enough to take the shorter route with the hardest kind of going.***

***My wife then became enthusiastic, and we started to write letters to people along this route, inquiring about roads and bridges and where gasoline could be located. We consumed two months getting this data together. We found that from Rice on to Fort Apache it was impossible to get gasoline. These places were located from 40 to 120 miles from railroad stations, so we arranged for gasoline packed in on burros from the railroad station to various points on the desert and mountain roads, which cost me seventy-cents a gallon.***

***I then called on Mr. James Barker, a Government civil engineer, who is now employed by the Department of Irrigation, and asked him if he would in his spare time make me a drawing of my trail across the thirteen States I had decided to pass through, and he favored me by laying out this map and made me a number of blue prints of it.***

***When this was done I immediately got in touch with Chairman of the F.A.M. and told him of my plans. He was then the fourth one in my secret. Mr. Donovan, before making a reply to my request for a sanction, found it was necessary to get in touch with all of the directors of the F.A.M., as he did not desire to bring any legal obligations upon the organization***

**Despite his large stature (6-feet, 2-inches) and weight (225 pounds), Baker was a successful track racer in the early teens against riders 75-90 pounds lighter. *Image: Indianapolis Motor Speedway Archives.***

Following his victory at the Indianapolis Motor Speedway in 1909, another noteworthy success came on July 4th, 1911 at the nearby Indiana State Fairgrounds. With President Howard Taft among the audience of 40,000 race fans, E.G.Baker won six races that day, including the special "President's race where he was matched against another local rider named Johnnie Sink. *Image: Indianapolis Motor Speedway Archives.*

***by issuing such a sanction, and I in turn guaranteed to him that I would live up to all the speed laws passing through towns and villages in my trip, which I afterwards did most faithfully.***

***I was then granted the sanction and after receiving it I wrote to Mr. Weschler of the Hendee Manufacturing Company, of my intentions and he replied: "Go to it. We will welcome you in New York whether you break a record or not."***

After waiting seven years to convince his wife he was in good enough financial shape to support the two of them, the news of a child on the way seemed to have an added impact on Erwin that he needed to get into even better financial shape. He realized that this needed to be more than a ride that only covered his expenses. So as he planned how he would put a transcontinental ride together, he crafted a proposal to get back to Weschler that would reward him well financially if he were successful.

According to early-day journalist J.J. O'Connor, who wrote about Baker's historic journey in the February 1944 issue of *"The Motorcyclist,"* Erwin put together a proposal that he personally presented at Indian headquarters to Frank Weschler. He asked for a bonus plan whereby he would be rewarded not just on the accomplishment of breaking the coast-to-coast record, but his clever concept was the more time he bettered the record of Volney Davis, the greater the size of the bonus. He estimated at the time that he would break Volney's record by three days.

Weschler agreed with the proposal and Baker had the financial incentive he was looking for to really go all out from coast to coast. He had a baby on the way and was looking to fill the cookie jar at home with the money he and Elenora would need to cover the many new bills that would be arriving in the coming months. But he knew there was a big risk. The big payday was based on actually setting the record. From this first trans-continental ride came a saying he used a lot in the coming years: "No Record. No Pay."

The Indian factory quickly went to work on a special machine built to Baker's specs learned in the 1913 San Diego to Phoenix race and it would soon be shipped to his starting point of San Diego, California. The 7-horsepower Indian V-twin would be one of the new "TT" models like Paul Derkum had ridden in the San Diego to Phoenix race that used an all-new electronic lighting system and also featured a new 2-speed transmission. The modifications from the stock model reportedly included installing a slightly larger 3-inch wide front tire, a heavy-duty 15-pound skid plate made from a boiler plate, as well as the expanded gasoline* and oil tanks for better range between stops.

**Editor's note:** *This contradicts somewhat his description of the motorcycle in writings for the Indian booklet where he says the only modification was the installation of the 3-inch wide tire, but its possible the marketing and PR department at Indian had the final say on the literature copy and deemed those other changes were not worth mentioning?*

With the motorcycle deal secured, Baker proposed various sponsorship deals with the many other makers of equipment that was on the motorcycle. On board were gasoline, oil, tire, seat, chain, lighting, carburetor, speedometer, clothing, goggle, puttee, shoe, watch, glove, battery, spark plug, handlebar grip and brake lining companies, most of whom would spend ad budget

The July 13, 1911 issue of *Motorcycle Illustrated* magazine showed this picture of President Howard Taft congratulating Baker after his victory in the President's Race. Taft said to Baker, "I congratulate you upon making a great race. I never saw such a race."

dollars in subsequent issues of enthusiast publications to promote Baker's success using their products.

Erwin kept busy riding the rugged desert terrain in events in and around the Phoenix area, while Elenora assisted with the letter writing duties to contact sponsors, Indian dealers on the route and others involved in logistics about the trans-con record plans. In her writing she often referred to Baker as "E.G." or "Bake."

On February 9th, he was one of six riders who scored a perfect 1000 points in a 77-mile endurance type ride from Phoenix up to Roosevelt Lake, one of the locations he would pass through in May on his ride to New York. His confidence level about his motorcycle obviously improved following that successful ride.

In early April, the exact start date of the transcontinental ride was not decided yet, but Baker knew it was approaching. There was a 100-mile race in Phoenix that he entered, surely feeling the track time would be good. It turned out, however, to be a very close call that could have delayed or ended his plans completely.

The April 7, 1914 edition of *The Bicycling World and Motorcycle Review* wrote: *"Erwin G. Baker, the Indianapolis Indiana rider, played the role of runner up for the greater part of the century (100 miles), but was seriously hurt when his rear casing proved unequal to the strain which the high speed imposed upon it and let go; the ruptured tire locked Baker's rear wheel and he skidded for a considerable distance, just in front of the grandstand, until the fabric was ground in two and the free end whisked around and flailed Baker across the back and shoulders, knocking him from the machine. While not unconscious, Baker was badly battered from the fall and his machine was so badly damaged that he could not continue in the contest."*

Baker fortunately did not suffer any broken bones in his crash in Phoenix and was able to keep all plans moving ahead. Not long afterwards he was contacted by his weather expert who told him that May 3rd was the date he should leave on the ride.

Baker wrote,***"My friend Brant (the weather clerk) decided that I should get to San Diego and be ready to start May 3, in between the storms. I then took an automobile stage and rode from Phoenix, Ariz., to San Diego, which consumed three days of my time. The day I left Phoenix my wife also left, for Indianapolis, and while waiting in San Diego for my machine I received a wire from my wife saying: "Don't start, as it is impossible to get through." This wire was due to the fact that while passing through Kansas and Illinois she met terrific rainstorms, bridges being washed out, fields flooded and streams swollen. This verified my friend Brant's prediction, and I was all the more anxious to get started and trail after that storm.***

***I then hunted up the Indian agents at San Diego, C.A. Sheppard & Co., and asked them if my machine had arrived. Sheppard smiled and said it had and wanted to know where my eyes were that I didn't see it stuck in the window together with a large display of a map, showing my proposed route across the continent. I took the machine out of the window, a mount I had never seen before, and took a little ride on it. I took a trip into the mountains to be sure of my adjustments before starting, and then returned to the agency. It then struck me that I could make faster time over my rough going in the desert and on rocky trails if I put on larger tires, so I put on three-inch Goodyear tires, both front and rear, and this was the only change that was made to the machine.***

***I hung around the agency and began to realize that a lot of the boys were stacking up their dollars in betting as to the number of days I would do the trip in, and I began to figure I was going to fool the whole bunch."***

**In late-1911, Baker was contracted by the Indian Motocycle Company to put their bikes to the test in long distance rides. He found he had good strength and stamina for such strenuous rides and this got him to begin planning for his first transcontinental motorcycle ride. He competed in numerous long distance events in the desert areas of the southwest, as well as an amazing 12,000-mile adventure ride to Florida, where he then ferried over to Cuba, across to the west and ferried again to the mainland of Mexico. He then rode north and made his way to San Diego. The seeds were now sown for the record attempt of 1914.** ***Image Indianapolis Motor Speedway Archives.***

# CHAPTER 3

# SAN DIEGO TO YUMA / THEN & NOW

## His Ride Begins

Baker took an automobile stage to downtown San Diego from Phoenix on Thursday, April 30, 1914. Upon his arrival he made his way to C.A. Sheppard & Company, the Indian agency there, where he was shown the Indian motorcycle that was sent out from the factory for him to ride on his record attempt. He spent the rest of that day and Friday mounting the wider tires and then giving the bike a short break-in ride to make sure everything was in proper working order. He was all set to depart Sunday morning, May 3, 1914.

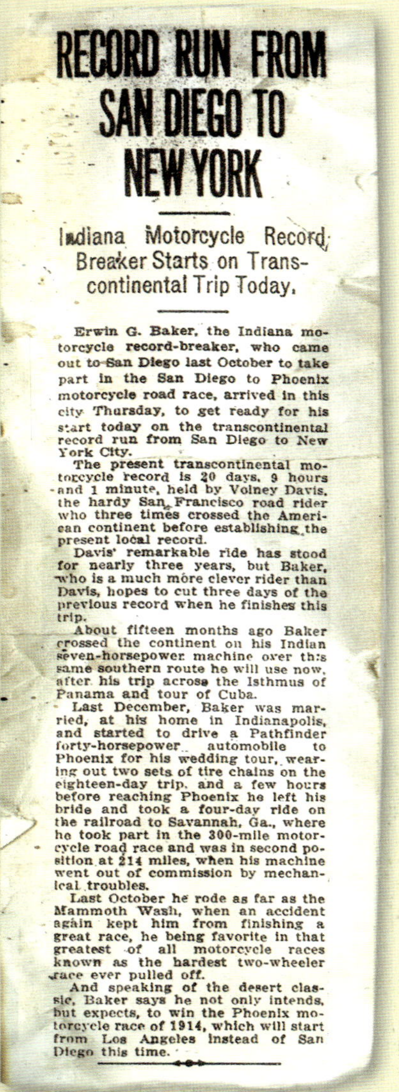

RECORD RUN FROM SAN DIEGO TO NEW YORK

Indiana Motorcycle Record Breaker Starts on Transcontinental Trip Today.

Erwin G. Baker, the Indiana motorcycle record-breaker, who came out to San Diego last October to take part in the San Diego to Phoenix motorcycle road race, arrived in this city Thursday, to get ready for his start today on the transcontinental record run from San Diego to New York City.

The present transcontinental motorcycle record is 20 days, 9 hours and 1 minute, held by Volney Davis, the hardy San Francisco road rider who three times crossed the American continent before establishing the present local record.

Davis' remarkable ride has stood for nearly three years, but Baker, who is a much more clever rider than Davis, hopes to cut three days of the previous record when he finishes this trip.

About fifteen months ago Baker crossed the continent on his Indian seven-horsepower machine over this same southern route he will use now, after his trip across the Isthmus of Panama and tour of Cuba.

Last December, Baker was married, at his home in Indianapolis, and started to drive a Pathfinder forty-horsepower automobile to Phoenix for his wedding tour, wearing out two sets of tire chains on the eighteen-day trip, and a few hours before reaching Phoenix he left his bride and took a four-day ride on the railroad to Savannah, Ga., where he took part in the 300-mile motorcycle road race and was in second position at 214 miles, when his machine went out of commission by mechanical troubles.

Last October he rode as far as the Mammoth Wash, when an accident again kept him from finishing a great race, he being favorite in that greatest of all motorcycle races known as the hardest two-wheeler race ever pulled off.

And speaking of the desert classic, Baker says he not only intends, but expects, to win the Phoenix motorcycle race of 1914, which will start from Los Angeles instead of San Diego this time.

*San Diego Union* May 3, 1914

Altogether his list of "spares" and other items he would carry included: two inner tubes, a short and long chain, Graflex camera and some film, a half-gallon water canteen, .38-caliber revolver (presumably, but not mentioned: some bullets) and a spare light bulb. Unlike latter-day motorcycles that would have saddlebags and numerous other means to carry luggage, the 1914 Indian TT, like virtually every other motorcycle at the time, had minimal means to carry anything. A small metal toolbox over the gas tank held a few tools and the spare parts, everything else would need to be carried in his jacket pockets, plus his canteen and camera were each held around his shoulders with straps.

A headline in that morning's edition of the *San Diego Union* newspaper read: "Record Run From San Diego to New York. Indiana Motorcycle Record Breaker Starts on Transcontinental Trip Today." The story went on to tell how Erwin G. Baker from Indianapolis, Indiana was leaving that day on his record attempt, and other details including his ride to Central America in 1912, how he had gotten married the previous December and had to cut short a "honeymoon" drive to Phoenix to jump on a train to Georgia to be in a motorcycle race. The story also pointed out how he had broken down in Mammoth Wash – almost 150 miles from the start – the previous October in the San Diego to Phoenix race. Baker also stated that he would be back in the Fall for the 1914 running of that grueling race and despite the 1913 machine failure, as well as two crashes, he boldly predicted that he would win it.

Baker chose to start his ride at the Carnegie Public Library at 8th and E Street in downtown San Diego. One of many public libraries funded by philanthropist Andrew Carnegie, it served the city well for many years, but was torn down in 1952 and replaced by a larger library. Since the F.A.M. was prepared to certify his record if Baker achieved it and followed other agreed-to requirements, the F.A.M. Competition Chairman had appointed Charles Fuller Gates, a west coast representative, to serve as an official starter of the ride. With local press, friends and staff of the Indian dealership and others looking on, Gates fired a starter's pistol precisely at 9:00 a.m. to signal Baker to begin his ride.

Baker noted the following in his journal about the beginning of his great adventure:

***"The morning of May 3 found me dressed in leather riding trousers, short raincoat and a khaki shirt, while I had a special canteen made to hold a gallon of water to help me across the desert. A beautiful rainstorm made its appearance, going south on the coast, and my good friends who were putting their money on me as a winner tried to prevail on me not to start, and those who were figuring on me to lose seemed to be very anxious for me to get on my way. But none of them knew I was using science in this thing and one of them figured this was only a local storm which I knew I was going to start out in, and at 9 a.m. Pacific time, I made my start before a battery of cameras and moving-picture machines."***

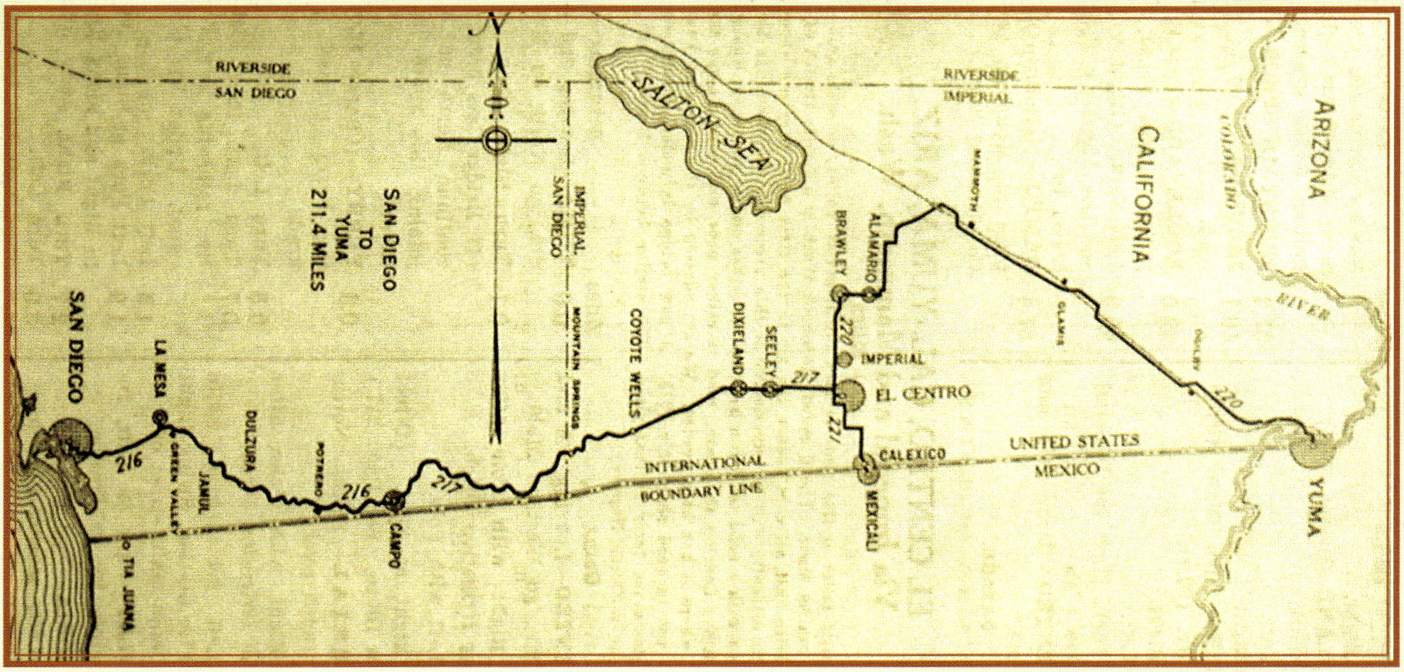


The road map seen at the top was available in Baker's day. It was published by the Pacific Coast Blue Book Publishing Company. This was prior to the wooden "Plank Road" that was eventually built, connecting El Centro to Yuma, AZ. It shows how travelers in 1914 had to go north from El Centro to Brawley, navigate the challenging Mammoth Wash, then southeast alongside the railroad tracks to Yuma. Our modern map below shows Baker's 1914 route in purple to green line, as well as the alternative we worked out (purple to red) after running into a roadblock and bad roads explained in this chapter. The purple line shows where we followed his same route on our "Mapping Rides" in 2012 and the Centennial Ride of 2014. The green line shows where Baker had ridden and the red line is our alternate route that we took. This same map format will be used throughout the book.

*Map by Bill Tipton / Compart Maps.*

**In 1914, the Carnegie Library at 8th and E Street in downtown San Diego served as the city's main public library. Baker departed from this location the morning of May 3rd.**

From the Carnegie Library in downtown San Diego, he rode east approximately 12 miles to La Mesa. From there he would head towards the desert on what is today Campo Road / Calif. Highway 94. Since he had ridden in the San Diego to Phoenix race the previous October, he knew the route out of town and made good time.

Erwin mentioned in his journal that as he rode east on Campo Road, he passed two regiments of U.S. Army troops. The United States was then embroiled politically in the Mexican Revolution that had begun in 1910. While no military actions had been taken yet, the tensions between the two countries were running very high. Campo Road was actually very vulnerable, as there was, and still is, a road that leads in and out of Tecate, B.C. Mexico just a few miles away. So any attacks of the San Diego area by the Mexican forces would likely have come there, at least partially.

He wrote,

***"Thirty miles out from San Diego, in the Cottonwood Mountains, the sun came out in all its glory, together with a strong wind, While passing along here I met a regiment of U.S. Infantry hiking along the Mexican border. The road where I met them was in a mountain pass and they formed in line and gave me enough room to pass through them on the mountain trail, all cheering and waving their hands. About five miles further on I came on to another body of soldiers, who were all at rest. It certainly did seem as if war had begun with the Mexicans, for it looked as if the boys had enough cannons and ammunition to blow up the whole of Mexico. From that time on I had sunshine with a very strong wind. I stopped for dinner at Mountain Springs, at the mouth of Devil's Canyon. The dinner was served at a slab-boarded shanty, where I had a handout of sour-belly beans and a cup of coffee, for which I paid liberally."***

At the time of his ride, there was a company in San Diego called Grist Auto Service that ran an Auto Stage service from San Diego to the Imperial Valley. It was basically like the old horse-drawn stagecoaches of the 1800s, except in large multi-passenger gas-powered cars. The full trip from downtown San Diego to El Centro was 7 hours.

While Baker no doubt made better time, for comparison, the Grist Auto Stage would arrive at Jamul from San Diego in 1 hour, Cottonwood in 2 hours, Campo in 3 hours, and Mountain Springs in 5¾ hours. In Baker's journal he mentioned making a stop in Mountain Springs for what he called dinner, but this would actually have been more like a mid-day lunch stop. While he may not have considered the light helping of sour-belly beans and a cup of coffee they served him at his Mountain Springs stop a bargain, he at least was surely relieved to have made it through the Mountain Springs in Devil's Canyon without any incidents. He had crashed twice there the previous November in the San Diego to Phoenix race, which led to him ultimately dropping out of the race a few hours later.

Mountain Springs was where the constructed road leading out of San Diego County ended and turned into a soft, two-track trail heading into the desert. The food wasn't great there, but the primitive early day "Truck Stop" did have some water piped in from the mountain above into a stone tank that auto travelers could use to top off their radiators before they headed into the desert, or for motorcyclists like Baker to top off their canteens.

One other significant point about Mountain Springs is this is where the weather would begin to change

**Postcard of Downtown San Diego in the early-teens.**

**Heading east from San Diego towards the desert, the first taste of the sand and loose dirt came at Devil's Canyon. Through the years there were numerous improvements to the road and today this section of road is the eastbound lanes of Interstate 8. *Photo: San Diego History Center.***

**Between El Centro, CA and Yuma, AZ lies the Algodones Sand Dunes, a huge area of sand which for many years had no easy way to navigate straight through. Motorists were forced to drive around it until 1915 (a year after Baker's record ride) when a road made of wooden planks was installed over the deep sand. It was only used that way for a few years until U.S. Highway 80 was cut through.**

**This grainy photo from the 1914 Indian Motocycle booklet was taken by Baker himself. It shows his Indian motorcycle in one of the two grooves used by automobiles as they navigated the punishing Mammoth Wash.**

**This postcard shows the train station at Yuma, AZ where Baker crossed over the Colorado River and stayed the night there at the hotel. From Mammoth Wash where he got onto the railroad tracks, he rode 64 miles between the metal rails to Yuma.**

dramatically. It is not unusual by May to have cool and sometimes rainy weather along the coast in San Diego, while at the same time the temperature out in the desert can be 100+ degrees. Such was the case in 1914. Baker encountered some light rain as he left downtown which followed him to La Mesa and up towards Dulzura. He reported that he eventually got ahead of the precipitation, saying, *"The sun came out in all its glory."* That was typical San Diego weather. It likely stayed very pleasant, except for some strong winds that are common there, as he rode through the mountains past Campo, which sits at 2,620 foot elevation.

As he began to descend down the mountain in Devil's Canyon, however, he would begin to feel the heat from the desert. He refers later to temperature of 119-degrees between Yuma and Phoenix, so it was likely somewhere in the 100-105-degree range when he stopped at Mountain Springs, and would have just gotten continually hotter as he rode east.

Baker continues: ***"From there I started through Coyote Wells, which was a stretch of 15 miles knee-deep with sand, cactus, sage brush and mesquite bushes, which was nothing more than a trail to Imperial Valley. This point is 250 feet below sea level. Then I found good roads from the end of this sand stretch into Brawley and from there on I was riding silt, which was axle deep for 19 miles to Mammoth Wash."***

## FIGHTING THE DEMON THIRST

***"At this point I decided to do the camel act and go without drinking water. I picked up a small black pebble about the size of a dime and placed this in my mouth under my tongue—same as the desert Indians do—in order to keep from drinking water. About one quarter of the way onto New Mexico I decided I would have just one swallow of water, and after going a little bit further found I would have another one. By the time I reached the railroad track I decided on taking one more swallow of water, and one more only until I reached Yuma, Arizona, which was the stopping point for the night. However, had I not carried the little pebble in my mouth my stops for water would have been multiplied many times.***

***The riding from Mammoth Wash was sand for five and one-half miles across, and when I got halfway across I met a sandstorm which followed me a considerable distance. I began to think that I would never reach the Southern Pacific railroad tracks, but I managed to do so without being affected or held up by the sandstorm. On reaching the railroad tracks I rode 64 miles on them into Yuma, Ariz.***

***That night I spent in Yuma. I left word before retiring to be called at 5 a.m. as my intentions were to make Phoenix the next night, and having been over this road before I knew the hard going I was up against. I sure did have silt sand to plow through, and rocky gulches to bound over, to say nothing of the mesquite bushes and cactus that I would have to dodge and all the time riding in that terrific heat, which makes a man feel that he is just about six inches from h---."***

Baker arrived at the Yuma train station just before 7:00 pm, which meant it took him about 10 hours to make the ride from San Diego. He has averaged 22 miles per hour for the 211-mile ride. He obviously felt very satisfied with how the first day had gone, especially compared to the difficulties on that same route in the 1913 San Diego to Phoenix race. At least he had ridden his motorcycle all the way to Yuma this time instead of having to hitch a ride on a train!

# FAST FORWARD TO 2012:
## The Mapping Work Begins

Joe Colombero and I had taken possession of our loaner KTM 990s back in May of 2011 and had done a few break-in rides on them. But by the time we got all of the accessories installed we were into the heat of summer in the Imperial Valley. By June the daily thermometer readings can hit 100-degrees there, and it climbs to 115 and even 120 at times. So while we waited out the return of cooler weather, I continued to work the Internet pretty hard trying to connect the dots on various sections of the route east.

Finally, in mid-January of 2012, Joe and I were ready to begin what we called the "Mapping Rides" to get the route bookmarked on our Garmin GPS and figured the best place to start was at the waterfront of the Pacific Ocean in San Diego.

On January 19th, we rode to downtown San Diego and located a parking area in front of a long-time San Diego seafood restaurant called Anthony's Fish Grotto. It is next door to where the historic 1800s *Star of India* ship is located. This was pretty much our starting point for mapping purposes, and as learned later, we were actually only a few blocks off from the original Carnegie Library that Baker actually departed from in 1914.

We proceeded on the KTMs on Highway 94 to La Mesa, and headed east on Campo Road as Baker had. After passing the town of Campo, Highway 94 merges with Old Highway 80 which later merges into Interstate 8. Not far after getting onto I-8 we entered the historic Devil's Canyon area. Mountain Springs Grade is a divided highway now with the east bound lanes the original old road. For a few miles numerous variations of the old road can be seen.

After stopping to check out Mountain Springs and finding nothing really useful that remained there, we continued on I-8 to the Ocotillo exit, and onto Old Highway 80 heading to Plaster City and Seeley. We made a quick stop in Seeley. My grandparents lived there at the time of Baker's ride, and five years later my father was born there.

From Seeley we rode to El Centro, then headed north to Brawley where we found a hotel to stay the night.

The next morning was a very exciting one for me. While I had done a lot of studying and map work to locate Mammoth Wash, I was really looking forward to actually riding it. We departed Brawley and headed north on Highway 111 and we had a few possible turn-offs that looked like they would take us to the wash. I already knew, however, that there was some kind of farm indicated in that area and it looked like Mammoth Wash might not be accessible

**Our mapping work started at the waterfront in San Diego in January of 2011. With the historic ship *Star of India* in the background, Joe Colombero organizes his gear before we mounted up on the KTM 990s and headed east to the California desert.**

When we finally got on the right road it took us right to the entrance of the farm which had a couple of signs at the gate that reads "Stay Out" and "Trespass and Loitering Forbidden by Law." It didn't take a lot of thought to get the message we needed to find another way to go, so Joe and I rode north about a quarter mile or so and finally got past all the fencing and an aqueduct until we came to a sandwash that headed directly east. This looked promising!

I had recalled what Baker said about Mammoth Wash, that it was axle deep sand and sure enough, as I took off to see where it would lead I did find the sand to be plenty soft. It was my first time in the dirt on the big KTM 990 and my instincts told me to "gas it up" a bit and it did feel more stable as the speed came up a bit. I

## CANNON BALL'S HALL OF FAME MEDAL

**When the AMA created its Motorcycle Hall of Fame in 1998, Cannon Ball Baker was elected in the first class, but he had no family to accept his medal and it was filed away at the museum in Pickerington, Ohio. When the project started, I asked them if I could borrow the medal to take with us as we retraced his 1914 route and received a positive response. I carried the medal right in my tank bag, so anytime we were at the same exact location where we knew Baker had been, it was quick and easy to take a photo with it.**

**East of San Diego, parts of the original old road to and from the desert can be seen from the current Interstate 8 as it carves its way through Devil's Canyon. It was a dirt road in Baker's day, later cemented over when it officially became part of U.S. Highway 80.**

**Farther east from the photo above is this stretch of road near Mountain Springs. There was once a roadhouse here with some gasoline, water and food, as well as a toll station to collect fees for westbound travelers to pay for the use of the road to San Diego. The current Interstate 8 freeway is just off to the left of the old road.**

rode maybe a quarter mile and came up to the historic railroad tracks that Baker had mentioned in his writing.

There was a road that paralleled the tracks, so Joe and I took it down to where my map and Garmin settings was telling me was Mammoth Wash. We stopped briefly to take a few photos. We were at the exact location where Baker had come up Mammoth Wash and then rode up onto the railroad tracks! This was our first "Cannon Ball Was Here" moment, one of many on our mapping rides.

It was a pretty warm day, in the 90s somewhere, and with our riding gear on, it didn't take too much action to start feeling some heat. So after taking in some fluids, we headed on the road that went south to the Glamis Store. We were on a two-track road not far away from the Great California Dunes at Glamis. That's Dune buggy country and the road we were on seemed like it was well traveled by the 4-wheelers and pretty chewed up. The road got softer and softer as we rode with lots of washboard ups and downs, which made it hard to get up the needed speed to keep from spinning the rear wheels and digging a trench.

It wasn't long until Joe and I were both stuck in the sand, so all we could do was get off and start scooping the sand out with our hands until we could get the bikes freed up and rideable. It was really our only way out.

Luckily we had been in the worst section of the road, so once we both got going again we were able to get our speeds up and made it back onto the hard packed trail. That road took us to the Glamis store at California Highway 78 and we rode back to Orange County from there. We make a note to add to our "To Do"

On our first "map ride" we encountered this dead-end on the road that Baker had ridden in 1914. The once highly-traveled Mammoth Wash is now a farm with a wide water aqueduct now cutting through what was once a road. The signs at the gate couldn't have been more clear. We knew we needed to find an alternative route to get around it.

Joe and I took a break on a 90+ degree day as we explored some options for a rideable route around the farm at Mammoth Wash. This section of Ted Kipf Road was used to continue our ride to Yuma, Arizona.

list to buy some lightweight plastic shovels to carry in the saddlebags!

When I returned home, I tried to assess what had actually happened to Joe and I with Mammoth Wash. I figured we would be doing some kind of group ride in the centennial year of 2014, and publicizing his actual route of 1914 might not be a good idea. There was, of course, the private property blocking the entrance to the sandwash on the west side that needed to be respected, but if riders took the next one to the north like Joe and I did, it would lead them right onto the soft road where we got stuck. We needed some options for that section. Lesson #1 of the Cannon Ball Project learned: It's one thing to *find* Cannon Ball's Trail, and might be another thing at times to *ride* it.

By late-March 2012 I had done quite a bit of online map research and located a route that could be accessed a couple of miles farther north of the actual Mammoth Wash crossing, then take it over to the east side of the railroad tracks and ride south past the "bad section." It then crossed back over the tracks and joined the same road that Joe and I had ridden when we were back on the hard packed dirt. It looked promising, but of course it needed to be ridden to confirm that we had an alternative.

On March 28, 2012 Joe and I had a ride planned to go back to the desert to check this alternative route. Our friend Perry King, an actor and member of the AMA Board of Directors, let us know he would be interested in going along with us. So now we were a three-some, actually four if we include another friend Scott Cox who rode along just part way the first day.

This time we rode north from Brawley on Highway 111, went past our previous turn to Mammoth Wash and kept going to a remote town on the southeast corner of the Salton Sea called Niland.

We turned onto the road that I had found on the map and proceeded east. The pavement soon ended and we were now on a wide dirt road which was easy riding for the first few miles. We successfully navigated my "possible" alternate route over one aqueduct and the train tracks and were feeling pretty good as we got onto a road called Ted Kipf Road. According to the map, this was the road that would take us about 65 miles south to Ogilby Road, then over to Interstate 8 and into Yuma, AZ.

As Joe, Perry and I pulled into Ted Kipf Road, that road quickly got very rough, with some areas very hard, washboard surface, but then we hit some deep sandy sections that would go for about a hundred yards or so. This went on for about five miles and I was feeling pretty shot when we finally got onto hard ground again. Other than my previous ride through Mammoth Wash, this was my first real run through rough terrain on the KTM 990. Loaded up with accessories and a tank of gas, it was 500+ pounds and I was finding things I knew how to do on a 250-pound dirt bike weren't working for me on the 990.

In Erwin Baker's journal of his ride, he noted the riding conditions going east from Brawley. He wrote, *"From there I was riding silt, which was axle deep for 19 miles into Mammoth Wash."* When I left the pavement in that area and headed up the sandy wash, it gave me goose bumps to experience what he was talking about. There I was "axle deep!" I knew we were truly on "Cannon Ball's trail"

Baker's medal first came out for a photo at this bridge at Mammoth Wash where he had ridden through the sand from Brawley. He got up onto the railroad tracks here and rode 64 miles south to Yuma.

One of the routes that Joe and I explored got even more than axle deep. This section of road was just too soft and too deep to be suitable for motorcycle riding. Luckily after we dug ourselves out, we found another road to the left of the trees in this photo that got us through the area.

But the good news was that the road did in fact go around the super-soft road that Joe and I had gotten stuck in a few months earlier and we had a great ride from there all the way to where the dirt road ended at Ogilby Road. We then cruised into Yuma where we stayed at a hotel that night.

Our plan the next morning was to ride home, but before we left we decided to see if there were any museums in Yuma where we might obtain some historical information. So I "Googled" Yuma history and found the website of their Historical Society with an address. So after breakfast, Joe, Perry and I rode there and went inside unannounced where we met Tina Clark. She is Yuma's City Archaeologist, Historian, Grants Writer and also serves as curator of the Yuma Crossing National Heritage Area. It was great luck for us that we got to meet Tina, as anything to do with history in that city or the surrounding area involves her.

We explained what the Cannon Ball Project was all about and she was on board right from the start. She ran us a few photo copies of some old maps in their files, gave us some other information and offered her assistance for whatever else we needed to know. We also planted the seed of a ride coming through in 2014 and that maybe we could work with her on some kind of reception, which she was very excited about.

Next, we were back on our bikes, heading home, now with a route identified that we could make work to "connect the dots" from Brawley to Yuma for the Centennial ride, and a new contact to work with for future activities over there.

This is Mammoth Wash today, running east and west. It is just north of the massive Algodones Dunes near Glamis that can be seen on the left of this photo. For many years in the early 1900s it was the only route available to travelers going to and from Yuma and San Diego.

Looking north, this is the same railroad track that Baker had ridden on in 1914 from Mammoth Wash south to Yuma.

Despite some challenging deep sand, there were parts of Ted Kipf Road like this that we found to be great for modern-day adventure bike riding.

Joe is seen here pointing out one of our early discoveries in Yuma. These are the remnants of the old train station shown on page 32 where Baker stayed at the end of his first day of his 1914 ride. The railroad tracks through Yuma were actually relocated in the 1920s. The town kept a short section of track in its original location with the period locomotive in the background to honor the many years of service the trains had in that location crossing over the Colorado River.

# CHAPTER 4

# YUMA TO PHOENIX / THEN & NOW

The first day of Baker's 1914 ride had ended at 7:00 p.m. just across the Colorado River at the Yuma train depot. There were sleeping rooms available there at the depot and a café nearby.

This postcard shows what downtown Yuma, Arizona looked like in 1914. Baker wasn't there very long to do any sightseeing though. After a good night's sleep at the hotel at the train station, he was off and running the next day at 6:00 a.m.

He was up at 5:00 a.m. the next morning and took off from the train station at 6:00 a.m. with his first goal for the day to locate the local postmaster. The deal he had made with the F.A.M. (Federation of American Motorcyclists) was that if he did indeed set a new transcontinental record they would certify it as long as he obeyed all the speed laws along the way, and that he could show proof that he was where he claimed he was each day. He wrote that he was able to send a few telegrams along the way on his ride, but his paper backup he carried with him was a logbook that he would have signed and date stamped at a post office each day.

The Castle Dome Mining Camp, northeast of Yuma, was in full operation at the time with over 3,000 miners living and working there. There was a post office at Castle Dome Landing that served that location. Its not a far distance from the Yuma Crossing Station to Castle Dome Landing, so it would not have taken Erwin too long to get to the postmaster's office, maybe an hour. That would have put him there about 7:00 a.m. Hopefully the postmaster was an early riser, because Baker wrote that he got his logbook stamped there. He was then on his way on Day Two and everything started well.

He noted in his journal: ***"The next morning, May 4, at 6 a.m., I was ready to start my journey to Phoenix. Knowing there would be no 'corner saloons' to stop off at, I made sure that my canteen was loaded right up to the cork. I rode to a station called Dome, there getting a post mark registration from the postmaster. Crossing the Gila River, from there I started over a road of deep washes, but outside of this there was fairly good going. Then I came into the Castle Dome Mountains and passed through this wonderful desert mountain range, which was nothing more than a series of mammoth flat-faced rocks, having the appearance of city skyscrapers, church spires or capitol domes, but without one sign of life, which could be seen from points of 80 to 100 miles. From then on I rode a very bad stretch of desert, made up of rocky gulches, deep washes and quantities of sand, all the while through intense heat."***

He was having a fairly routine ride that morning with an equal mix of amazing Arizona scenery and challenging sandwashes that taxed his years of motorcycle riding experience. But before he got to his first planned gas stop of the day, his tank ran dry and he had to push his motorcycle 4 miles in the 119-degree heat. There was a hotel in Agua Caliente, which luckily had everything that was necessary (gasoline for the motorcycle; food, water and ice for the rider) and a bed to relax on until he was back in shape to resume his ride. Without the services available at Agua Caliente, Baker could easily have suffered a heat stroke or even died that day.

After leaving Yuma, Baker's next destination for gas, food and water was this hotel, hot springs and roadhouse at Agua Caliente. Originally the hot springs were used by local Indians for therapy until the 22-room hotel was built in 1897. It was a popular stop for travelers between Yuma and Phoenix for many years and for Baker, a life-saver. On a 119-degree day, Baker ran out of gas four miles short of Agua Caliente and pushed the bike the rest of the way through the sand. Luckily there was plenty of water and ice at the hotel to cool him down. Four hours later he was re-fueled and revived enough to continue his ride over to Phoenix.

The map below shows Baker's 1914 route (purple to green to purple) versus some differences we needed to take (purple to red to purple) based on circumstances detailed in this chapter. The red dotted line shows where we were "off-course" as explained in this chapter.

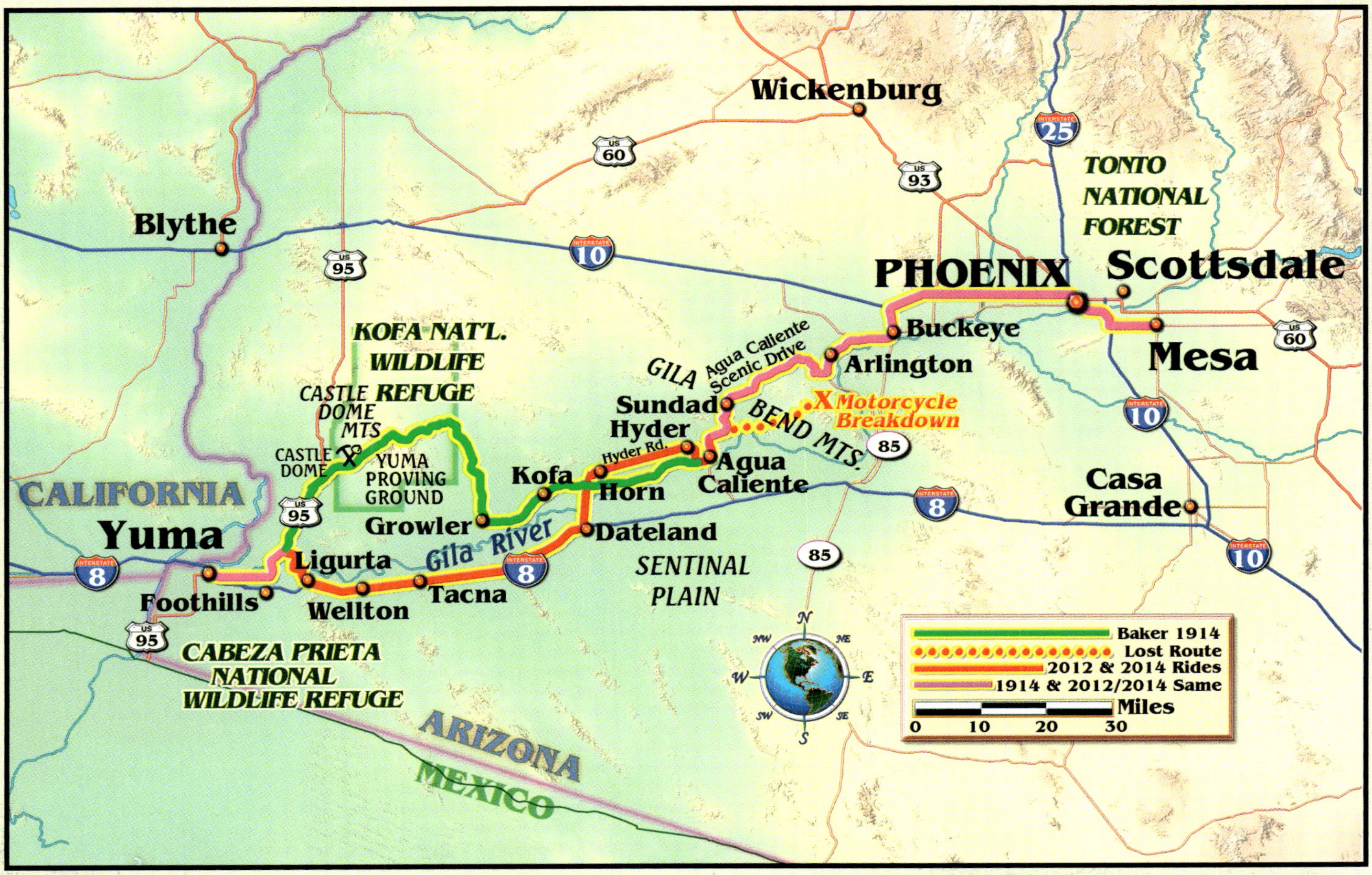


Map by Bill Tipton / Compart Maps.

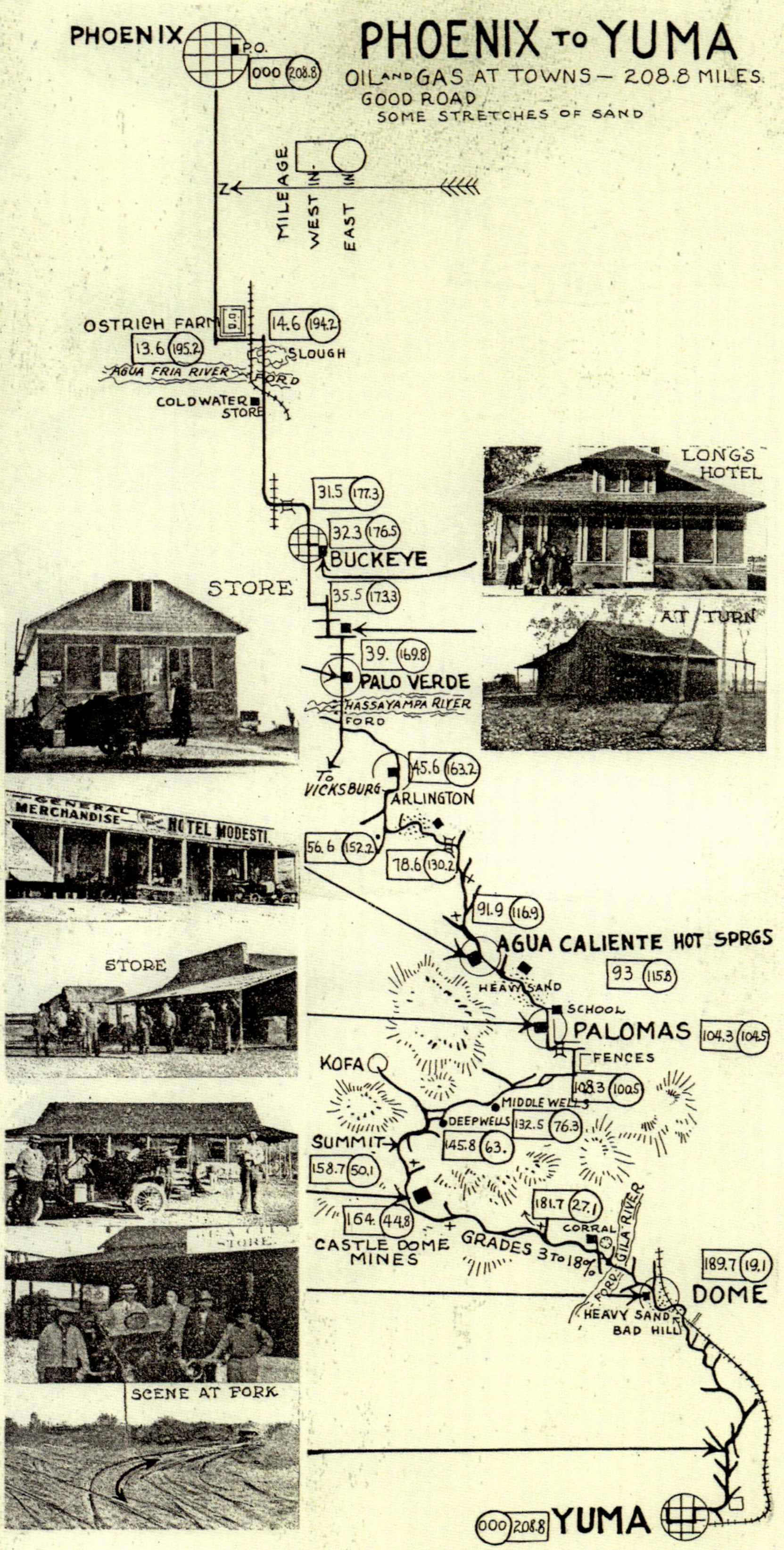


In his notes he mentioned how much the ice helped to revive him so he could get going again, ***"Four miles before reaching the town of Agua Caliente (called by the natives Water Springs) I ran out of gasoline while in deep sand, and from there I had to push my machine along until I reached the springs, with the thermometer standing at 119 degrees in the shade. There I spent four hours, having dinner and then resting up from the exertion of pushing my machine through the deep sand in the intense heat. I was so exhausted when I reached the Spring house that someone suggested pouring ice-cold water right down my spine, which certainly did revive me. I was fortunate in hitting this Spring house, because they had a little ice machine there and I think if it hadn't been for that ice machine I would never have seen the bright lights of Broadway. If I could have got a moving picture man to take pictures of the things I saw on that desert in my imagination after the heat hit me, they sure would have some moving picture stunt.***

***I found fairly good going for 14 miles from there on, and then struck sand and silt for 32 miles, riding rocky gulches and sandy washes in to Arlington. At this point I was met by Lorenzo Boido, one of the "crack" motorcycle riders of Phoenix, who escorted me into Phoenix. I was given a right warm welcome reception when I entered Phoenix by all my friends. This was 441 miles from San Diego, and I had covered the distance in two days. My friends saw to it that I had a good square meal and a soft, downy place to sleep."***

It took Baker 13 hours and 10 minutes to make the 210 mile ride to Phoenix, an average of only 16 miles per hour, but considering he was parked for four hours in Agua Caliente, that was still a productive day.

**This is a period map for travelers going to and from Yuma and Phoenix circa 1914. Note that it does not display the towns and routes with "Due North" at the top. The true route is actually more diagonal. It shows that in those days travelers went out of Yuma past Dome to the Castle Dome Mines. From there the road continued through a mountain range that today is closed for the KOFA National Wildlife Refuge. At Palomas the road was back on flat ground and ran parallel to the Gila River towards Agua Caliente. The map indicates "Heavy Sand" about where Baker ran out of gas in 1914. *Map courtesy of Arizona Historical Society.***

# DOUBLE, DOUBLE TOIL AND TROUBLE

It turned out that the ride from Yuma, AZ to Phoenix would be a very troublesome one for Erwin Baker. What are the odds that 98 years later Joe and I would also have trouble at about the same location between Yuma and Phoenix?

With San Diego to Yuma all worked out, we next were ready to tackle Baker's "Day Two," the ride from Yuma to Phoenix. Since our last trip there a few weeks earlier, I had studied the Google maps on the internet and thought I had the "overland" route figured out. It was easy to find the ghost town of Agua Caliente where Baker rested for four hours after pushing his motorcycle in 119-degree heat.

North of the Agua Caliente ghost town was the route that Baker took in 1914 to reach Buckeye, and then on to Phoenix to conclude his second day of riding. Today, that road is known as the Agua Caliente "Scenic Route" going into the west side of Phoenix. "A piece of cake," as some might refer to such an easy undertaking. When talking to one of the ladies with the Arizona Historical Society about the route, she said a person could drive a motor home through there.

So Joe and I planned our next mapping ride to knock out just the Yuma to Phoenix section. Since it was just another up and back trip, we decided to trailer the bikes over to Yuma, and brought one of Joe's friends, Michael Bryant, to drive my truck and trailer. We planned to drive to Yuma and stay at the Hilton Gardens there, unload and ride the bikes to Phoenix, while Michael drove over and met us there, then trailer everything home. That is what happened, but it turned out to be a "little" more complicated than we were expecting.

We got loaded up and drove to Yuma on April 18, 2012. The next morning, we were up early and unloaded the trailer, put our riding gear on, checked that our Satellite phones were talking to each other (100+ degree day and we were riding over 100 miles of dirt roads, at least 50 miles in some places from the nearest piece of civilization). Soon we waved goodbye to Michael and headed north on Arizona Highway 95, while he drove eastbound on Interstate 8 heading to Gila Bend, then north to Phoenix. We planned to meet up on the other side in Buckeye.

Approximately 20 miles out of Yuma, we came to where the Gila River passes under the highway. That is very near where the old Castle Dome Landing used to be where Baker got his logbook stamped. There is an unmarked road leading off to the right and my Garmin GPS was pointing it out as the Butterfield Stage Route, which once carried the stage coaches, mail carriers and others in and out between Yuma and Tucson.

**In my pre-ride studies, a paper map of the area made it look to me that Joe and I needed to proceed down Hyder Road to get to Phoenix. Listed as the "Agua Caliente Scenic Route," I plugged "Hyder Road" into my Garmin GPS and when we got there, it appeared that we were on the right route. We would realize many miles later that we were not. Joe is seen here as we headed east after stopping at the Agua Caliente ghost town.**

A look back at the road Joe and I had taken heading east. After approximately 60 miles, it was becoming obvious that we had taken the wrong route. A road that was supposed to be wide enough for a motor home, was becoming more like a Jeep road. All we had to go with now was that we were, in fact, heading in the direction of Phoenix.

This was where we knew we would be taking a diversion from Baker's 1914 route. In his journal he wrote that after he got his logbook stamped, he rode north into the Castle Dome mountains. There was a massive lead ore operation running then and it used a huge wagon that could carry up to 20 tons of ore down that road to Castle Dome Landing where it could be loaded on trains. It took 40 horses or mules to pull the wagon.

Baker make good time riding up to the Castle Dome Mine and then followed a road northeast into the mountains, then south to Palomas. From there he hit some deep sand and is where he ran out of gas about five miles short of Agua Caliente.

For Joe and I, the road north to the Castle Dome Mine is still there, in fact there is a little ghost town there that has been recreated for tourists. But in my research I learned that the road that Baker took going past the Mine goes into a restricted area for the Yuma Proving Grounds, a U.S. Army facility that is one of the largest military installations in the world. It didn't seem like a good idea to try to sneak though a place where they test artillery, rockets and bombs. But as if that wasn't enough of a reason to not take that route, the area that borders the Yuma Proving Grounds is the KOFA National Animal Refuge, which is totally off limits for any kind of motorized traffic. Baker's route essentially ended at the Castle Dome Mine. Disappointing, but as we learned back at Mammoth Wash, it was important to know what Baker's 1914 route was, even if it is not rideable today.

Instead of riding north from Dome as Baker did, we continued east on the Butterfield Stage Route, which was a fun dirt road for Adventure bikes. Then we came to Old Highway 80, which parallels Interstate 8 and rode that for about 50 miles until we got to a truck stop off I-8 at Dateland for gas, a snack and refilling our fluid supplies. We weren't too concerned about our gas range as our KTMs could go over 200 miles full, and it would only be about 95 to Buckeye. It was going to be a 100+ degree day, though, so I made sure my Camelback water pouch was full, and had some extra bottles of water in the saddlebags and granola bars, etc. We were all set for the Back Country.

From the truck stop we rode under Interstate 8 and north a few miles on a paved road (Ave. 64E) until we came to Palomas Road, and this put us back on Baker's 1914 course. We turned right and rode east until we came to Ave. 76E, turned right again, and that loops around to the old ghost town at Agua Caliente. In Baker's time this was a very active stop along the only route between Yuma and Phoenix. It's all boarded up now, so we couldn't do anything except stop and take a few photos.

## HYDER ROAD

After we had the photos taken we rode east to Agua Caliente Road, turned left and went about a mile until we came back to the road that we were on previously, now shown on the signs as Hyder Road. I will admit, my experience with GPS settings was a bit limited at that time. Since we were riding off-road its not easy to ask the Garmin to give you directions that takes you down a dirt road, so I was still referring to my paper maps for backup.

I had it all worked out in my head (and on my map) that we would turn right on Hyder Road and take that a few miles until we got to the Agua Caliente Scenic Route. We would go left there and that would take us all the way over to Buckeye. I could practically taste the Margaritas that awaited us.

So we turned right at the intersection of Agua Caliente Road and Hyder Road and proceeded east on the pavement for about a mile, then it switched to a dirt road. But it was a super-wide dirt road, the kind for motor homes like I had heard about, so I wasn't worried. And my Garmin said we were on Hyder Road. In a few miles we should come to the "Y" in the road just like Baker had done in 1914.

We rode farther than I was expecting, but finally after about ten miles we came to what looked to be the long-awaited "Y" in the road. There was even a road sign with an arrow pointing to the right that read: "Painted Rock Petroglyph." And below it there was an arrow that pointed to the left. It said: "Dead End. No Outlet." Hmm. All I knew was we needed to turn left. And the road to left, by the way, was just as well graded as the road to the right. Joe and I were connected with Cardo helmet radios, and when he asked me why they would say "Dead End," I said something like "They probably don't want people out here in cars getting stuck." Good answer, I thought at the time.

So we took off to the left with our spirits a bit higher. I can't speak for Joe, but I was pretty sure we were finally on the right road. We went about another ten miles and then we took a sharp right. The dirt road ended and dumped us down onto a two-track trail and into a pretty deep and loose sandwash. In an instant we went from checking out the tall cactus and other scenery to the "Charge of the Light Brigade." It was obvious we had to get on it and motocross those big 990s through the wash until we could find some solid ground. We eventually did get to the other side. It was hot and after that exercise we started going through our water. Joe also mentioned that his 990's dashboard was going off and then back on again. We both commented that our temperature warning lights for the bikes were flashing as we came out of the sandy wash.

We rested just a few minutes, but it was so hot by then—105-degrees that day—that we decided we'd be cooler if we were moving and it looked like good trail ahead, albeit a two track. I wondered how a motorhome could possibly have driven through that wash, but was sure in my mind that we had not missed the left turn for the "Scenic Route." In retrospect, this is probably where I should have turned around, but there was no "Plan B" in my head if this wasn't the right road. We would just have had to ride back the way we came to Dateland.

**A few miles after the previous photo the "Jeep road" suddenly became a single track trail up a steep hill. Joe is seen here having a good look at it before he made his attempt to ride up it. No fault of his, but he didn't make it.**

So we continued forward about another 10 miles following very closely most of the time a railroad track that went east and west. It was getting late in the day and we didn't have a clear view of Phoenix yet. In fact we were starting to approach a range of low mountains that were a little concerning since we were on the big adventure bikes. We stopped at one point and took a look at the map, drank about all the water we had left, and talked about Joe's flashing dashboard. After checking out one road that went up the mountain, we opted for a second route that just had a few rolling hills to get over. But that trail only brought us to an even steeper mountain than the first one and the two-track trail turned to a single track.

The crazy thing was that even though it was beginning to sink in that we were on the wrong road, the map on my Garmin still said it was Hyder Road. What hadn't sunk in yet was that just because a road or trail has a name that shows up on your Garmin doesn't necessarily mean it is passible in, or on a motor vehicle.

My feeling then was that we just needed to turn back. We were riding bikes that were approximately

A broken battery bracket shorted out Joe's KTM and there we were with only one working motorcycle as the sun was beginning to set. I was beginning to have thoughts that we might be spending the night out there in the Arizona desert, but Joe and I decided to ride out two-up in the dark.

double the weight of most MX or Dual Sport bikes and I thought it was too big a risk trying to get them up the hill without a crash. And even if we got up this side, we didn't know what we'd have to do to come down the other side? And if we didn't make it up and fell over, picking them up would be really hard to do on the side of a hill. But Joe was still optimistic. He sold me on the idea that he could take a run up the hill just to see how close we might be to Phoenix. His point was: "What if its just on the other side of the hill?" To turn around would mean riding back about 50 or so miles to Dateland. Okay, so the plan was he would go up there, and then come back down and report on what he saw.

That sounded okay to me, so I found a good tree with some shade while Joe motored off and headed up the hill. He hit the throttle hard at the bottom and was going like a true hillclimber until about halfway up when I heard the motor die. I figured he would either get it re-started and try to continue up the hill, or more likely turn it around and ride down. There was a tree on the hill that blocked my view of what was going on, but it was just silent for a few minutes. Finally I see Joe walking down the hill and the KTM was still where it was on the hill when the motor cut off.

When he got back where I was he said everything on the dash was out, and the motor would not re-start. He had spent those extra minutes looking at a few possibilities and concluded that most likely the electronics system on the bike had melted down. After all the reports of his dashboard going off and on that afternoon in the heat that was a hard theory to argue with. Didn't matter really.

So there we were. It was about 5:00 in the afternoon, we were out of water, about 50 miles from anywhere and everywhere and we had one dead motorcycle. Our first move was to relocate back where we were earlier checking out that alternate way over the mountain. We had a better view of the overall desert there, and figured if someone might be coming to look for us we'd be easier to spot. It wasn't a long distance so Joe just walked it and I rode my bike over. We would have to deal with Joe's 990 later.

Our first thoughts were that we needed to get picked up. We had some cell phone coverage that came in and out, and also a satellite phone. So we were able to contact Michael Bryant and told him about our dilemma.

So he made some calls and finally found a towing business in Buckeye, Hamilton Towing Service, who said they had a 4-wheel drive tow truck that could come out there. I got on the phone with their driver, Rick, and told him where we were and he was on his way. We weren't sure yet if he could get Joe's 990 out, but knew help was on the way for Joe and I. He said it would take at least an hour to get there.

Well, it turned out we were having some problems getting our correct location explained to Rick, as he did not have any GPS equipment. He knew the area and was thinking the only possible place we could be was on the "Scenic Route." So he drove up and back along that route and of course never saw us because we weren't on it.

By now it was pretty well dark. At one point I was telling Joe that if we had to spend the night out there I did have some emergency stuff with me, like space blankets, matches, etc. etc. Joe wasn't having it. No way were we spending the night out there.

After about an hour had passed I talked to Rick again and he then asked if we were north of the railroad tracks, or south? When I told him we were on the south side, he let me know that he could not get there in his truck. But he knew where that spot was with the sign to the Painted Rock Petroglyph and said if we could get there he could meet us there. So that was the plan... except there was Joe and I, with one running bike, and it was now dark. Real dark.

So the game plan was we needed to start heading back the way we came, and obviously we needed to pack double. Fortunately I had the Garmin GPS and it marks a blue line wherever you go. So to backtrack I just needed to follow the blue line on the screen, and my Warn spotlights added a little extra help to the stock headlight to brighten the trail.

At first Joe was hesitant about the idea of us riding double. He knew how hard it had been riding solo through those sandwashes when the sun was shining, and figured nothing productive was going to come from trying it two-up in the dark. Joe suggested we try to have me blaze the trail with the lights of the bike and he would walk it. Well, that didn't work out. For starters we were about twenty miles from where we would meet the truck driver, and also it was was pretty unrideable going at a pace that Joe could keep on foot.

I had the KTM set up with a Saddlemen fabric travel trunk strapped to my seat, so we unstrapped it and left it behind. Now Joe could get on and ride on the back and we'd take it slow and easy. Getting through those two sandwashes in the pitch dark with Joe on the back was, for sure, a challenge. Don't ask me how, but we never crashed. If anything, Joe's extra weight on the back helped us get traction in the soft sand, but it was pretty "squirrely." Once we got through the last sandwash the road immediately was back to the wide dirt road and we cruised at a decent pace to that cutoff and Rick from Hamilton Towing was there waiting for us. By then it was about 9:00 p.m. and both Joe and I had gone for about 5 hours without anything to drink. Rick's desert experience was obvious when he welcomed us with cold bottles of water. I never knew water could taste so good!

We also had been keeping Michael Bryant up to date on the Sat phone, so he knew the plan that we'd throw my bike on the tow truck and ride back in the cab with Rick and meet him at Hamilton Towing in Buckeye.

## DRUG DEALERS AND MOUNTAIN LIONS

That night when Joe and I were stuck out in the hills, we had friends and family putting out the call for people who knew the area in case a rescue was needed the next day. We were out of water and another 105-degree day was in store. But we were also trying to figure out how we were going to get Joe's KTM out of there. Early the next morning, a friend of my son-in-law Ryan made contact with a man in the Phoenix area named Bryan Glider who was in a Toyota Four Wheel Drive club. Luckily we had SPOT GPS units with us, and had them on SPOT Share, so others could see where we were. Joe's SPOT was still putting out a signal, so Bryan went online and said he saw right where the bike was at, knew that area and could go get it. He said he had a Toyota 4Runner converted into a Rock Crawler with a winch on the front. He let me know he'd had to basically carry it out on the winch, but I had nobody else in line with any other ideas.

So the plan was he would go get it and bring it back to a designated area out in the hills. I had my truck and trailer, but we felt the road in would be too rough, so I got back with my guys at Hamilton Towing and arranged to go out there with Rick in the tow truck to get the bike and he'd then bring it out where my truck and trailer was parked.

As we were driving along, Rick asked me if when Joe and I were waiting for him the night before if we saw any mountain lions? Surprised, I said "No," then asked if there are any out there. He laughed and said, "Oh yeah, lots of them." Then he added there's also lots of drug dealers out there too. He said they wait until after dark so the helicopters can't see them like they can in the daytime, then come out and do their deals. At that point I realized it was a very good thing we didn't camp out.

**After Joe and I made it back to civilization the previous night, one remaining problem was that the KTM he was riding was still out where we left it in the desert. Thanks to a great effort by family and friends to put out online calls for help, we were able to connect with Bryan Glider from Phoenix, who volunteered to take his 4WD Toyota 4Runner out the next day to fetch the bike. Thanks to SPOT Share, we were able to broadcast the location of the motorcycle for him.**

Once we had the bikes all loaded in the trailer, it was back to Orange County to get Joe's 990 fixed and figure out what went wrong with my map work. We had Baker's trail confirmed to Agua Caliente, but there was a broken link to be solved later on regarding how to get from there to Buckeye and on to Phoenix.

## KTM REPAIRS AND LESSONS IN READING MAPS

When we got back from Arizona, I took the KTMs over to Boyko Racing for service and to see why Joe's 990 died out on the trail. It turned out we didn't melt the electronics after all. A KTM 990 has the battery mounted in a box below the motor and a bracket had broken and allowed the battery to move around. The bouncing on the trail was apparently enough to cause the dashboard to go on and off, but it was his attempt to climb the hill that let it move all the way to where it made contact with something metallic and everything shorted out. Ted Boyko fixed the bracket, in fact modified it so it couldn't move around like it did, and also updated my bike as well. We

## WHAT WENT RIGHT ON HYDER ROAD

**I have been a fan of SPOT GPS for many years, but never has it ever come in more handy than it did when Joe and I were stuck in the desert. Despite our dilemma of a broken motorcycle, and no water or food, in the back of our minds we knew we had SPOTs signaling our location and if necessary we could have hit the 9-1-1 feature to request a helicopter rescue.**

If I had done a better job researching the maps, both in paper form and online, Joe and I would not have gotten stuck out there in the desert. And yes, maybe I trusted my route plan longer than I should have before deciding to turn around. But so it goes sometimes out on the trail. Mistakes can happen and the outcome is often dependent on how prepared you are for unplanned situations.

It was a 105-degree day when all this happened, and being 50 miles from the nearest assistance it is possible that Joe and I could have died from heat exposure if it were not for some things we did right. Here are the main ones:

1. SPOT GPS: I am big fan of the SPOT GPS Personal Trackers. If you ride motorcycles or otherwise travel to remote locations, I think a SPOT is a must-have product. If you are not familiar with them, you can go online and see all the features and options they offer. But in a nutshell you carry the GPS unit on your bike, or in a pocket or backback. You can set it into a full tracking mode if you want to record a full route you take. There is also an online feature they have called SPOT Share and you can post it when you go and others can view it. Or, you can leave it in a mode where you can hit an "OK" button and people on your designated message list will get a text or email that everything is okay where you are. Family members like to get that one. Should you encounter some mechanical problem or have a non-serious injury that would involve someone driving out to your

never had any problems again with the batteries.

It actually didn't take very long to figure out where we got sidetracked. As soon as I could get back online I checked Google Maps and zoomed in super close. Ouch! Did I ever feel dumb when I realized that I had put too much faith in my paper maps. Where it appeared on the map that the turnoff was 5 or so miles down Hyder Road, I actually needed to go straight at the intersection of Agua Caliente Road and Hyder Road!

Now I could see where we needed to go. The problem was that it needed to be physically ridden to get that section onto our Garmins for the final GPX file we would give everyone going on our ride the following year. After what Joe and I had just experienced, I knew we had to make sure everyone got that section correct. But because we had so much of the country yet to be mapped, we moved on with our mapping rides and it would be mid-February, 2014 until we got back and rode that section. Ha! It turned out to be one of the best roads for Adventure bikes on the whole ride.

**location you can hit a HELP button. And finally, if there is a serious injury or other life-threatening situations, you can hit a 9-1-1 button and you literally are calling for a helicopter or related emergency pickup virtually anywhere in the world. It is not a free service for that last one, but SPOT does have an insurance policy you can buy to cover that expensive level of coverage.**

**In the situation that Joe and I were in, we were able to direct Bryan in the Toyota 4Runner to my SPOT Share page and he was able to see exactly where Joe's KTM was. We had two SPOTS, by the way. Joe's was in the tracking mode to show our route. The other we used for "tagging" our route with "OK" signals. If, however, we had not gotten picked up that night and were going to be out there in the desert the next day without water, we could have, and would have used one and hit the 9-1-1 button and emergency help would have been on its way to get us.**

**Since this all happened, SPOT has improved its product even more and now has a model where you have the ability to include a brief text line with a help message, such as "Broken Chain" or even "Broken wrist, but OK" if you were close enough that someone could come get a friend within a reasonable distance, and it wasn't really a Life Flight situation. SPOT also has some reasonably priced Satellite phones now as well. And by the way, I have no relationship with SPOT or means for financial gain by giving you this information about them.**

2. **Satellite phones. In addition to SPOT GPS units that we each carried, I bought two Satellite phones, one to carry and another for our support vehicle. Once you get out of cell phone range you are pretty helpless without a way to communicate. Might be a little extreme for most kinds of trail riding situations, but very welcome when you really need them.**

3. **Its one thing to have Satellite phones, but do they work? Way back in Yuma at the start of the day, not only did we test the two Satellite phones to make sure they were both working, we also checked to make sure we both had the numbers to call each other if necessary.**

4. **We also had a pre-ride discussion in Yuma about what our emergency plan was, so Michael had our home numbers, etc in case family needed to be reached.**

5. **Social Media. As Joe and I awaited the arrival of the tow truck, I made some calls and one was to my daughter who got the word out quickly on Facebook and to numerous people that we needed help on the west side of Phoenix. That's how we made the contact with Bryan in the 4Runner who went and picked up Joe's KTM.**

6. **Water! We carried as much water as we could in the KTM saddlebags and I was wearing a Camelback water pack. In 100+ degree heat you have to drink as much water as you can to keep from getting dehydrated.**

7. **Lastly, we didn't use them, but if we had needed to camp out there that night, I did have an emergency pack with me that had a flashlight, space blanket, pocket knife (for fighting off mountain lions or drug dealers!) and a few other essentials.**

CHAPTER 5:

# PHOENIX TO SPRINGERVILLE / THEN & NOW

In the early 1900s, hard-packed, graded roads were the exception and not the rule, but that is exactly what Baker found when he sped up the Apache Trail on Day 3 of his ride. The 64-mile road had just recently been built to transport construction equipment from Phoenix to build a dam at Roosevelt Lake (see sidebar: Building The Apache Trail).

After his unplanned four-hour stop the previous day at Agua Caliente, Baker finally did get going that afternoon and rode uneventfully after that and was greeted by friends in Phoenix. After a good night's sleep, he was up early the next morning and ready to get back on the trail.

What was in store for him was a full day of riding that would put both rider and his 7-horsepower Indian motorcycle to the test. His plan was to ride from the desert town of Phoenix (near sea level) up to 9,647 feet in the mountains and over to Springerville. In all, he would travel 265.5 miles and unlike some places he had ridden where he could get some speed up, he would be tackling many miles of twisty turns with steep hills to climb and descend. He noted, ***"On the morning of May 5 I told the boys that I was going to Springerville. Ariz., and that I was going to do it that day before sundown. Everyone gave me the laugh, because they knew I had some riding before me."***

Baker rode due east from Phoenix to the town of Mesa, then took the road past the stage coach station at Tortilla Flat. He then proceeded approximately 60 miles up what is now known as the Apache Trail. Baker referred to it as the "Roosevelt Route" and added that it was ***"similar to the picturesque Grand Canyon of Arizona."***

## BUILDING THE APACHE TRAIL

### Excerpt from Arizona Centennial: A Century of Cooperation

Construction of Roosevelt Dam was a logistical nightmare because the site was so remote—nearly 60 miles from Mesa and 40 miles from the copper mining town of Globe. Although dam construction commenced on August 24, 1903, a supply/construction road first had to be built, along an old Indian pathway, in order to haul men, equipment, building materials, and supplies from Mesa to the dam site. The route presented challenges due to steep gradients and narrow right-of-way, challenges that required more money than originally thought. Through special bond issues authorized by the Congress, Salt River Valley towns were able to borrow the money needed to complete the road.

Apache Indians from the San Carlos Reservation provided the bulk of the labor for road construction. While there was initial skepticism about their ability to do the difficult road work, they soon demonstrated that they were up to the task. Louis Hill, Supervising Engineer, first said they were undernourished and too weak to work hard. He paid them only $1.50 per day ($2.00 was the average) until they became stronger. But it was not long before he rated Apache workmen above the Mexican and Anglo workers. The Apache workmen lived apart from the other construction crews (who also lived in separated camps) and often had their wives and children living with them. Their talent and skill for building with dry-laid masonry resulted in a roadbed that endures and portions of it can be seen today.

The new 64-mile-long road was finished in December 1904, at a cost of over $200,000. Apache workers also built a sawmill road in the Sierra Ancha Mountains where lumber for construction of the dam was cut and milled, as well as roads towards Globe and Payson. By the time Roosevelt Dam was finished in 1911, nearly $500,000 was spent building 112 miles of roads to the dam site at a cost of roughly $4,500 per mile. Today this road is known as the Apache Trail.

Once Baker arrived at the Roosevelt Lake Dam, he had the 40-mile ride to Globe, which was the seat of Gila County. The current Arizona Highway 60 was not built yet, so he would have continued east on what became Arizona State Highway 73. From Globe he went through Cutter and on to a town then called Rice, which eventually was absorbed by its neighbor San Carlos. This was the gateway to the San Carlos Apache Indian Reservation and the section of road from Cutter to Rice (San Carlos) later became Indian Route 6.

Baker turned to the north there and rode what became Indian Routes 4, 9 and 10. His next planned stop was Fort Apache, a ride of about 60 miles into the mountains, which had to be some of the most challenging roads yet for his 7-horsepower Indian. He commented, ***"I will say right here that it is absolutely impossible for a motorcycle to go over this route without a two-*** *speed, for after I started out of the lower sea level to go up into the higher altitudes, I used my two-speed every inch of the way. The ride of this day was a continuous one over narrow, dangerous cliff roads and the change of climate from the hot desert sands to the snow-peaked mountains was enough to give a man the shivers and shake him off his machine."*

**This period postcard shows what a nice, wide road the Apache Trail was back in Baker's time, and it is actually still much like this today. Now listed as Arizona Highway 88, it was originally named after local Apache Indians who provided the manpower to construct it in the early1900s.**

**The map below shows how we followed Baker's route from the Mesa, AZ area up Arizona Highway 88 (purple line), also known as the Apache Trail, then southeast to Globe. The current AZ highway 60 was not built yet in 1914, so Baker rode to San Carlos (green line), where he picked up a road in the Apache Indian reservation to Fort Apache, then northeast to Springerville. Because of travel restrictions on Indian lands, we took AZ highway 60 (red line) for our rides in 2012 & 2014.**

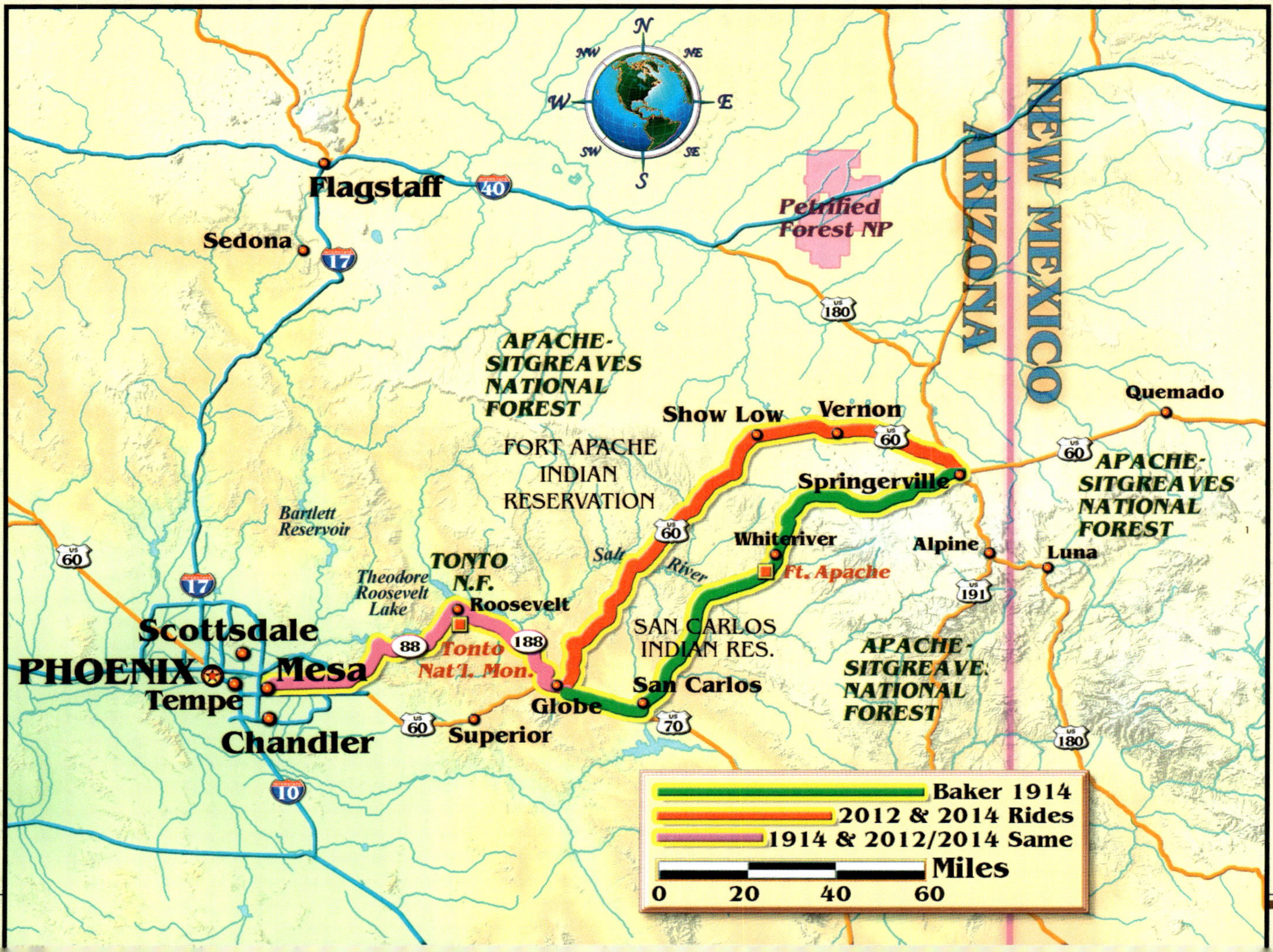


*Map by Bill Tipton / Compart Maps.*

Since he traveled alone most of the time, Baker did carry a pistol with him for protection. His only reported use of this 38-caliber Smith & Wesson was at the Indian reservation at Fort Apache when a swarm of wild dogs angrily encircled him when he arrived and he had to shoot and kill two of them to get through. *Photo from 1914 Indian booklet.*

## INCIDENT AT FORT APACHE

On his way north to Cooley's Ranch Baker made a stop at Fort Apache. Before he had left Phoenix that morning one of his friends noted he didn't have much in the way of pistol power to be heading off into the remote Indian lands. It turned out the friend's advice was accurate. He had an unfortunate incident there with some wild dogs, but was able to handle the situation with his upgraded armaments.

Here are Baker's notes on his stop at Fort Apache: *"I also had some very unkind comments made to me regarding the little "pop-gun" I was carrying, and Doc Boido stepped up to me, took the toy away and snapped a real "cannon" on my handlebars—a Smith & Wesson 38-caliber long, for which I was mighty glad afterward. The gun looked all right to me because it had three notches on the butt of it. It proved afterward that I sure did have use for this gun, for while coming through the Indian reservation at Fort Apache I was given a big welcome by more dogs than Indians, and I had to put this gun to use. These dogs were worse than wolves and I had to drop two of them in their tracks to get by. I stopped at the Indian agency (not Indian Motocycle agency, but the Government Indian agent) and some of the Indians gathered around making noises that sounded to me like: 'Ugh! Heap fine pony! Heap fast pony! Ugh! Go get 'em pony.' "*

After his brief stop at Fort Apache, he rode north through the White Mountains and made a stop at Cooley's Ranch (now McNary, AZ.), which was a large spread of land south of what today is called Show Low. That town reportedly was named for having changed hands due to a legal dispute back in the 1800s. The issue was decided over a simple card draw, "Show low and you win." The winner was Mr. Cordyon E. Cooley. His ranch, known as Cooley's Ranch, was located approximately where the current Hon-Dah Indian casino-resort-convention center lies today in Pinetop, just west of the town of McNary.

The mountainous terrain between Cooley's Ranch east to Springerville was some of the twistiest and challenging that Baker had encountered yet. It was also his longest day so far. He rode for 12 hours and went 265 miles, an average of approximately 22 miles per hour. He wrote: ***"When I reached the top of these lofty mountains I felt as if I had been down on a visit to "Old Nick" and had used my excursion ticket back to heaven, because that good cold air revived me, gave me new life and spurred me on my way. I could have ridden further, but I felt as if I was getting cross-eyed from making the twists and turns through those paths on the cliffs. Some of them made me feel that I could almost shake hands with myself so I rested the night at Springerville over night."***

It would take Baker 12 hours to ride from Phoenix to Springerville on Day 3. He stopped to take this photo of the road through the mountains north of Fort Apache. This photo from the 1914 Indian booklet shows a slightly downhill section, but he had also encountered uphill sections like this, a real test for his 7-horsepower, two-speed Indian motorcycle.

## 2012:

By June of 2012, Joe and I had gone back and forth between Orange County and various parts of California's Imperial County and Arizona six times. It was now time for us to hit the road and get the route bookmarked. Because of some other commitments I had with my business, I needed to cut the run across the country into two parts. In June we would ride from California to Ohio, return home, and come back to Ohio again in July to resume the mapping to the east coast.

We took off from Aliso Viejo, CA. on June 10, 2012. Since we knew we would later be riding the Agua Caliente-to-Phoenix link that we did not complete in April, we just rode straight out on Interstate 10 and checked into a hotel in Goodyear, a suburb of Phoenix. It was 104 degrees when we arrived.

The next morning we made a few stops at some hotels that looked promising as lodging for the 2014 Centennial ride. We wanted to make it to Santa Fe that night, so we decided to ride across the Phoenix valley straight to Globe on Arizona Highway 60. This meant on this ride we needed to bypass AZ88, the Apache Trail or what Baker called the "Roosevelt Route."

We returned, however, in March, 2013 to ride and bookmark it on our Garmin GPS. We were joined on that ride by Pete Pfeifer, a local rider from Tucson, who I had been talking with often about the route through Arizona. Joe, Pete and I had a great ride and agreed the Apache Trail would be one of the highlights of the whole Centennial ride. It was just as Baker had described.

**Nowhere in Baker's journal from his 1914 ride did he express so much amazement at the terrain as he did on Day 3 when he rode from Phoenix to Springerville. This scenic overlook shows the route of the Apache Trail as it carved its way north to Roosevelt Lake. Our excitement when we rode it in 2012, and again in 2014, was that it is the most unchanged part of the whole 3,000+ mile route that Baker traveled in 1914.**

It was always so exciting when we knew we were on the very same road that E.G. Baker had ridden on a century ago.

For our ride, Pete brought along a note for me to carry.

Many people like Pete who live in and around the Indian lands tend to have, and show, their respect for America's first inhabitants, the Indians, and we appreciated him providing background material such as the blessing.

Thanks Pete Pfeifer.

## Apache Blessing

- May the sun bring you new energy by day,
- May the moon softly restore you by night,
- May the rain wash away your worries,
- May the breeze blow new strength into your being,
- May you walk gently through the world and know its beauty all the days of your life.

On our first ride east, Joe and I stayed on Arizona Highway 60 from Globe north to Show Low, then east to Springerville. This modern route bypassed the actual route that Baker would have taken. Something that I spent a lot of time studying were the current roads within the Apache Indian Territory. Baker would have ridden on them in 1914 after passing through Globe and on to San Carlos, then north to Fort Apache. I also consulted with Pete Pfeifer and we talked about riding through the Indian country, about permits, gasoline and other issues and concluded it was better that we stick to the current U.S. Highway 60 through the towns of Globe, Show Low and over to Springerville, where Baker had stopped for the night in 1914. Another case of *riding* Cannon Ball's Trail being different than *finding* it.

Travelers today through that area actually need to purchase two separate permits to travel through the Apache Indian Reservations: the White River Apache Reservation on the north side, and the San Carlos Apache Indian Reservation on the south side.

We still weren't sure if the 2014 ride would stop in all the same cities that Baker had, or not, so we stopped in Springerville to have a look at their hotel accommodations.

Our June mapping ride continued to Santa Fe, New Mexico.

**Here I am getting ready to start a new day as Joe and I rode east in June of 2012 to map out the route of Cannon Ball's Trail.**

**Unlike the twisty and rough dirt roads in Indian country that Baker rode in 1914, AZ Highway 60 north of Globe is a great stretch of road with some amazing views.**

**Baker wrote in his journal how the terrain became much like the Grand Canyon and we certainly found plenty of examples of that on our ride.**

**The White River canyon on AZ60 offers some spectacular views, and also gives us an idea of the altitude change that Baker encountered on his ride in 1914.**

# CHAPTER 6

# SPRINGERVILLE TO SANTA FE THEN & NOW

**After riding the day before from near sea level in Phoenix to over 9,600 feet in the mountains north of Fort Apache, Baker had better conditions on Day 4 on the road east from Springerville. He started out with a 125-mile dash to Magdalena, NM, got gas, and rode to Albuquerque where he had a dinner stop. He then continued on to Santa Fe to end a 350-mile day of riding.**

When Baker arrived in Springerville, Arizona the night of May 5th, he had accomplished one major aspect of his journey: he had reached the highest altitude of his coast to coast adventure. All of the major hillclimbing that needed to be done since he left sea level back in Phoenix was now behind him. In a few days he would descend off the upper mesa at Raton, New Mexico down to the "flat lands" of Kansas and the central Prairie.

His main challenge would be to keep his equipment working and to not run out of gas. He was heading into cattle country and there were not a lot of towns directly ahead. When he left Springerville, it was about a 125-mile ride to Magdalena, New Mexico to get to the next gas stop. That's about the same distance he rode in Arizona on Day 2 when he ran out of gas heading to Agua Caliente, so he was likely a little concerned about making it to Magdalena.

He noted in his logbook: ***"On the morning of May 6, I started down the mountain, making sure that my brakes were limber and ready for work. I left Springerville with an early start, the next station I had in mind being Magdalena. From Magdalena I rode to Secur, New Mexico and from there started for Albuquerque."***

The route from Springerville to Magdalena to Secur (now known as Socorro) was a long dirt road, running east, winding slightly at times. It was originally used mainly for cattle drives into that portion of New Mexico but was gaining notariety as a key roadway in the new "Ocean-to-Ocean Highway network, linking the Santa Fe Trail with roads to and from the west coast.

Once Baker arrived in Secur, the climate and landscape changed a lot. The Rio Grande River runs north and south through the valley that includes Secur, then Albuquerque to the north, and farther yet is Santa Fe. The valley he was now in had a sandy base alongside the river. There were (and still are) some Indian villages he would have passed along the way as he headed north on the old Indian road. After getting gas in Magdalena, he had a ride of approximately 105 miles to Albuquerque.

Baker demonstrated a very descriptive writing style when he noted his feelings of successfully getting through that valley. He knew that from that point forward he would have a better defined route, especially as he approached the beginning of the Santa Fe Trail that would lead him all the way to Missouri and beyond.

He wrote: "***At this point I started on a desert stretch, which was exceedingly hard going, passing through 90 miles of alkali desert. Scattered here and there over this trail were the bleached bones of cattle and old-time prairie schooners, and to me it seemed like passing through the 'Valley of Death,' after seeing these, the monuments of pioneers who had started out like many others to make history. These sights did give me a creepy feeling, because I figured if I ran out of water or gasoline, or if my machine should break down, that the Indian motorcycle would be the monument that would mark my last resting place.***

***I finally landed at Albuquerque, breathing easy because I knew I had placed almost the worst of the route behind me. I stood on the edge of the desert with my hat in hand, bidding it good-bye, and hoping that***

*I could stick up a record which no one else would attempt to pull down, because no matter how often one crosses the Great Desert, he is apt to go among the missing. And yet—should this record of mine ever be lowered, I will again stand ready to cross the desert on an Indian.*

*That day I had gone without dinner, and in Albuquerque I made up for it with a big square meal, and feeling so fine after this meal, I decided to continue on and make Santa Fe, New Mexico before turning in. The road between these two points was over mountain cliffs, but it was just like a boulevard, and I certainly did burn up the gasoline. This hung up a record of 350.3 miles for that day's riding and at Santa Fe I put up for the night. Before I went to bed at Santa Fe I had another good meal."*

**When Baker got to Socorro (then called Secur) he crossed the bridge over the Rio Grande River. He would now turn north and follow the river to Santa Fe, passing through some Indian villages along the way.**

**Baker got someone to snap this photo of him as he began his journey through one last stretch of desert, about 90 miles long, between Socorro and Albuquerque. In his journal he noted "it seemed like passing through the Valley of Death" seeing "bleached bones of cattle and old-time prairie schooners."**

Map by Bill Tipton / Compart Maps.

**The map here of Day 4 shows how similar our route to Santa Fe, NM in 2012 and 2014 was with Baker's. Other than now being widened and paved, the section from Springerville to Socorro (purple line) was virtually the same as Baker rode in 1914. We used the red line from Socorro to Santa Fe because, in reality, today's Interstate 25 runs parallel to the old road -- which still today passes through some inhabited and active Indian villages dating back to Baker's time. Also, he was not specific which route he took from Albuquerque to Santa Fe, so the one we chose was our best guess.**

## 2012:

ther Joe or I even saying a word, we just put our bikes in gear and headed over to the other place. And it was closed too!

What a cruel trick had been played on us. I later saw Pie Town featured on the CBS *Sunday Morning* television program and one of the two owners said that rather than compete for the pie business, they alternate days that they are open "so everyone can get some pie." I guess they must have had their calendars mixed up the day Joe and I came through?

We were so bummed out after getting locked in about the pie, but we carried on. The next planned stop was for gas at another tiny community called Datil, about twenty more miles. When we arrived there was just one row of gas pumps, and they were the type where you had to go inside to pay. When Joe and I were at the cash register we noticed they had a restaurant, the kind with lots of framed photos on the walls, plus a huge buck deer head with antlers mounted on the wall. It was about 4:00 in the afternoon, and we thought why don't we go ahead and get our pie and some coffee here?

Soon we had menus, but Joe noticed on a chalkboard the Special of the Day was a steak sandwich. That sounded great, so we quickly changed plans and ordered steak sandwiches. Turned out to be the most amazing steak sandwich either Joe or I could ever remember having...the steak was way bigger than the bread and had a flavor that was incredible. We talked to the people there and learned they have their own cattle there on the ranch, so they control everything from the field to the plate. In my notebook that night I wrote in the Eagle Guest Ranch Café for a gas stop and dinner for the group on the 2014 ride. Steak sandwiches, of course.

When we left Datil, we just needed to bring it in to Santa Fe. We had already ridden roughly 300 miles that day and still had another 200 to go. Highway 60 was a four-lane highway that continued from Datil to

**When Joe and I rode through Springerville in 2012, we spotted this section on the map called "old Highway 60" making its way east from town. We went to check it out and it only runs a few miles, apparently not part of a road improvement project bringing AZ60 right through the downtown section. It does seem likely that Baker would have used this stretch of road in 1914.**

Springerville is the last Arizona stop on Highway 60 heading east towards Socorro, New Mexico. When Joe and I were on our mapping ride in June 2012, we were keeping the Centennial ride in mind for 2014. We made a stop in Springerville to check possible hotel rooms, then continue riding east on Highway 60. It was going to be a long day for us, started in Mesa and we had reservations for that night in Santa Fe.

The highway becomes a pretty straight stretch of road and while we had not experienced the physical wear and tear that Baker had back in Arizona, it felt good to stretch our legs and start to enjoy the ride touring-style.

One light moment we had began about 40 miles past Springerville when we started seeing road signs for a place called "Pie Town" and pictures of homemade-style pies. There were a few more signs as we got closer and at one point I said to Joe in my helmet radio: "I could sure go for a piece of pie." He agreed and we now had pie on the brain. Funny the kinds of things you think about riding down the road.

So finally we arrived at Pie Town and we saw two restaurants...one on the right and another across the street. So we pulled off to the right, and I started to think of what flavor pie I was going to order. And then we saw a "Closed" sign in the window. I don't recall ei-

Socorro, then we connected with Interstate 25 North. One last highlight of things to see and note on Highway 60 was what is called the "Intergalactic Array" of huge satellite dishes that fill out a large field not far from the highway. "Supposedly" all that happens there is they listen for transmissons from around the galaxy, but it was hard to not start thinking about episodes of the *X-Files* as we rode by.

It was a real windy night as the sun went down and Joe and I were now just on a "speed run" for Santa Fe. We had reservations at the Santa Fe Sage Inn, which turned out to be a very nice and "motorcycle friendly" hotel for our overnight stay. As we rode, I thought it was exciting that we would be spending the night in another town that Baker had stayed at. He was there the night of May 6, 1914.

We were always interested in local knowledge, so the next morning we met up with Roger Pattison, a local, and avid motorcyclist who puts on tours in his area. He had volunteered to be our guide that day as we tried to work out our routes and points of interest.

**The road though Springerville is part of a 1911 route designation called the National Old Trails Road, created by the National Society of the Daughters of the American Revolution. It became the basis of America's first identified network of highways. In Springerville, one of twelve "Madonna of the Trail" statues can be found that were erected by the NSDAR to honor the role of women in conquering the wilderness and establishing homes as America moved west. Interestingly, seven of the twelve statues are in cities on Cannon Ball's Trail. This one was built in 1928.**

**After making it to Santa Fe, New Mexico on our mapping ride of 2012, Joe Colombero (seen here) and I prepare to continue our ride east. We didn't have any support vehicle with us on this trip to haul any parts, extra luggage, etc., so we carried everything for the trip with us in our saddlebags and tank bags. A true road trip.**

# CHAPTER 7

# SANTA FE TO WATROUS / THEN & NOW

So far, Baker had only experienced one delay of four hours to recover physically after pushing his motorcycle in the Arizona sand for four miles in 119-degree heat. Everything else had gone well and he was making great time. As this was the beginning of the well-known route called the Santa Fe Trail, it could be expected that he felt his pace would pick up at this point and it would be smooth sailing from here. But it would turn out to be his least productive day of the whole ride...one where he was fearing his well-planned cross country adventure might come to a halt.

Baker wrote that he departed Santa Fe, New Mexico at 5:45 a.m. and by 8:00 a.m. had already covered 86 miles, so he was making good time. He added: ***"... then my road through these mountains brought me to a mountain stream on which I had not figured. It was so swollen that it looked to me as if my journey was at an end. There was no means of crossing at this point and I spent almost an entire day locating a safe point to ford the stream with the machine. Finally I found a place in the river that was shallow enough to take the machine across without immersing the entire motorcycle in the river. In order to do this I waded back and forth across the stream many times to locate the shallow ford and by the time I finished this job it was 5 o'clock in the evening. I dried my clothes and then started for a little town called Watrous, which was about 18 miles distant, making a complete run of 94.8 miles. I rode up to the postmaster at Watrous and had him put the post office stamp in my book, as this was a point from which I could not telegraph to the officials of the F.A.M."***

THE SANTA FE TRAIL

I found it confusing to determine exactly where Baker encountered that deep stream. He kept excellent notes, especially considering his minimal capacity to carry anything. But despite his efforts to offer plentiful details, there are some things about his ride route that requires a look at what his options were, and consideration of them all as being possible.

The modern highway tagged as the Santa Fe Trail goes southeast from Santa Fe before turning north and the first major town one comes to is Las Vegas, New Mexico, for many years one of the biggest and liveliest towns in the southwest. Baker's journal reveals that he rode 86 miles that morning where he then encountered an unexpected stream that he was unable to immediately cross. He later did cross it after many hours of searching and said he then rode 18 miles to the town of Watrous. Looking at a map, if he were traveling on what is generally considered the Santa Fe Trail, then that would have put him in, or near Las Vegas.

Something wasn't adding up based on what information Baker had given us. Roger Pattison, one of our New Mexico resources, studied some New Mexico maps of that period of time and what troubled him about just following the Santa Fe Trail as it is listed now, was that he didn't believe that any of the rivers that cross there would have been impassable. The Santa Fe Trail was at this time an established route so it didn't seem likely that the road would be under that much water to submerge a motorcycle.

Baker also made a couple of references to riding through the mountains, so Roger's theory was that he had ridden north that morning from Santa Fe to Chimayo and into the mountains that today includes the Santa Fe National Forest over to an area known as Golondrinas, then southeast down the road from there to Watrous. It is more likely, according to Roger, that he could have encountered the washout up in those mountains before finally getting across and down to Watrous and onto the Santa Fe Trail. It is approximately 20 miles from Golondrinas.

We can't be 100% sure which way he did go, but whatever route he did take to Watrous, that was the end point of that day's ride for him. It would be his shortest ride of the whole journey, logging only 94.8 miles on the odometer of his Indian. Despite losing almost the whole day trying to cross the river, he was able to make it into town before the hardware store closed. We learned that it housed the post office, and Baker got his logbook stamped and signed there by the postmaster.

**As detailed in this chapter, Baker did not specify his exact route leaving Santa Fe on Day 5. Using local knowledge, we accepted the theory that he rode north, which is where he encountered an undocumented river, costing him many hours trying to cross. He eventually did get across and ended his ride that day in Watrous, NM. It was his least productive day of his entire ride. Interstate 25 runs today on what was once the historic Santa Fe Trail.**

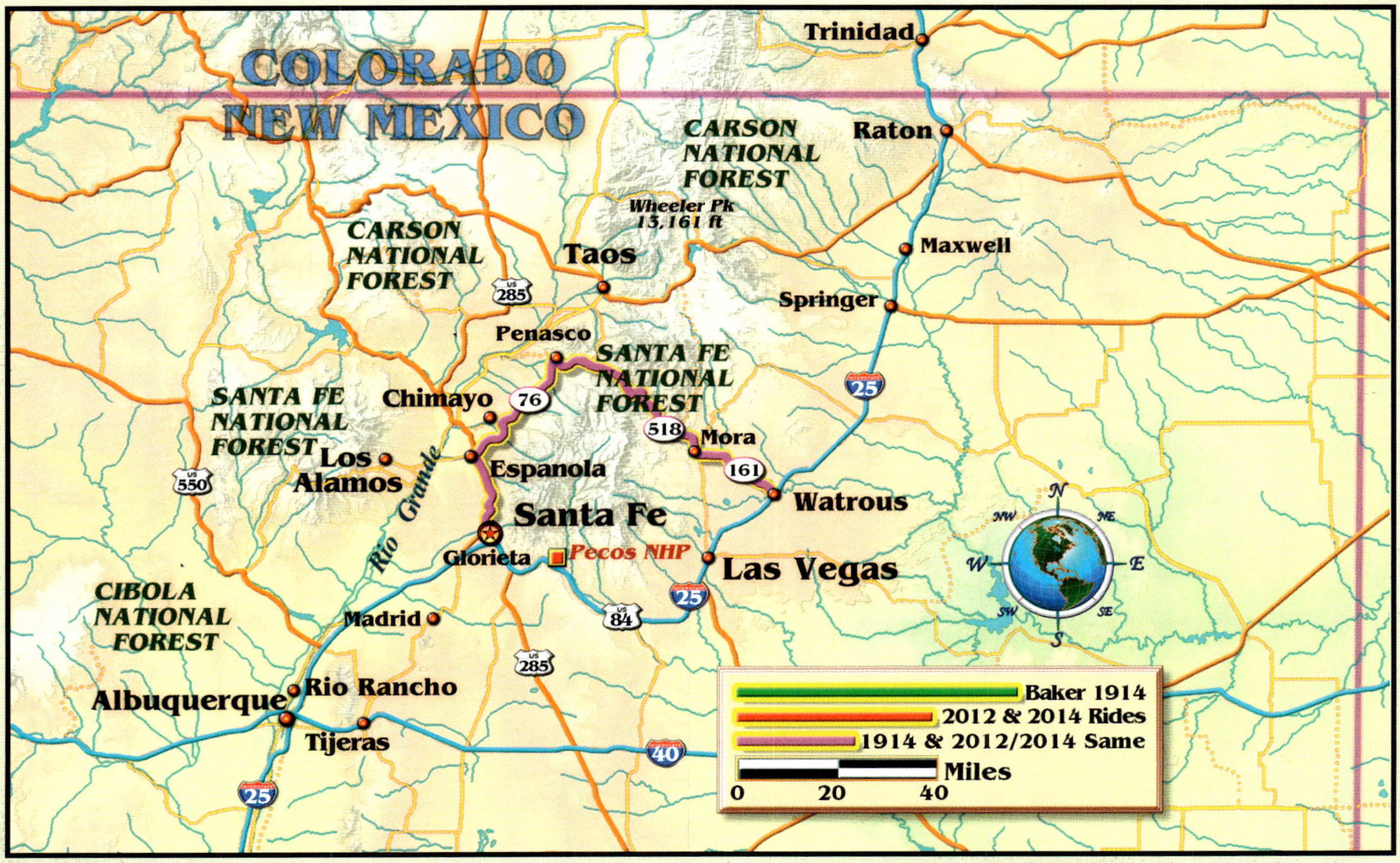


Map by Bill Tipton / Compart Maps.

## THE SANTA FE TRAIL

In the mid-1800s, a couple of writers, including Horace Greeley, used the phrase: "Go West, young man and grow up with the country." Thousands followed their advice and the movement began. In the Kansas City area, there was a junction of three routes: the Oregon Trail heading northwest, the California Trail continuing straight west, and the Santa Fe Trail, which angled southwest through Kansas.

While the other two routes attracted many settlers bound for San Francisco or the Northwest, the Santa Fe Trail was initially more of a commercial route serving the Southwest. Coaches and wagons hauled products to be sold or traded in and around Santa Fe, the capital of the area previously known as Northern Mexico until statehood was granted in 1912. It was renamed New Mexico (Arizona became a state the same year).

Merchant wagon trains would assemble at places like Arrow Rock, Fort Osage, Independence, Westport Landing and other locations at the Kansas/Missouri border. They would then begin their slow, laborious journey across Kansas through Fort Dodge, taking the mountain route to Trinidad, Colorado and up to Raton, New Mexico, then southwest to Santa Fe. Later, there was a "Cimarron Cutoff" that went more southerly through the northwest corner of Oklahoma down to Santa Fe. It was more direct, but a lack of reliable sources of water was problematic.

There was never anything easy about travel on either option of the Santa Fe Trail, with challenges through the years that ranged from severe weather, lack of water and food, as well as vegetation to feed their working draft animals, attacks from unfriendly Indians and/or robbers who stole mail bags, money and even the horses and oxen pulling the wagons.

Because of these many great difficulties in transporting people, mail, supplies and merchandise, the railroad companies saw the opportunity to showcase their abilities to haul much larger payloads in a single trip, thus making it more profitable for business and safer for the travelers to use the trains. The race was on, primarily between the Atchison, Topeka and Santa Fe Railroad company and Denver, Rio Grande and Western Railroad company, to lay down track from Kansas City to Trinidad, Colorado, up the steep mountain climb to Raton, New Mexico and over to Santa Fe. The Atchison, Topeka and Santa Fe Railroad prevailed in that race primarily by doing a better job negotiating property purchases and land-use arrangements and on February 16, 1880 its first train rolled into Santa Fe.* The headline of its newspaper read, *"The Old Santa Fe Trail Passes into Oblivion."*

While the year 1880 is generally known as the end of the "Old" Santa Fe Trail," it was also the beginning of what would become the "New" Santa Fe Trail. The rail service had been built right on what had been the previous dirt road through that part of the area. Despite the long-haul benefits of the railroads, there was still a need for travelers on horse back or horse-drawn vehicles to travel along the way. In most cases new roads were built that paralleled or generally followed the railroad tracks between Santa Fe and Trinidad, Colorado via Raton Pass.

For the next twenty-five years there were not a lot of upgrades or attention paid to the dirt roads around the country, including New Mexico. But the increasing use of automobiles and motorcycles after the turn of the twentieth century added great pressure on the government and communities to maintain a roadway through the state. This became a very busy and exciting time in the history of roadways in New Mexico and the rest of America.

One major push was coming from the three principal coastal cities of California: San Francisco, Los Angeles and San Diego. They all understood the importance of having a reliable route to their city from the east. San Diego also hosted the Panama-California Exposition beginning in 1915 to celebrate the opening of the Panana Canal. So the route through New Mexico was vital to the success of the exhibit if people living in the Midwest or East coast wanted to travel there by automobile.

Magazines began to appear that addressed the growing interest in traveling the country by automobile, and in some cases, by motorcycle. The many articles provided route information and other tips, and products could be purchased, such as Travel Log Books produced by A.L. Westgard, considered the leading travel writer of his time.

As the roads improved and travel seemed less risky, the numbers of travelers began to grow. The slogan that created much of the fever was "See America First," a term meaning that yes, many people will take vacations to Europe, but people were encouraged to first get out on the roads of America. And it worked!

The American Automobile Association (AAA) had a magazine at the time called *American Motorist*. In an article in 1914, writer W.D. Rishel wrote that transcontinental tourism would surpass baseball as the National Pastime. He said, "the movement started in 1912 when an estimated 5,000 crossed the country by automobile," albeit at a much more leisurely pace than Erwin Baker had.

Baker surely enjoyed the areas where the roads were graded, but its a big country and the government funding for new or more "Good Roads" programs was just getting started. As a result, he had his share of roads that were far from ideal even in good weather. When it rained, of course, one was in for a *very* challenging ride.

In the years to follow, the dirt road from the south that passed through Socorro, Albuquerque and Santa Fe, New Mexico north to Raton and on to Trinidad, Colorado was paved and with the creation of the Interstate Highway System became part of Interstate 25.

**Note: Another historic significance of this accomplishment was that construction of rail tracks continued west from Santa Fe and in 1881 were linked with the Southern Pacific Railroad tracks at Deming, New Mexico to open the nation's first transcontinental rail service.*

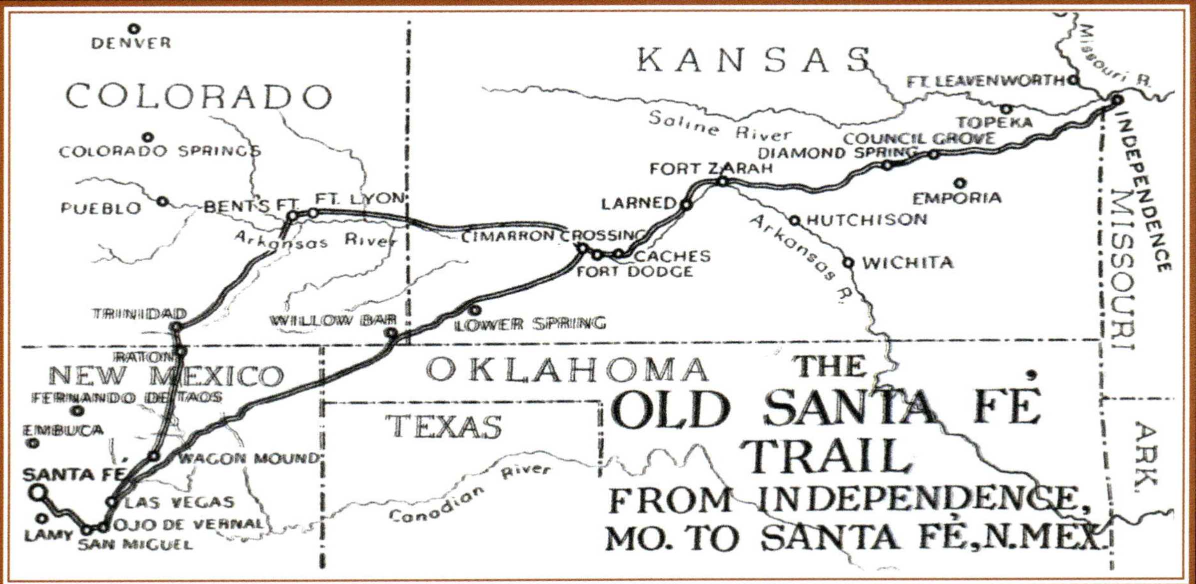

## 2012:

**After stopping at the current post office in Watrous, where a lifelong resident of the area told us about the old hardware store, we rode over to check it out. Not much of the store, which also served as the post office in 1914, is still standing these days. Our local "guide," Roger Pattison (left) and Joe Colombero get a close up look.**

When Joe and I met up with Roger Pattison at our hotel in Santa Fe the morning of May 7th, our main goal was to go check out Watrous, which now looked on the internet like it was a ghost town. After breakfast, we got on our bikes and headed north up Interstate 25. We made a stop to have a look at the historic town of Las Vegas, New Mexico and then continued on until we saw the exit sign for Watrous.

As we entered what would loosely be called "the town," we noted a lot of old cars, some buildings in various states of repair and a few trailers. We were just putting along and saw a sign marked with an arrow and "post office" in it. What luck. Sure enough, after we parked our bikes and went inside, a young lady named Sandra at the counter greeted us and we told her about the Cannon Ball Project and that we were searching for any applicable information we could obtain. She pointed across the room to an older gentleman who was sitting reading his mail. She said he was in his 90s and had lived there his whole life.

Our conversation got his attention and pretty soon we were talking to Mr. "Dogie" Jones, who raised quarter horses on his nearby ranch. He confirmed what Sandra had said, that he had lived there his whole life. What I was most curious about was where the post office was where Baker got his logbook signed – obviously they didn't operate out of the trailer we were in that day –and I was also curious what hotel would have been here that he would have stayed at?

Dogie was quick to point out that the post office used to be inside the old hardware store there in town. "You would have passed it on your way into town," he said. "It's the building with just the one wall standing and everything else fallen down." That sounded familiar and we would go check it out. He wasn't 100% sure what hotel Baker would have stayed at. The town had suffered a major fire back in 1901, which destroyed most of its business district and several homes, and it never again had a real thriving economy.

We thanked Dogie for his help to locate the post office, and also Sandra too, and we let her know we'd be back in a year with a group and would be stopping by again. We then got on our bikes and rode over to the building that Dogie told us about. Sure enough, it was easy to spot. One big wall of large white bricks, and everything else had all fallen into the center. Roger, Joe and I took various photos of each other at the location, and since we knew we were at an exact location where Baker had been, we pulled out Cannon Ball's AMA Hall of Fame medal and took a few photos there with it.

With our business done that day, we bid adieu to Roger who rode south, and Joe and I continued on I-25 north. We still had a fair amount of the day left and hadn't made any hotel reservations and figured we'd see how far we could get.

When we confirmed that we were at another location where E.G. Baker had been in 1914, we pulled out his Hall of Fame medal for a photo.

There is not much left of Watrous these days, just a few houses, a post office and one business that appeared to be an active auto shop.

# CHAPTER 8

# WATROUS TO SYRACUSE / THEN & NOW

After his frustrating day on May 7th, spent mostly trying to get across the river, Baker was up extra early the next day and ready to hit the road long before the sun came up. He put his Indian's new electric headlight to the test that morning in the pitch dark when he left Watrous at 3:00 a.m. His notes were brief, but even though he was now riding on the actual Santa Fe Trail, he makes it clear for the first time that wet weather was now a factor. The Santa Fe Trail was unpaved, so the rain changed most of the 350 miles he would travel to mud. For anyone who rides modern dirt bikes, they will surely agree that Baker will never get enough credit for the many miles of muddy roads he covered on that 7-horsepower Indian.

He wrote: ***"I left Watrous at 3 a.m. coming through Wagon Mound. From Watrous to Wagon Mound the going was fine, as this was all prairie land, and from Wagon Mound to Springer, New Mexico, the roads were good. I then hit Raton. The going here was rough in spots, but I crossed through the Raton Pass to Trinidad and found this part of the going rougher, due to the severe storm I was trailing across the continent. This was most particularly due to washouts."***

To have Baker say the going was "rough in spots" no doubt meant it was very muddy and would have been a great challenge for a lesser skilled rider. He added, ***"I stopped and had dinner (mid-day lunch) at Trinidad and then continued on to La Junta to get gasoline and oil. After getting another square meal and a little rest, I continued on good Kansas roads, riding on the Santa Fe Trail, and finally reaching a little village which had met with a severe storm which had washed out all the bridges. I therefore found it necessary to go a roundabout way, 25 miles back on to the Santa Fe Trail, riding to Syracuse, Kansas, that night, a distance of 348.9 miles. I put up there overnight."***

**This period postcard shows an automobile navigating its way through the Raton Pass area of New Mexico. As explained in the previous chapter, the original Santa Fe Trail through this area had been taken over by the railroads and track was laid over the dirt road. That major change resulted in a new road being built for use by automobiles, motorcycles and what horse-drawn vehicles were still in use.**

**The most economical way to construct roads in the early 1900s including going around as many obstacles as possible, rather than carve thru as would be done today. This photo looks west from Raton Pass back to the town of Raton, NM circa 1914.**

Travelers heading north on the Santa Fe Trail achieved an elevation of 7,835 feet at Raton Pass, then began a steep 2,000-foot decline by the time they reached the next town of Trinidad, Colorado, 20 miles away.

SCENIC HIGHWAY, RATON PASS. RATON, NEW MEXICO.

Our route of the 2012 and 2014 rides from Watrous, NM to Syracuse, Kansas were the same as Baker took in 1914 (see purple line)—the difference being it was all paved for us and all dirt for Baker. He rode the Santa Fe Trail north from Watrous, to Raton, Colorado. He wrote that the going was rough from there as there had been rain very recently and the downhill road from Raton Pass was not in very good condition. At Trinidad the riding conditions improved as he made his way to Syracuse, Kansas.

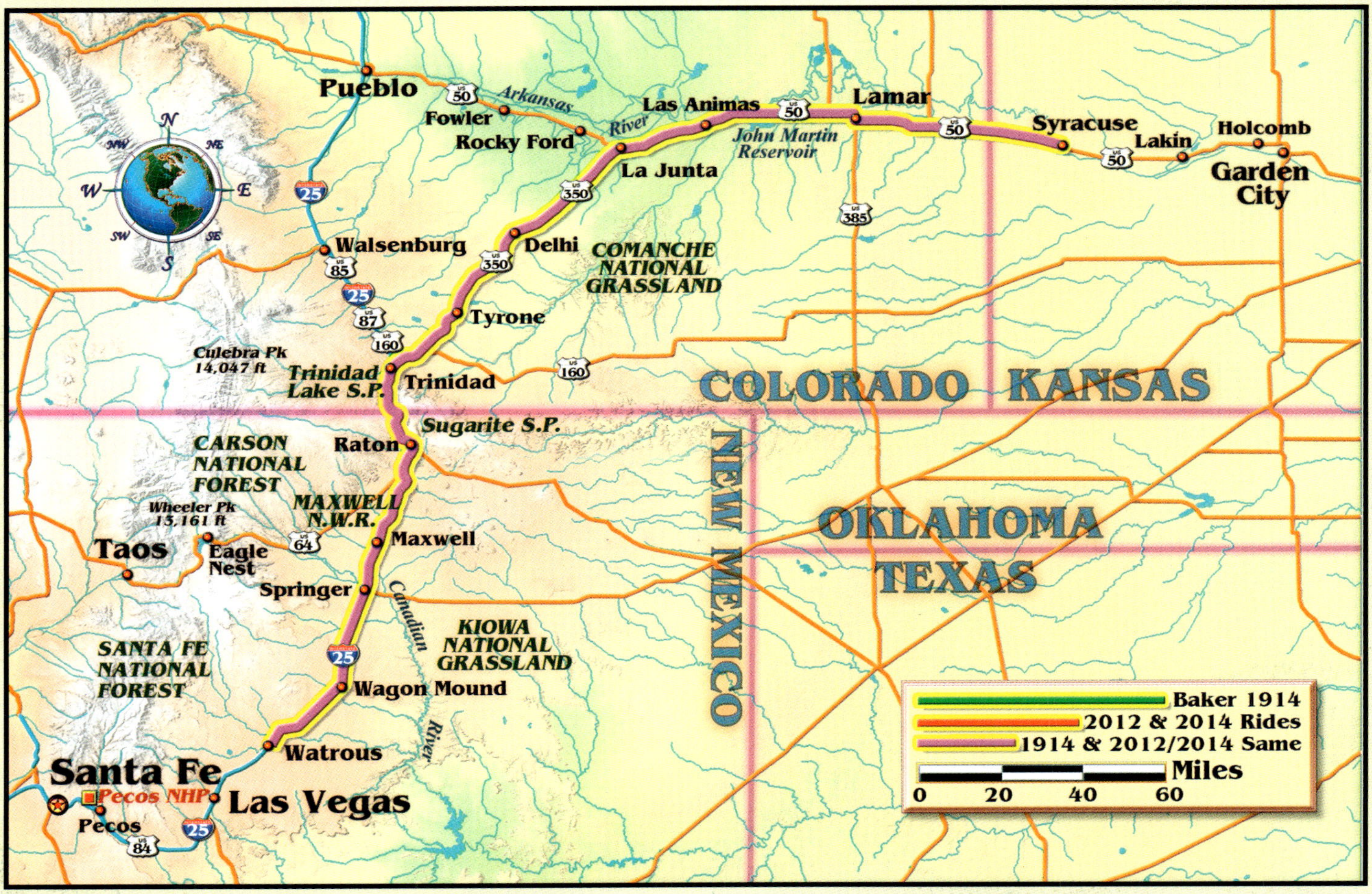


Map by Bill Tipton / Compart Maps.

**This period postcard shows a view of the towering 10,280-foot Fisher's Peak that we enjoyed just as Baker did in 1914 coming down the grade from Raton Pass. It is about five miles east of Trinidad.**

**By the time eastbound travelers reach La Junta, Colorado the elevation is 4,078 feet, although it is relatively flat all the way across Kansas. Originally the home of some Indian tribes, La Junta served in the 1800s as one of the fur trading stops along the Santa Fe Trail, and grew from there into a major commercial hub in the region.**

## 2012:

On our 2012 mapping ride, Joe and I had stopped at Watrous on June 12th. We then headed north on Interstate 25 towards Wagon Mound, as Baker had done on May 8, 1914, and continued on to Raton, New Mexico. We noticed the wind was beginning to pick up and the temperature dropping. It looked like it could rain in the direction we were heading, so for the first time on our trip we pulled out our rain gear. Ironically, this is about where Baker first mentioned in 1914 getting into some "weather."

We got back on the road and headed north again on I-25 towards Raton Pass (elevation 7,835 feet). At Raton Pass, we dropped about 2,000 feet by the time we got to Trinidad, Colorado, which is 20 miles down the hill. We did hit some rain on our descent down the hill there, as Baker had in 1914. The difference there for Joe and I was that we were on pavement compared to the dirt road he was on. Also the current Interstate is one long six-lane highway with long sweeping curves. Baker had to navigate down the twisty and historic Raton Pass road downhill with many left and right hand turns. The fact that he was able to achieve 350 miles that day is quite incredible.

Joe and I were following the Santa Fe Trail and after a lunch stop in Trinidad (same as Baker did!), our next stop was La Junta, Colorado where we got some gas. We didn't have any hotel reservations and were just enjoying the ride, so we decided to keep going and figured some hotel would turn up that we could stop at. Wow, the fun and freedom of a road trip! I am not sure I ever felt more "unplugged" in my whole life than I was right then. I am usually the one who has to have all the details in place, and here I was just riding along with no clue where I'd be sleeping that night.

We noted that Syracuse, Kansas was the next town, a little over 100 miles and that was where Baker had stopped on his ride. It was a little after 6:00 p.m. by then and the sun was going down.

We pulled out of the gas station and headed east on U.S. Hwy 50. It couldn't have been ten minutes out from the gas station when suddenly it got real windy. Luckily, there wasn't much traffic on the road. As we rode along we had two lanes going in each direction and were having trouble keeping our bikes just in one lane. I was trying to stay in the slow lane, but a few bursts of wind moved me clear over into the fast lane. Once I came within just a few feet of running off the left side of the fast lane. In my fifty years of riding a motorcycle, this had to be the closest I ever came to getting blown completely off the road.

I was quickly having doubts if we should continue or not. I got to thinking what if it got worse as we went along and if we got blown off the road in the dark? We might be out there all night. So I decided to try to get turned around, but it was a divided highway with a guardrail in the middle. It was so windy I didn't want to take an arm off the bars to signal Joe, and so noisy we couldn't talk on the communications system. I finally spotted a turnaround coming up between the lanes and I put my turn signals on and got back in the left hand lane so Joe could see that I was heading over for that. Safely stopped and in the turnaround area, we talked and agreed it would be smarter to head back to La Junta and find a hotel for the night. So that's what we did, although the ride west back to La Junta was just as challenging as the ride we had going east.

We stopped at the first hotel we found in La Junta and at check-in told the lady at the counter about our encounter with the wind. With the Rocky Mountains to the north and the big elevation change from Raton Pass to La Junta, she said the winds are almost always something to deal with there. Her recommendation to us was to get rolling as early as we could, saying the winds die down at night, but the heat of the sun puts it all back in motion as the day goes on.

So that's what we did. The next morning Joe and I were suited up and rolling before the sun came up and the lady at the hotel was right, it was much calmer, and we were on our way. We even skipped breakfast there and decided to get down the road a while before stopping.

**While the modern highway, now Interstate 25, is wide and paved, there are many signs posted along the way reminding travelers of the great history of the Santa Fe Trail.**

It was still windy that morning, but much more manageable than the night before. We finally stopped for breakfast in Syracuse, the town that Baker had stayed the night in 1914. I don't know what they had back then for hotels, but its mostly grain silos there now, but we did find a nice little coffee shop where we relaxed a little, hoping to get a good day of riding in. It was a lesson for us, for sure, to respect the winds of the Great Plains. Yet another lesson awaited us as we learned the meaning of the term "Kansas Lean."

**This photo from the 2012 mapping ride shows best what we remembered about our ride across Kansas: the wind. After aborting a planned ride from La Junta the previous night due to high winds, we got an early start the next day and while windy, it was rideable. On this day, we experienced what is known as the "Kansas Lean," a sustained ride leaning into the wind.**

# CHAPTER 9

# SYRACUSE – ELLSWORTH / THEN & NOW

**Few towns, if any, provide the history and atmosphere of the Old West as Dodge City, Kansas. It was built in the mid-1800s as a stop to provide shelter, refreshment and protection for early American settlers traveling along the Santa Fe Trail. The town grew into a lively, and at times, wild community famous for its saloons, gunfighters and lawmen such as Wyatt Earp. Remnants of the original town still exist, including the famous Boot Hill Cemetery.**

Baker had endured two challenging days of riding over the mountains of New Mexico with considerable rain falling on the road just ahead of him. Departing Syracuse, Kansas the morning of May 9th, with weather improving, he welcomed the opportunity to pick up some speed as the Santa Fe Trail was now flat and straight much of the way as he began his run across the Great Plains.

His ride plan for the day was a lunch stop in Dodge City, then a departure from the Santa Fe Trail to ride north to Great Bend to see a friend and fellow racer, Paul "Speck" Warner, who had an Indian motorcycle dealership in Ellsworth, Kansas. From there, Baker planned to get on an improved roadway known as the Golden Belt route into Kansas City. But things didn't go exactly as he planned that day. He wrote, ***"I started out with the intention of making Kansas City that night. The roads were fine and I began to feel at home. I continued riding until within 40 miles of Dodge City, when I was brought to a sudden stop by picking up my first nail in the rear tire. Within the next 20 miles I picked up six nails and lost a lot of time repairing tubes. I continued five miles further and then the boys from Dodge City, about 25 in number, met me with a good Indian yell, and you can just bet I was pleased."***

He continued. ***"I got into Dodge City O.K. and had dinner, and the boys fixed me up with gasoline and lubricating oil. They wanted me to stop over and look at their new racetrack, but they forgot I was out knocking minutes off a record. However, this track was on my way out of the city going east and I managed to get a good view of it. The boys continued on with me until they had gone about ten miles east.***

**Great Bend, Kansas was a cattle town along the Santa Fe Trail in the old days. Baker rode through it in 1914, where he continued northeast on to Ellsworth. This period postcard shows how it would have looked to Erwin Baker when he rode through on his Indian motorcycle.**

*From Dodge City I rode right for Great Bend. "Speck" Warner, the Indian agent at Ellsworth, Kansas, met me 30 miles west of Great Bend, riding with me into Ellsworth, 80 miles. While covering this distance we had an interruption caused by a large shepherd dog, which came very near putting me out of my transcontinental trip. This dog seemed to have a great desire for the Goodyear tire on my front wheel, but my desire for this tire was still greater. The dog took a fall out of me, which put me in bad shape, as I slid along the road on my elbows and knees. I kept the tire and the dog lost his life. At Ellsworth I had a good meal, then sent for a doctor to get bandaged up, and went to bed."*

Despite his shortened ride, Baker still logged 253 miles that day.

**One of E.G. Baker's friends in the motorcycle sport was Paul "Speck" Warner, of Ellsworth, Kansas. Warner for a time was a U.S. mail carrier and reportedly delivered the mail with his personal motorcycle. He also was a respected racer, and luckily for Baker, had an Indian motorcycle dealership at the time of the 1914 cross-country ride.**

**As we had done the previous day on our 2012 mapping ride, Joe and I followed Baker's same route of 1914 (see purple line), branching off the historic Santa Fe Trail at Great Bend, Kansas and heading to Ellsworth.**

*Map by Bill Tipton / Compart Maps.*

## THE FIRST INTERNATIONAL 300-MILE RACE AT DODGE CITY • JULY 4, 1914

In Baker's journal he wrote that when he rode through Dodge City on May 9th, "they wanted me to stop over and look at their new racetrack, but they forgot I was out knocking minutes off a record." There was in fact a new racetrack being built there at the time in preparation for a 300-mile motorcycle race on the 4th of July. Baker actually came back and raced in the event that July.

In 1914, the Federation of American Motorcyclists, the same sanctioning body that was being asked to certify Baker's transcontinental record if it was achieved, also had a hand in the planning, organizing and sanctioning of an all-new race to out-do any motorcycle race that had ever been held. Likely seeing the success in the automotive world with the relatively new Indianapolis 500-mile car race, the F.A.M. organized a 300-mile dirt track race for motorcycles to be held on the 4th of July in Dodge City, Kansas. Working in conjunction with local officials, a 2-mile race track was carved out of a large open field not far from the center of town there.

The event captured great attention of the industry and sport. The Indian factory was a huge supporter, entering ten factory riders, while Excelsior entered eight. Other companies with factory support included riders of Flying Merkel, Pope and Thor motorcycles, and even the Harley-Davidson Motor Company, to date not very supportive of motorcycle racing as a way of promoting its products, saw four Harley-Davidson riders entered. Some of the company's management attended the race, including founders William S. Harley and William Davidson.

The Harleys did not fare well in this event, with a best finish of 15th. But Mr. Davidson was quoted in Motorcycling magazine, saying: "We are glad we came, even if we didn't win. We got the experience we needed, and which is to be obtained only by getting into the game. A lot of our Western dealers are clamoring for speed, and we satisfied them that we have it. Next year we will know how to get it right." Davidson was correct. Otto Walker would win the great 300-mile Coyote Classic for Harley-Davidson the following year.

As for Erwin Baker, in his notes of his transcontinental ride, he wrote that the locals wanted him to go over to see the track they were still working on in preparation of the 4th of July event. Time only allowed for a quick glance, though, as he rode out of town. He never mentioned if he already had any plans or intentions to race in the 300-mile event at Dodge City, but when the entries were announced, the Hendee Manufacturing Company listed him as one of its factory-entered riders along with other top stars of the day including Glen "Slivers" Boyd (eventual race winner), 1913 San Diego-to-Phoenix winner Paul Derkum, Indian factory engineer Charles Gustafson Jr., Baker's friend "Speck" Warner (who finished 4th) and others.

Baker did, in fact, return back to Dodge City for the 300-mile race event and not only raced in it, but turned in a very respectible 7th place finish. The inaugural race was considered a big success, with over 10,000 fans braving the 100-degree 4th of July heat.

*Photos and materials from Don Emde Collection.*

Baker is easy to spot on the far left side of this photo taken at the Dodge City 300-mile race on July 4, 1914. He stood about a head higher than his Indian teammates. He would go on to finish 7th in the grueling race, which was run in 100+ degree heat.

(Left) This photograph was taken at the Dodge City motorcycle races on July 4, 1914. From left to right: Goodyear employees W.J. Cameron, F.H. Ferguson, Ernest Brunswick (co-developer of the first Goodyear Blue Streak racing tire), Sales manager Shelby Falor and his young son George.

(Above) The 2-mile Dodge City oval track was located less than a mile from downtown. Three riders are seen here kicking up dust and smoke around the large sweeping turns in 100+ degree heat. Only 6 of the original 36 riders were credited with going the full 300-mile distance in the 1914 race.

## 2012:

After a breakfast stop in Syracuse, Joe and I continued on the KTMs on Highway 50 with a lunch stop planned for Dodge City. Funny how, despite our modern machinery, we had many occasions on our cross-country ride when we would cover the same distances as Baker had. Syracuse to Dodge City was one.

It was definitely windy as we rode along, but not as bad as the evening before out of La Junta. But even so, as we rode Joe and I noticed that we would need to lean the bikes into the wind to go straight. We didn't know there was an actual name for this until we mentioned it to someone a few days later and they nodded and said, "That's called the Kansas Lean." We rode pretty much that way from La Junta to Dodge City, a distance of 200 miles.

Dodge City has so much history from the days of the "Old West," we planned to take a little extra time after lunch to check out the legendary Boot Hill and the adjoining museum. We were there for two hours altogether.

As we came back to where we had our motorcycles parked, we were greeted by a friendly lady who was reading the logo on our windscreens out loud... "Finding Cannon Ball's Trail," she said, and added, "I know about Cannon Ball. We're having a centennial here next year of our Dodge City 300." She then introduced hereself as Colleen Hastings, the Visitor and Community Coordinator of the Dodge City Convention and Visitors Bureau.

So we talked a while and she told us what they were planning for a motorcycle rally in 2014 to celebrate the first Dodge City 300 motorcycle race held July 4th, 1914. And we told her about what we were doing and how we hoped to be back through there in May of 2014. We exchanged business cards and she told us how Jim Johnson from Dodge City was someone we should contact to coordinate regarding our trip the next year. We thanked her and resumed our journey. Over the next few months I did have quite a bit of contact with Jim, who helped us arrange many things, including accommodations in towns for our Centennial ride.

**When Joe and I did our mapping ride in 2012 we tried to keep a good pace going, but we took a little break when we got to Dodge City to soak up the great history of the town.**

**The historical centerpiece of Dodge City today is where buildings along Front Street, the main section of the bustling old town, once stood. This entrance area has a gift shop and leads to what is left of the old Boot Hill cemetery where numerous outlaws and peace officers alike were buried in the heyday of the Wild West days that Dodge City is remembered for.**

The Santa Fe Trail continued in a pretty straight shot from Dodge City to the southwest side of Kansas City, but since Baker had turned north just outside of Dodge towards Great Bend, we of course followed his 1914 route. The wind had come back up that afternoon with the heat of the sun and while not as bad as La Junta, it was getting challenging again. What made it rideable was the fact that we didn't have any big highway speeds, there were a lot of slower country roads to cover.

So we made it through Great Bend and north to Ellsworth, the town where Baker had crashed. We made a brief stop there to have a look around and get gas, but didn't find anything applicable or meet anyone who looked like they would remember when Baker slept there.

Our journey to the east coast continued…

**Relics from the early days of Dodge City can be seen inside the reconstructed buildings on Front Street. Seen here is printing equipment from the old Dodge City newspaper office.**

**On this sign at the entrance, it reads: *"Boot Hill began as a resting place for the departed who did not have enough money to be afforded the luxury of being laid to rest at Fort Dodge. Few had ceremonies, none had coffins, and since most died, and were buried with their boots on, the cemetery gained its name."***

**A devastating fire destroyed the buildings along Front Street in 1885, including the historic Long Branch Saloon, one of 16 saloons in the town. In 1947, this reconstructed version of the street was built and it provides a view of what the street looked like back in the days of Wyatt Earp. Numerous artifacts from the early days are on display inside.**

# CHAPTER 10

# ELLSWORTH TO LEXINGTON THEN & NOW

## HALF WAY!

When Erwin Baker woke up in Ellsworth, Kansas the morning of May 10th, he surely was in pain. He apparently didn't break any bones when he hit the dog the previous day, but his injuries were serious enough that he did request a doctor to patch up some cuts and scrapes. Any repairs needed to straighten out his motorcycle could be done there at the Indian dealership of his friend "Speck" Warner.

Baker had now ridden for a full week since leaving San Diego and traveled approximately 1,740 miles – roughly half the distance to New York City. For anyone keeping score as Baker went along, on paper it looked like he was definitely on pace to smash the current transcontinental record by 6 days or more.

**After riding for a week through the deserts of California and Arizona, the mountains of Arizona and New Mexico, then across the prairie of Colorado and Kansas, the scenery changed dramatically for Baker when he got to Kansas City. This was the first big metropolitan area he would pass through since leaving San Diego.**

Despite his good pace so far, though, it would seem Baker was well aware that it could all come to a screeching halt at any time. There were no better examples than the dog that brought him down just the day before, the ongoing rain storms that were creating some very dangerous and physically-draining riding conditions, and the new problem he encountered in Kansas with the many flat tires.

Thousands of horses had taken those same dirt roads in the last hundred years and the nails falling out of the horse's shoes no doubt littered the roadway. They were never a problem for the settler's wagons with the wooden wheels, but pneumatic motorcycle tires were another story. Baker of course had to stop and fix each flat as it occurred and refilled the tire with a hand-pump that he carried with him.

Apparently both rider and machine were patched up well after he hit the dog, and the weather was cooperating. Fortunately, he was soon riding on the Golden Belt route towards Kansas City, a wide graded road that was part of the "Good Roads" projects that were happening in various parts of the country. It was by far the best stretch of road he had experienced yet since leaving San Diego and he was finally able to crank the Indian up and really make some good time.

Fortunately he did not encounter any more punctured tubes and had an uneventful ride on the Golden Belt to Kansas City and continued on to Lexington, Missouri, approximately 50 miles east. His brief notes of this day: ***"I got an early start and rode clean through to Kansas City on the Golden Belt route, a distance of 175 miles. I had a late lunch at Kansas City. From Kansas City to Lexington, Mo., all the roads were good and all along the Indian dealers had the boys out to meet me as I passed through the various towns. At Lexington, Mo., which was a distance of 293.7 miles, I put up for the night."***

As sales of automobiles and motorcycles grew through the early 1900s and into the teens, so did the frustration of many drivers and riders who got caught out in storms, or sometimes even a brief rain shower that would turn the roads into muddy quagmires. This photo of the National Road was taken sometime in 1914 and could well have been in this condition when E.G. Baker rode through. *Ohio Historical Society photo.*

On Day 8 Baker rode east from Ellsworth where he picked up an early-day "highway" into Kansas City known as the "Golden Route." It was a well-manicured stretch of road, the best road yet of his 1914 trip. He rode past Kansas City and ended the day in Lexington, MO.

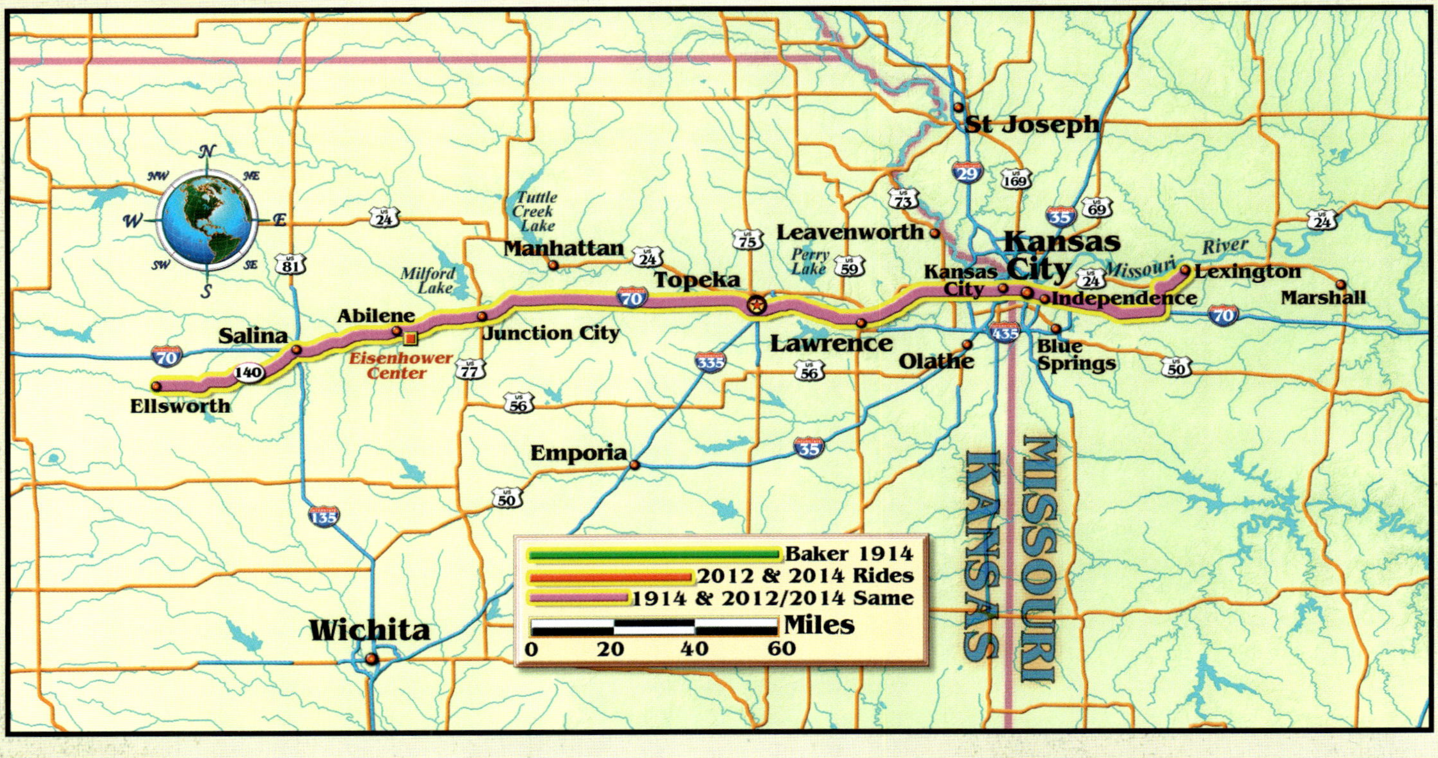


*Map by Bill Tipton / Compart Maps.*

## THE GOOD ROADS MOVEMENT

### How America's First Highway System Was Created

President Thomas Jefferson signed the Congressional act for the establishment of a road to connect Cumberland, Maryland with the Ohio Valley. Known as the National Road, construction began in 1811 at Cumberland and extended initially as far west as Wheeling, West Virginia. Through the years, contruction continued off-and-on as the road snaked its way west through the states, with priority given to cross through the major cities and/or capital cities of each state.

By 1838, the road had been established 620 miles west to Vandalia, Illinois. With construction costs covered in the latter years from both Government and State funds the National Road extended to St. Louis and finally Jefferson City, Missouri.

Farther west, however, Kansas City and nearby Independence at the Kansas/Missouri border were a major intersection of roads and trails of the Old West that served the growing needs of expeditions and wagon-train caravans moving westward from the east coast. The area became a major hub where travelers would stock up with provisions they would need in the months to come, hire guides and repair wagons and other equipment.

The Santa Fe Trail began there for travelers heading more southwesterly, and ended for those heading east. Other routes to the west connected there, including the Oregon Trail, and the Golden Belt route, a generally smooth and wide route to and from Denver that featured numerous posted road signs to direct travelers.

As motorcycles and automobiles became more popular in the early 1900s, demands for better roads, signage and maps grew rapidly. The needs for the motorized travelers concerned both the conditions of the roads, as well as some defined routes that the public could use with confidence. There became two primary efforts that competed for the attention of government and private funding and support. One was spearheaded by Carl Fisher, who also conceived and built the Indianapolis Motor Speedway, and it was based on the transcontinental highway that would become the Lincoln Highway from New York to San Francisco.

A second concept extended the historic National Road further south with outlets planned at Los Angeles and/or San Diego. In April of 1912, a convention was held in Kansas City with numerous individuals from various aspects of the industries, government and related interested parties to discuss a way of making the National Road ideas come to fruition. The result was the creation of a highway system called the National Old Trails Road, also called by some the "Ocean to Ocean Highway."

The purpose of the National Old Trails Road organization was to identify the key route from the east coast to points on the west coast. The National Road was clearly the established main route from the east to its conclusion

## 2012:

Ellsworth is not far from Interstate 70, so after Joe and I looked around there we jumped on I-70 East and headed towards Kansas City. I was keeping an eye out for where we could pick up signs for either the "Golden Belt Route" that Baker had noted, and/or U.S. Highway 40.

We hadn't traveled very far that day before we noticed that now that we were riding due east, instead of north,

**The National Road, Lewis & Clark Trail, Santa Fe Trail, and more. The historic names are different, but the actual roads are the same in many places across the Midwest, as was the case in Lexington, Missouri.**

In April of 1912 a convention was held in Kansas City that resulted in the creation of an organization called the National Old Trails Road Association. Its initial work was primarily to establish an "Ocean-to-Ocean" route from Baltimore to Los Angeles and San Francisco. That route utilized the National Road to Kansas City from the east and connected it with the Santa Fe Trail into New Mexico. The route from Albuquerque to Los Angeles became the basic western portion of what later became Route 66.

**at Jefferson City, and a preferred Missouri route through Booneville and Lexington onward to Kansas City was identified. From there, much of the road system was an overlay in certain areas of the Santa Fe Trail, Oregon Trail and a route that would ultimately help establish the legendary Route 66 to Los Angeles in later years.**

**With the key routes now identified, the way was clear for directing funds for massive building projects to actually create wider and smoother roads, and in places certain methods of paving the roadways began.**

**In 1926 the National Old Trails Road network was replaced by a new National highway identification system, and the highway from Colorado through Kansas City and onward to the east coast on the historic "National Road" became U.S. Highway 40. The Lincoln Highway, which also paved the ways to the west coast became U.S. Highway 30.**

we were bucking those dangerous winds again, much like we had coming out of La Junta. All of the strong buffeting made it pretty scary to share the Interstate at 60-70 mph with lots of cars and 18-wheelers. It was late enough in the afternoon by then and Joe and I decided to find a hotel and call it a day at Salina.

The next morning we got going early, but unlike our departure from La Junta where it had calmed down overnight, on this day the winds continued to blow hard. We rode straight towards Topeka, where not only did the winds die down slightly, but we also picked up the first signs designating an exit off I-70 for Highway 40. There are exceptions, but from that point clear into Pennsylvania, Highway 40 is the primary route that Baker would follow. It links up with the historic National Road in Illinois.

Pulling off of I-70 and onto Highway 40 was very exciting for me. Yes, we needed to get to the east coast, but riding the interstates was not what we wanted to be doing. Being now on what was once the National Old Trails Road for the first time put us back in our "detective" role to uncover pieces of history and information about Baker's route. Said another way, we were again literally on "Cannon Ball's Trail."

About mid-day we were getting to Kansas City and made a stop for lunch, then rode east on the old road to Lexington, where Baker had, as he called it, "put up for the night."

# CHAPTER 11

# LEXINGTON TO GREENVILLE THEN & NOW

Fair weather and familiar roads allowed Baker to really get rolling on May 11th. The man from Indianapolis had an uneventful day as he made his way from Lexington to Jefferson City and on to St. Louis. He was able to make a stop at the Indian dealer there and also got a good meal in as well. He then rode over the mighty Mississippi River into Illinois and rode over to Greenville on the National Road (which was later renamed U.S Highway 40.)

He noted, ***"In the early morning started for St. Louis, where the natives of Lexington thought I would arrive about midnight, but I fooled them. I was at Hurck's, the Indian agent in St. Louis, at 4:30 p.m. There I had my dinner, having covered a distance of 250 miles, and after stopping there 1½ hours for something to eat, I continued on to Greenville, Ill., where I put up for the night—304.3 miles that day."***

Upon his departure from St. Louis, Hurck sent off a telegram to his fellow Indian dealer in Indianapolis to alert them that Baker was on his way and would arrive the next day.

**(Right) This period map shows how the National Road was a straight shot east from St. Louis over to Greenville, Illinois. Baker stopped there the night of May 11th, then the next day headed on to Indianapolis and east from there. The relatively straight and flat road allowed him to make good time and cover a lot of territory each day.**

**The map on the right shows Baker's route from Lexington. MO. to Greenville, IL. (see purple line). As he rode east he was riding on the National Road (now US Highway 40) that once served thousands of early-day settlers in horse-drawn caravans. US 40 is the same stretch of road as Interstate 70 in some places.**

**The city of Greenville, Illinois got a new post office in 1910. E.G. Baker stopped for the night in Greenville in 1914 and got his logbook stamped by the Postmaster there before leaving town.**

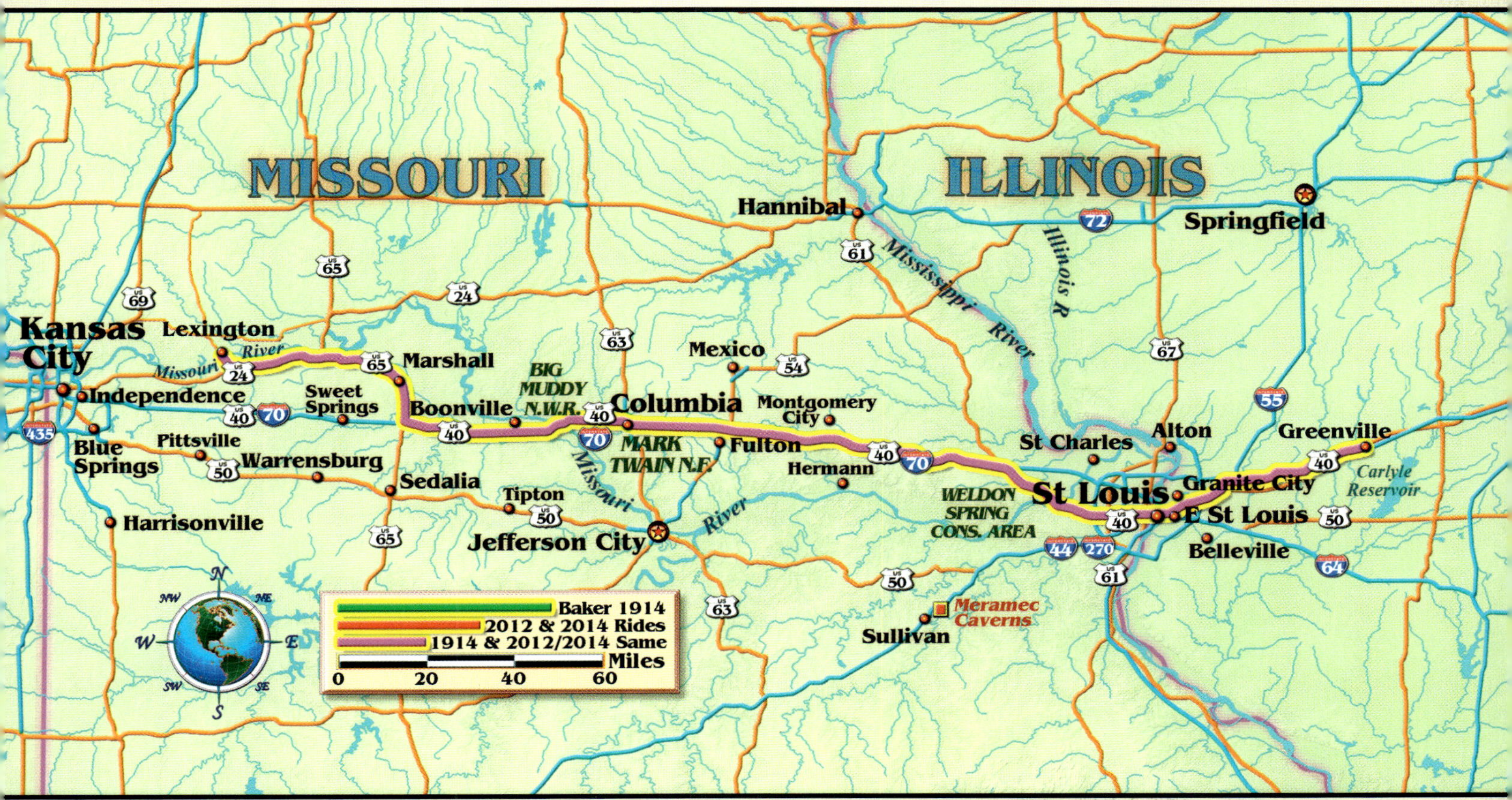


*Map by Bill Tipton / Compart Maps.*

## 2012:

**Missouri and Illinois is Lewis & Clark country. This was a dirt road in Baker's time, and obviously prior to that when horses and oxen pulled coaches and wagons there for settlers and commercial traders. U.S. Highway 40 is a great road today for a modern motorcycle ride.**

Joe and I made it to Lexington late in the afternoon of June 14, 2012 and continued eastward to U.S. Highway 40 which shares the same highway with Interstate 70. We knew there were some details about his route through Missouri that we didn't have all figured out, but I was now becoming a bit pressed for time as I had an airplane flight home booked for the morning of 16th from Columbus, Ohio to take care of some business matters back home. (We would fly back there in July.) So we got on I-70/US 40 and booked it all the way to St. Louis, then over the Mississippi River bridge into Illinois just as Baker had the night of May 11th in 1914. It was getting late, so we stopped for the night in Collinsville, Illinois where we saw signs for the National Road for the first time.

When we did get rolling the next day we backtracked a few miles to see where the National Road started in that direction on the east side of the Mississippi River. The only notable thing we spotted was the "World's Largest Bottle of Catsup" along the road on the property of the old Brooks Catsup Co. It's actually a 70-foot high water tower made to look like a catsup bottle.

Next we turned around and just started following the signs for the National Road and GPS directions

**Heading east to Greenville, Illinois on US 40. This was an exciting destination for us as we knew that Baker had stayed the night there in 1914. We had high hopes to learn something about his stop there.**

for US40. After a leisurely, one hour ride through the countryside, we came up to the town of Greenville, Ilinois. After what we called a "bomb run" the day before on I-70, Joe and I were enjoying the scenery and mellow pace of Highway 40.

I knew from Baker's journal that he had stopped for the night there, so when we came into town I was hoping we might learn something, like where he stayed, or maybe got his logbook stamped. The first thing we came up on was a small building that looked like it was once a train station (our first clue was that it was right alongside the tracks!) There was a lady there watering some plants and the sign said it was a real estate business there now.

Joe and I stopped and took our helmets off, and we asked her if there was a museum or history center there in town? Georgia Shank was her name and she asked what we were looking for? After I told her the story of Erwin G. Baker and the record ride...and that he had stayed the night there in 1914, she pulled out a cell phone and said, "Just a minute."

Georgia then made a call, told the person on the line about what we told her, and then put me on the phone with John Goldsmith from their Chamber of Commerce. He is the Tourism Director there and was very excited to hear what we had going on and invited us to ride over to his office on Main Street. While we headed there, he called Jeff Leidel from *The Greenville Advocate,* their local newspaper, to come over also to take some photos and put a story together. We shared with them the story about Baker getting his logbooks stamped at the post offices and it turned out we finally found one that Baker would have been in. So we all headed to their post office, which was built in 1910, and Jeff took some photos of Joe and I with Baker's Hall of Fame medal on the steps there.

We talked with John for a while and when we were done, it was pretty well set up that the town would like to do something for us when we came through on the Centennial ride in 2014. Depending on the time of day, they would have something planned. Maybe an ice cream social or something like that, he said.

As it turned out, a year later Greenfield would really roll the red carpet out for us...

**When Joe and I rode into Greenville the first thing that caught our attention was what looked like a train station alongside the railroad tracks, and we spotted this lady, Georgia Shank. We stopped and asked if there was a museum in town with information about the history of the town? There wasn't, but we got the next best thing. She introduced us to John Goldsmith of the Greenville Chamber of Commence.**

**Of all of our "close encounters" we had along the way from San Diego to identify places where Baker had been, none were better than Greenville. We learned that its post office had been built in 1910, so he would have gone through this doorway in 1914 to get his logbook stamped. Jeff Leidel of *The Greenville Advocate* snapped this photo of Joe and I holding Cannon Ball Baker's Hall of Fame medal.**

# CHAPTER 12

# GREENVILLE TO COLUMBUS THEN & NOW

Taken from the Indian booklet, Baker being welcomed at G.H. Westing's Indian dealership in his hometown of Indianapolis on May 12th. Baker spent 2½-hours enjoying a lunch with friends and family until he had to get back on the National Road heading east.

Baker was now getting back into his home area on the east side of the Mississippi River where he knew the roads best and he planned to make some really good time. But he ran into more rain, which turned the roads to mud. Lesser skilled riders would have dove for cover, but he pressed on to Indianapolis where family and friends were expecting his arrival. There he took a rare break from his record-pace riding and enjoyed a 2½-hour mid-day visit with family and friends at Westing's Indian Agency in Indianapolis until he finally "excused himself" and sped off on the Indian.

Despite the terrible weather conditions and the long stop, he still managed to chalk up 376 miles, the most in a day since he had started in San Diego. He did have a little help in his cause when the local police lifted the speed limit in Indiana just for one day...May 12, 1914.

He noted, ***"With thunder storms all around me, I was somewhat worried during the night, as I was getting near to the point where my friend Brant (the weather clerk at Phoenix) had predicted I would have a storm overtake me. I knew I never would get through even with a team of horses over the mudholes if I was caught in heavy rain, so bright and early in the morning I mounted my machine and rode for dear life, not even stopping for breakfast. I rode for Casey, Ill., which was about 90 miles from Greenville, and the rain started to pour down on me and I found then that the roads were getting so slippery it was necessary for me to ride seven or eight miles on the railroad ties in order to reach a well-known gravel road, which led into Terre Haute. I entered Terre Haute, Ind., in torrents of rain.***

***I was informed then that I could pass through with no limit to speed. Being a native of Indiana, everyone was out to welcome me and the message was sent along the way: "Clear the road; I am a-coming." As I passed through small towns and villages the natives***

*were standing on the roadsides with umbrellas up waiting for me.*

*I rode from Terre Haute to Indianapolis—a distance of 72 miles—in a downpour of rain, in an hour and 55 minutes, reaching Indianapolis, which is my hometown, at five minutes to 12. At last I was at home in my native city with my folks for the mid-day dinner, and I found that they had a regular banquet arranged for me. I remained there two hours and a half.*

*Mr. Westing, the Indian dealer, telegraphed ahead to Dayton, Ohio, the fact that I was on my way. I reached Dayton, rode up to W.B. Schaefer's, the Indian agency, and found a crowd of motorcyclists ready to start out to meet me in an hour or two, as they expected that I would take at least five hours to ride the distance of 112 miles. I had accomplished it in three hours and twelve minutes. They had my machine filled up with gasoline and oil and I continued on my way and rode from there to Columbus, Ohio, having finished a ride that day of 376 miles. As I approached the city of Columbus, Mr. Barr, with a number of motorcyclists, met me and escorted me into the city, where I put up overnight."*

**A 1914 National Road photo shows how bad the conditions could get for a motorcyclist when it rained. Baker reported in his journal that heavy rain that started about 70 miles west of Indianapolis made the road so bad that he rode on the railroad tracks for a time near Terre Haute, Indiana.** ***Ohio Historical Society photo.***

**The historic National Road that Baker rode in 1914 was later designated as US Highway 40. It parallels Interstate 70 through Illinois all the way through to the east coast. The only place Baker departed from the National Road on this day was to visit an Indian dealer in Dayton, then back to Springfield, and east to Columbus.**

*Map by Bill Tipton / Compart Maps.*

This old postcard shows a covered bridge in Indianapolis that spanned the White River and gave passage to travelers on the National Road. It was built in 1831 at a cost then of $18,000 and was in use for sixty years until it was torn down and a new bridge took its place. ***Indiana Historical Society photo.***

Baker's home town of Indianapolis was a large, bustling city when he passed through on his record ride. ***Indiana Historical Society photo.***

This covered bridge was built in 1834. Because of the cost to build them, most bridges across the rivers charged a toll for all travelers, with various rates for walkers, those on horses, and eventually motor vehicles. The option was to take a ferry. ***Indiana Historical Society photo.***

Meridian Street in downtown Indianapolis in 1914 looking up at Monument Circle. The tower is the Indiana State Soldiers and Sailors monument that was built in 1888. The brick-lined streets of downtown Indianapolis were a welcome sight to Baker. Once he made it past the city limits, it was again a dirt road. ***Indiana Historical Society photo.***

Downtown Columbus, Ohio as it was when Baker rode through in 1914. ***Ohio Historical Society photo.***

## 2012:

**Getting ready to cross through the Jackson Truss Covered Bridge--built in 1832. Finding this great old covered bridge was the result of watching for "Old" National Road signs on US 40. As we approached the town of Greenup (between Effingham, IL and Terre Haute, IN) we took Cumberland Road, a brief departure from our main route.**

**Just west of Brazil, IN there is a split where US 40 goes to the right and the National Road goes left. Its just a short section of road and soon after meets back up with US 40.**

Joe and I had a great time on the June 2012 mapping ride when we were in Greenville, Illinois, but our time there meeting people and telling them about the Cannon Ball Project put us a little behind schedule. As mentioned previously, I had other business commitments back at my office in California and we had airline reservations that day from Columbus, Ohio.

We had arranged with Katy Wood from the AMA Motorcycle Hall of Fame Museum to hold the KTMs there for us for a few weeks while we returned to California. For that reason we needed to get back to Ohio that day. By mid-afternoon, we had mapped Highway 40 and the National Road to the border of Indiana at Terre Haute. We were still 270 miles from the hotel though, so we could see that there was no way we'd be able to finish our mapping work that afternoon. So at Terre Haute, we stopped our GPS tracking and made another "bomb run" on I-70 straight over to our hotel in Pickerington, near the AMA headquarters.

Our plan worked great, and we appreciated the kindness of Katy and everyone at the AMA for housing the two bikes and gear for a month. On July 16th, Joe and I flew back to Columbus and the next morning were back in Katy's office at the Hall of Fame Museum picking up our riding gear and then off we went on the KTMs again. Since we had cut off our mapping back in Terre Haute, we had to ride back on I-70 to the place when we had left Highway 40 and picked up the GPS mapping there. Weather was a factor for us on this trip. The heat index was 100-degrees, yet we'd get rain from time to time.

Riding Highway 40 in Indiana was very enjoyable. We had it marked on GPS, but we also let some road signs guide us when some special alternatives presented themselves. We were directed to some covered bridges and other interesting "Alternate National Road" sections we could take.

We eventually made it to Indianapolis, Erwin Baker's hometown. One thing I wanted to do was locate Baker's family plot at the Crown Hill Cemetery on the north end of town. All I had with me when we arrived was the Section and Plot numbers of his gravesite. As we started getting close I remembered seeing a photo of his large marker that had just "Cannon Ball Baker" on it. It was pretty easy to spot as we came up on it, so Joe and I parked our bikes and spent a little time there. We took some photos and just soaked up the moment at the final resting place of the man that this project was all about.

It was somber enough to see the actual grave marker on the ground for Erwin G. Baker, but alongside was the one for his wife Elenora L. Baker and we were surprised to also see one for a son, Sherman W. Baker. What especially caught our attention was Sherman's birth and death years...1914 to 1929. That meant that Sherman died when he was only 15 years old. I had not previously studied Erwin's family, but with a little

Both photos here show a section of the Old National Road near Putnamville (west of Indianapolis). The top photo shows how the road flowed through the countryside back in the day—the biggest difference of course was that in 1914 it was still a dirt road, and slightly narrower than seen here. In the lower photo, Joe and I check out an original bridge that can still be crossed over. We thought it was very cool to think that all of the travelers on the National Road in the early days passed over it as well.

The National Road (currently US 40) enters Indianapolis on Washington Street and follows through the town heading east.

searching learned that the boy died from a tooth infection. His death would prove to have a huge impact on his parents who were both emotionally devastated by their loss.

After stopping at the cemetery, Joe and I rode south and picked up signs for US Hwy 40 / National Road and headed east. We rode that day to Dayton, Ohio, as Baker had done, then got a hotel for the night.

Since we were staying very close to the Wright-Patterson Air Force Base and Air Museum, Joe and I stopped there the morning of July 19th and took a few hours to tour that fascinating museum. Then it was back on the bikes and we took the National Road to Springfield, Ohio and right to and through Columbus, coming out the other side and returning back to the Holiday Inn & Suites in Pickerington.

This was the weekend of the AMA Vintage Motorcycle Days at the Mid-Ohio Sports Car Course near Mansfield. So Joe and I enjoyed the weekend watching vintage bike races and concours judging, and we also gave a few talks to some attending riders who wanted to know more about the Cannon Ball Project.

The next day we got back to work on our mapping and rode east to stay on Baker's route…

One important stop that Joe and I made on our ride was to the Crown Hill Cemetery on the north side of Indianapolis, just down the street from the Indiana State Fairgrounds. This is the main headstone that overlooks where Erwin G. Baker and his family were laid to rest at that cemetery.

There are three markers at the Baker family plot. One for Erwin, one for his wife Elenora (not shown) and to our surprise, there was a marker for a son, Sherman. He was born in 1914 (the year Baker did his record ride) and he died in 1929. I later researched the son and learned that Sherman suffered an infection from dental surgery and died. He was just 15-years-old.

A brief shower passed over when Joe and I were stopped in Richmond, Indiana (east of Indianapolis). At least I had my rainsuit on!

It wasn't part of Baker's 1914 ride, but since he had taken a detour to Dayton, Ohio to visit the local Indian dealer, we followed his route and found ourselves virtually at the front door of the amazing Wright-Patterson Aviation Museum in Dayton. We spent a couple of hours there, could have spent a week.

In earlier chapters we pointed out the Madonna of the Trail statues that are found along the National Road. They were funded by the Daughters of the American Revolution to honor the women of the old west who supported the family's daunting task of crossing the country in covered wagons in the mid-1800s. This statue is in Richmond, Indiana.

CHAPTER 13:

# COLUMBUS TO GREENSBURG THEN & NOW

As Baker got closer and closer to New York City, he seemed possessed about not just breaking the existing record of Volney Davis, but beating it absolutely by as much as he was physically able. He also had some financial incentive with his Indian bonus, based on how much time he broke the existing record by. After riding for many hours in the pouring rain the previous day, Baker continued to ignore the cold and wet conditions that continued as he moved eastward through Ohio. He pointed out in his journal that the road conditions got really bad east of Columbus as he headed towards Wheeling, West Virginia and Pennsylvania.

**The Pennsylvania countryside has always been very picturesque. This period postcard is of the National Road, near Uniontown, where we believe Baker turned north to Greensburg.**

**In Baker's time there were usually two ways to cross the wide rivers, toll bridges or ferry boats. This old postcard shows both at the Ohio River near Wheeling, WV.**

His 7-horsepower, "two-speed" Indian that he rode had to be extremely challenging to ride in the deep mud that he mentions in his journal. He did not have the benefit of a clutch that operated like a modern day motorcycle, so how he kept the motor revving properly in deep mud bogs is difficult to imagine.

Yet despite the terrible conditions, and the fact that he had time to spare to establish the new record, it doesn't appear that he ever considered stopping for a day or so to wait for the weather to clear up and the roads to dry out. The muddy road between Columbus and Zanesville was particularly challenging.

His notes included, ***"The next day being May 13, I got some of this unlucky number wished on me. The boys in Columbus showed me through the city and finally led me to the end of the beautiful pavements they had there, and, as if chopped off by a knife, came the end of that good road. Before me lay roads that looked like newly-plowed fields, and I found on getting into them that it was mud almost knee deep. I had some real riding to do that day, my Indian acting more like a bucking bronco than a motorcycle."***

Baker's plan was to stay on the National Road through Ohio and West Virginia, but in Pennsylvania he would ride north to pick up the all-new (at the time) Lincoln Highway (which later became U.S. Highway 30). In his notes, however, he was not totally clear on what actual road he took north to get past Pittsburgh and over to Greensburg, Pennsylvania where he stopped for the night.

I felt a logical alternative would have been to continue on the National Road from Washington, Pennsylvania to Uniontown and then turn north on Braddock's Road, a famous road for moving troops in the Revolutionary War. Today, Braddock's Road is Pennsylvania Highway 119 and goes directly to Greensburg. Joe and I noted when we were doing our mapping rides that PA 119 ran parallel to a range of mountains near Greensburg like Baker says he "skirted" on his way there.

He wrote: ***"I arrived in Wheeling, W. Va., at noon, had some lunch there and continued on my way. It was my intention to pass through Pittsburgh but I began to figure that I would get into congested traffic in the Smoky City and lose a lot of time, so I didn't go directly down the main part of town, but switched at Washington, Pa., passing through West Pennsylvania, skirting the base of the mountains into Greensburg, Pa., and arriving there about 7 o'clock in the evening in a downpour of rain. I had covered a distance of 232.8 miles through rain and mud, so I put up at Greensburg that night."***

**The postcard shows downtown Greensburg, PA on a day with a nice blue sky and just a few clouds overhead. When Baker arrived there on May 13th it was actually pouring rain. He rode over 200 miles that day, all on muddy roads.**

**The map below shows the route that we *believe* Baker took in 1914 (purple line), and for sure it's the route we rode in 2012 and again in 2014. One thing Baker was clear about in his journal was that he didn't go through Pittsburgh. On the maps we researched, a route that stood out as being very likely was that from Washington, PA he could have stayed on the National Road to Uniontown, then taken Braddock's Road (now PA119) north to Greensburg. It's a historic Revolutionary War route and skirts the mountains in that area as he mentioned. My personal point of view was that with all of the rain that had passed through the area, Baker would not likely have taken to the hill country north of Washington, PA to get to the Pittsburgh area when there was a good flat road to Uniontown and then up Braddock's Road.**

Map by Bill Tipton / Compart Maps.

Except for the brick streets in the big cities, the National Road through Ohio was all dirt. On a nice day, travelers could usually enjoy a smooth ride, but rain quickly turned it into a very challenging adventure. The photos on both pages below were taken in 1914 (the year of Baker's ride) in the area near Zanesville, Ohio. *Ohio Historical Society photos.*

Knobby tires had not been invented yet when Baker rode through the muddy sections, but he sure could have used some!

This is how the National Road would have been on a good day...smooth and dry. Unfortunately, it rained the day he traveled across Ohio.

The National Road showing some ruts caused by vehicles traveling when the road must have still been wet.

(Above) Nice and straight, but relatively narrow. Motorists would be vulnerable to kids and dogs running out in the road in a section like this.

(Above) Wet, with ruts.

(Left) Another hazard for Baker would be encountering a buggy pulled by a horse that could easily get spooked by the sound of the motor.

# 2012:

**A place that Baker would have sped past on the National Road in 1914 is the Hedley Inn between Columbus and Wheeling. It was built in 1835 and served as one of ten stops for mail coaches to change horses.**

After spending the weekend of July 20-22 at the AMA Vintage Motorcycle Days event near Mansfield, Ohio, Joe and I were back in Pickerington that Sunday night, and the next morning (July 23rd) we departed east to continue our mapping. We were happy to be joined that morning by Mark Mederski, former Director of the AMA Motorcycle Hall of Fame Museum. He and I had worked together for a time when I was Chairman of the American Motorcycle Heritage Foundation, which oversees the operations of the Hall of Fame Museum. In addition to a solid motorcycle background (he was for many years the AMA's Membership Director), he has a great knowledge of Ohio history and could call out some points of interest.

So after meeting up at the AMA headquarters, Joe, Mark and I took off on U.S. Highway 40, not far from the AMA location. It wasn't long until he was directing us over to the side of the road to check out a historic house that was on the original National Road, as well as one of Ohio's famous "S" bridges.

**A marker identifying the Hedley Inn as being listed in the National Register of Historic Places.**

I'd have to say that eastern Ohio was one of my favorites of the whole route. That part of the country felt a little frozen in time. Except for the roads being paved and the modern gas stations, hotels and fast food restaurants, the rest of the scenery looked like it would have been just the same when Baker rode through, including some of the remaining mile markers from the 1800s that can still be spotted along the way.

When Joe, Mark and I got to Wheeling, we picked up two more friends who wanted to do some "mapping" with us, Rob Buydos and Tom Carson. We continued on the National Road and followed our belief that Baker had taken that route to Uniontown. This was the turnaround point for Mark, so we bid him adieu and Joe, Rob, Tom and I took Highway 119 towards Greensburg. Rob and Tom peeled off along that section to head back to Ohio, and Joe and I made it to Greensburg, as Baker had done in 1914.

Something unique to the state of Ohio are its "S-Bridges," a design believed to be stronger than a straight bridge and less vulnerable to being damaged by flood or high water. This one crosses over Fox Creek along the National Road. It was built in 1828.

Mark Mederski from the National Motorcycle Museum in Anamosa, IA was a willing guide for our ride across Ohio and into Pennsylvania. His knowledge of Ohio history was very useful.

(Left & Right) A pleasing sight for history buffs are the historic mileage markers that can still be found along the National Road. These markers date back hundreds of years and not only would they have been seen by Baker in 1914, but also by the thousands of settlers passing by in covered wagons during the 1800s.

# CHAPTER 14

# GREENSBURG TO NEW YORK CITY THEN & NOW

When Baker left Greensburg, Pennsylvania the morning of May 14th it was Day 11 of his ride and he was still over 400 miles from New York City. His plan then was to stop in Paoli (near Valley Forge on the west side of Philadelphia) for the night, then bring it in to New York the following day in twelve days, beating Volney Davis by eight days. Who wouldn't think that was a great feat?

He was now on the all-new Lincoln Highway that had opened only about six months before. It was America's first transcontinental highway built for motor vehicles and he made great time the entire day.

When Baker arrived at Paoli it was 6:00 p.m. and he had been riding for 14 hours. George Maslen, the Indian dealer in Philadelphia, was on call from Indian headquarters in Springfield, Massachusetts (known then as the Wig Wam) to help Baker with whatever he needed. Maslen was expecting Baker would be in for the night and back on the road the next day. But Baker had other plans. He wrote, ***"The roads began to look better to me, and I soon made up my mind that I would not stop until I had reached New York."***

Baker was greeted by Maslen and a small group of riders. After enjoying a dinner meal with them and relaxing a bit, Baker knew the clock was ticking and he let everyone know he had decided to keep going. He had come so far, and so fast, he was ready to go put his name on the transcontinental record as quickly as he could. So with a local guide, he was back on his way that night, bound for New York City.

He added, ***"I reached Philadelphia about 6 o'clock in the evening, or, rather, Paoli, which is 30 miles west of Philadelphia. There George S. Maslen, the Indian dealer at Philadelphia, met me with a number of riders and he elected one of them to show me the way into New York City. After having supper at Paoli, we started for New York City, and it being a very dark night, we were lost two or three times, even with the rider who knew the roads. He showed me the way to Weehawken, N.J., where I took the ferry to New York City. This ferry consumed over half an hour of my finishing time, and my feet touched the streets of New York at 10 minutes past 12, the night of the 14th. I landed at West Forty-second street. My race with time***

**After all of the challenges that Baker had along the way with sand, mud and rocks, he had to be overjoyed at the flat and smooth dirt roads that awaited him in Pennsylvania. The new Lincoln Highway was only six months old when he came through and it must have felt like a racetrack to him. Plus the weather stayed clear that whole day for him.**

***was then ended and I found that I had accomplished that which I had undertaken; that my trip had taken only 11 days, 12 hours and ten minutes."***

So Baker had reached the end of his journey. He had ridden 418 miles on that final day and the transcontinental record was his. Just as he was leaving San Diego back on May 3rd, he had been quoted saying that he was ***"...ready to make the transcontinental trip that would make them all 'sit up and take notice.'"***

And take notice they did. After receiving a telegram from George Maslen that Baker was on his way from Pennsylvania, representatives of the F.A.M. (including fellow racer, John U. Constant.) were waiting for him at the Manhattan landing dock of the Weehawken Ferry. Baker added, ***"Pictures were taken by flashlight at the ferry house, and then I proceeded to the Hotel Astor, where I was met by a delegation of New York reporters and Associated Press men, also by Mr. Sherman, of the Publicity Department of the Hendee Manufacturing Company."***

**Seen here is a postcard showing the Lincoln Highway some years after Baker's 1914 ride.**

**From Greensburg, Baker followed the new and well-traveled Lincoln Highway (later designated US Highway 30) through the hills of Pennsylvania. As noted in this chapter, following a dinner break in Paoli (west of Philadelphia), he and a local guide departed for New York City on what is now US Highway 1, where he completed his 11½ day adventure just after midnight.**

*Map by Bill Tipton / Compart Maps.*

It was dark when Baker made it onto Manhattan, but the next morning he surely got a good look at Lady Liberty. Thus he completed his "Ocean-to-Ocean" experience.

When Baker arrived on Manhattan there was some welcoming and press activities at the Weehawkin ferry landing. He then rode over to the prestigious Hotel Astor for additional interviews with reporters. He finally called it a night and went to bed at 2:00 a.m.

Indian's P.R man Sherman who was mentioned by Baker must have been a pretty good salesman, as he convinced numerous journalists to turn out after midnight to come and hear Erwin's story. Baker obliged all of the reporters and answered their questions until two-o'clock in the morning. One creative writer had an angle he was going with and came up with the line, "He shot across the country like a cannon ball!" It was a great story and the cannon ball reference stuck from that day forward.

In 1975 Russ Catlin wrote an article for ***Automobile Quarterly*** called "The Inimitable Mister Baker." He wrote that Baker commented at the time "After all, where would Barney Ofield have gotten without his cigar?" For Erwin Baker, it was the nickname Cannon Ball instead of a cigar that was his new icon and he had it trademarked.

He was now and forever more Cannon Ball Baker!

## BAKER'S OWN STORY

Baker's post-ride story ran twelve days later in the May 26, 1914 edition of *The Bicycling World and Motorcycle Review…*

*While I arrived in New York City at midnight, May 14, clipping approximately 9 days from the previous transcontinental record, according to my way of thinking I really achieved the feat four months before. What I mean by that is: Thorough preparation and endless calculation preceding the trip is what brought me through.*

*First, I laid out my route – a matter of no small importance in selecting roads and towns through which to pass. Then, having done this I enlisted the cooperation of a weather expert and together we examined weather conditions over my chosen territory for ten years past. Analysis showed that, contrary to general opinion, May was the best month for me to undertake a coast-to-coast ride on a motorcycle. So relying on the weather's past performances, I determined to start in May, leaving San Diego on the 3rd at 12 o'clock, Eastern time.*

### THE RESULTS OF HIS FORESIGHT

*The weather ran true to form, and I did not hit rain until after I had gotten east of the Mississippi Valley, at which point I struck gravelly roads which absorbed moisture readily and gave me minimum trouble. This was just as I had planned. I followed behind a storm area trailing from west to east and struck no storm until another one finally caught up with me. During the rainy period I covered one stage of 72 miles through wind and water in 1 hour and 55 minutes.*

*Another matter of foresight which helped me was the planting of tanks of gasoline ahead of me at remote spots, where I knew no gas would have been obtainable. Thus I avoided fuel troubles.*

*Still another factor, of course, was my machine. I rode a 1914 7-horsepower twin two-speed Indian, with electric equipment and cradle spring frame. In all the distance of 3,497 miles I had no mechanical difficulties whatever and I encountered all the different road conditions known to travel. Between Mammoth, Cal.*

The Holland Tunnel had not been built yet in 1914, so Baker needed to get onto Manhattan from New Jersey on the Weehawkin ferry. As soon as he landed there at 10 minutes past midnight, a small contingent of people were awaiting him, including a fellow racer named John U. Constant as well as representatives from the Federation of American Motorcyclists. His record ride was now complete.

*And Glamis I rode 64 miles on the railroad ties, crossing trestles and bridges. In a 1,027-mile desert stretch of sand, cactus, heat, thirst and desolateness, I traveled 115 miles without seeing a single living thing – except Gila monsters and snakes.*

## INDIANA GOOD TO HIM

*Four mountain ranges were negotiated. At one point at the northern end of Arizona I climbed from 200 feet below sea level to an altitude of 9,647 feet into the mountain snows. It was in this mountain work that the two-speed showed its supreme qualities. My brake power, too, in making the precipitous descent of the winding mountain trails, never failed me for a moment. If it had, I might not be able now to tell this story.*

*When I struck Indiana the authorities raised the speed limit for one day, so that I could do my best. And I did, making 376 miles in 11½ hours. I am a Hoosier, and the welcome and encouragement which the people of my home state gave me as I passed from town to town was a generous and appreciated demonstration.*

*From Columbus, Oh., to Greensburg, Pa. the going was bad. I ploughed my way through 232 miles of mud – and was mighty glad to get out of it onto firm ground again.*

*My final dash was a 418-mile one from Greensburg, Pa. to New York City. This I did in 20 hours, 16 of which was actual riding. Total time for the trip was 11 days 12 hours and 10 minutes, during which I took only 46 hours' sleep – about 4 hours per day. Average mileage per day was 304.*

## HOW HIS FITNESS STOOD UP

*I took along an extra electric light bulb, expecting to need it with such hard riding. But I arrived in New York with the original bulb still in its socket and burning brightly. My batteries were still in fine condition and needed no recharging or attention during the ride.*

*It is my estimate it was the cradle spring frame above all that contributed to my success. It absorbed all road shocks and vibration and this, of course, saved all my strength and, besides, enabled me to make speed over the roughest roads.*

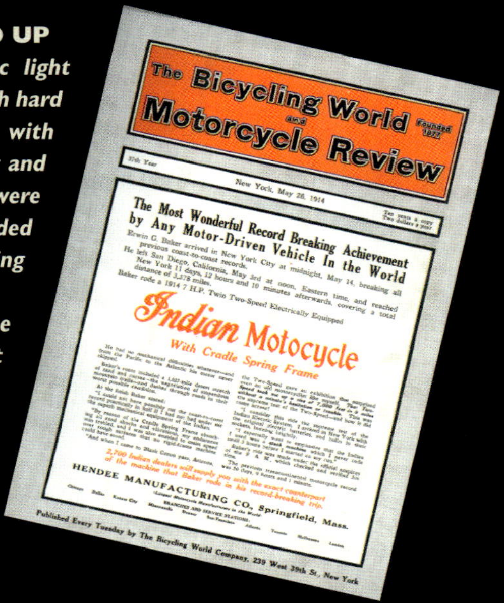

The Bicycling World and Motorcycle Review
Founded 1877

New York, May 26, 1914

Ten cents a copy
Two dollars a year

The Most Wonderful Record Breaking Achievement by Any Motor-Driven Vehicle In the World

Erwin G. Baker arrived in New York City at midnight, May 14, breaking all previous coast-to-coast records.
He left San Diego, California, May 3rd at noon, Eastern time, and reached New York 11 days, 12 hours and 10 minutes afterwards, covering a total distance of 3,378 miles.
Baker rode a 1914 7 H.P. Twin Two-Speed Electrically Equipped

Indian Motocycle
With Cradle Spring Frame

2,700 Indian dealers will supply you with the exact counterpart of the machine that Baker rode in his record-breaking trip.

HENDEE MANUFACTURING CO., Springfield, Mass.

Published Every Tuesday by The Bicycling World Company, 239 West 39th St., New York

As soon as the news broke of Baker's success, virtually any or all of the motorcycle equipment manufacturers with products on his Indian booked space in the next issue of the leading magazines to tout their involvement. We know Baker had already arranged deals with most of them for a bonus if he set the record, so many likely had the ads already created and were just waiting for the confirmation that the transcontinental record had, in fact, been broken.

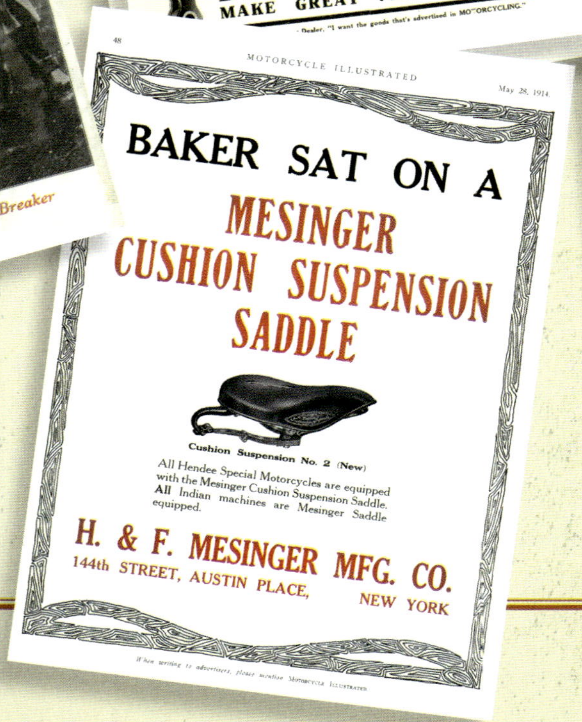


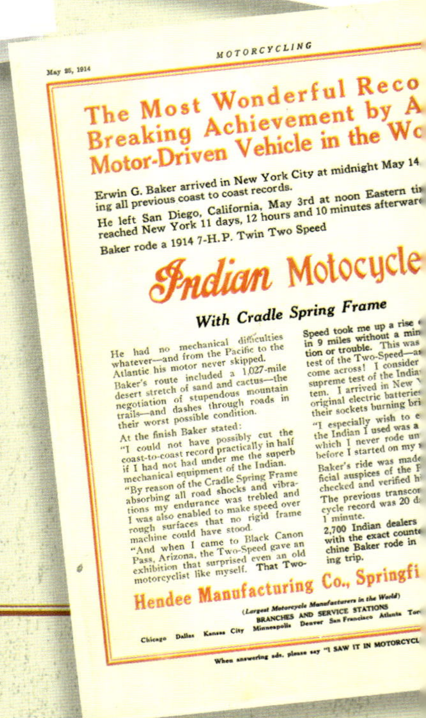

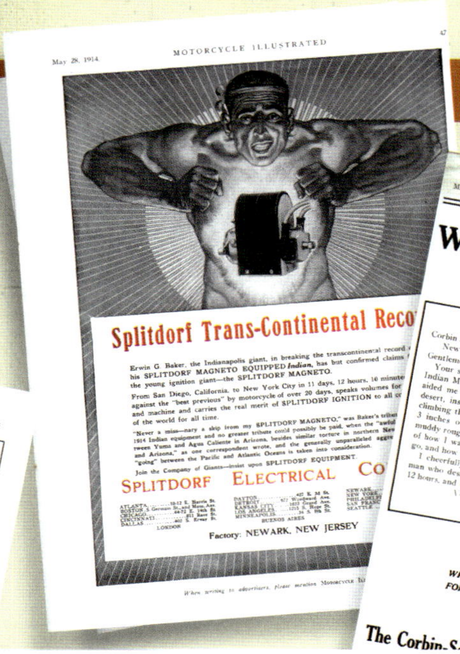
May 28, 1914.
MOTORCYCLE ILLUSTRATED
Splitdorf Trans-Continental Reco
SPLITDORF ELECTRICAL CO
Factory: NEWARK, NEW JERSEY

May 28, 1914.
MOTORCYCLE ILLUSTRATED
41
With Baker From Coast to Coast
Springfield, Mass., May 20, 1914.
Corbin Screw Corp.,
New Britain, Conn.
Gentlemen:—
Your speedometer, which was attached to my Indian Motocycle, was one of the factors which aided me in crossing 1027 miles of hot sandy desert, insuring me against losing my trail; in climbing the mountains where I passed through 3 inches of snow; fording streams, and over muddy rough roads; I found it telling me the tale of how I was diminishing the distance I had to go, and how fast I was accomplishing my task.
I cheerfully recommend it, especially to the man who desires to beat my record of 11 days, 12 hours, and 10 minutes.
Very truly yours,
(Signed) E. G. Baker.
THE
CORBIN-BROWN
SPEEDOMETER
"The Speedometer of Absolute Accuracy"
At an altitude of 7000 feet, in a temperature of 120°, on a desert-crossing of 1027 miles of sun-scorched sand, the Corbin-Brown Speedometer maintained an unerringly accurate register. A more rigorous test of a speedometer's value cannot be devised—a more conclusive proof of the superiority of the centrifugal Corbin-Brown can hardly be demanded.
WRITE TODAY
FOR CATALOG
The Corbin-Screw Corporation
IN, CONN.

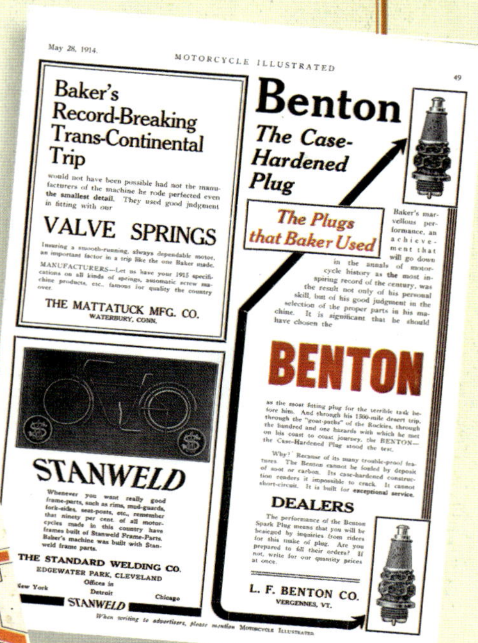
May 28, 1914.
MOTORCYCLE ILLUSTRATED
49
Baker's Record-Breaking Trans-Continental Trip
would not have been possible had not the manufacturers of the machine he rode perfected even the smallest detail. They used good judgment in fitting with our
VALVE SPRINGS
Insuring a smooth-running, always dependable motor, an important factor in a trip like the one Baker made.
MANUFACTURERS—Let us have your 1915 specifications on all kinds of springs, automatic screw machine products, etc., famous for quality the country over.
THE MATTATUCK MFG. CO.
WATERBURY, CONN.
STANWELD
THE STANDARD WELDING CO.
EDGEWATER PARK, CLEVELAND
Benton
The Case-Hardened Plug
The Plugs that Baker Used
Baker's marvellous performance, an achievement that will go down in the annals of motorcycle history as the most inspiring record of the century, was the result not only of his personal skill, but of his good judgment in the selection of the proper parts in his machine. It is significant that he should have chosen the
BENTON
DEALERS
L. F. BENTON CO.
VERGENNES, VT.

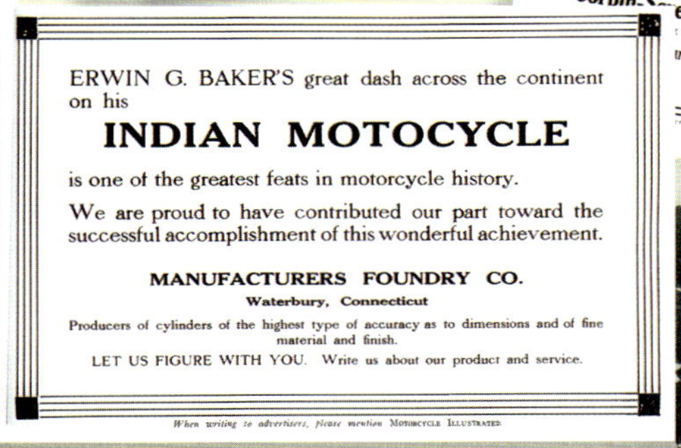
ERWIN G. BAKER'S great dash across the continent on his
INDIAN MOTOCYCLE
is one of the greatest feats in motorcycle history.
We are proud to have contributed our part toward the successful accomplishment of this wonderful achievement.
MANUFACTURERS FOUNDRY CO.
Waterbury, Connecticut
Producers of cylinders of the highest type of accuracy as to dimensions and of fine material and finish.
LET US FIGURE WITH YOU. Write us about our product and service.

ERWIN BAKER'S OWN STORY
Of His Record-Breaking Transcontinental Trip
MOTORCYCLE ILLUSTRATED
Thursday
SECOND MAY NUMBER
May 28
A Motorcycle Runabout for Two
Indian Motocycle With Side Car
HENDEE MANUFACTURING CO., Springfield, Mass.

May 28, 1914.
MOTORCYCLE ILLUSTRATED
43
Baker's Motor Had Good Valves
Baker used valves with cast iron seats in his trip across the continent and they came through in excellent condition, just as they stand the test of everyday service in thousands of motorcycles.
Any serious valve trouble would have lessened Baker's chances and probably spoiled a record breaking trip.
Cast Iron Seat Valves
will give any motorcycle manufacturer the same dependable service they gave to Baker. They will insure good compression and full power of the motor for months after the machine has left the factory.
Nothing is more important than good valves in giving satisfaction to the motorcycle rider.
Our engineers are at the service of any motorcycle manufacturer to help him find the best valve for his motor.
The Electric Welding Products Co.
"A Valve Department for Motorcycle Makers"
CLEVELAND, OHIO

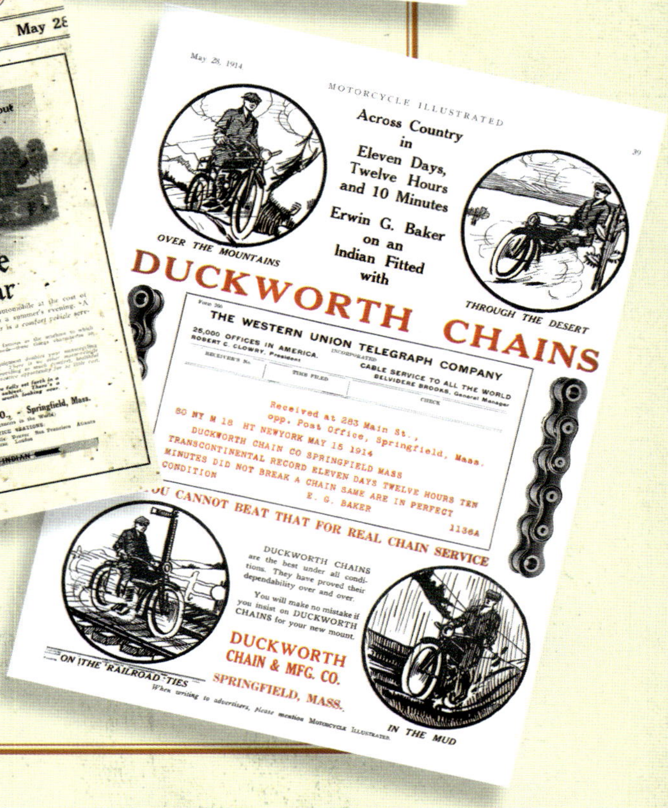
May 28, 1914.
MOTORCYCLE ILLUSTRATED
Across Country in Eleven Days, Twelve Hours and 10 Minutes
Erwin G. Baker on an Indian Fitted with
OVER THE MOUNTAINS
THROUGH THE DESERT
DUCKWORTH CHAINS
THE WESTERN UNION TELEGRAPH COMPANY
25,000 OFFICES IN AMERICA.
ROBERT C. CLOWRY, President
CABLE SERVICE TO ALL THE WORLD
BELVIDERE BROOKS, General Manager
Received at 283 Main St., opp. Post Office, Springfield, Mass.
80 NY M 18 HT NEWYORK MAY 15 1914
DUCKWORTH CHAIN CO SPRINGFIELD MASS
TRANSCONTINENTAL RECORD ELEVEN DAYS TWELVE HOURS TEN MINUTES DID NOT BREAK A CHAIN SAME ARE IN PERFECT CONDITION
E. G. BAKER
1136A
YOU CANNOT BEAT THAT FOR REAL CHAIN SERVICE
DUCKWORTH CHAINS are the best under all conditions. They have proved their dependability over and over.
You will make no mistake if you insist on DUCKWORTH CHAINS for your new mount.
DUCKWORTH CHAIN & MFG. CO.
SPRINGFIELD, MASS.
ON THE RAILROAD TIES
IN THE MUD

The background map (without the Cannon Ball details) originally appeared in the February 24, 1912 edition of *The Bicycling World and Motorcycle Review.* *Don Emde Collection.*

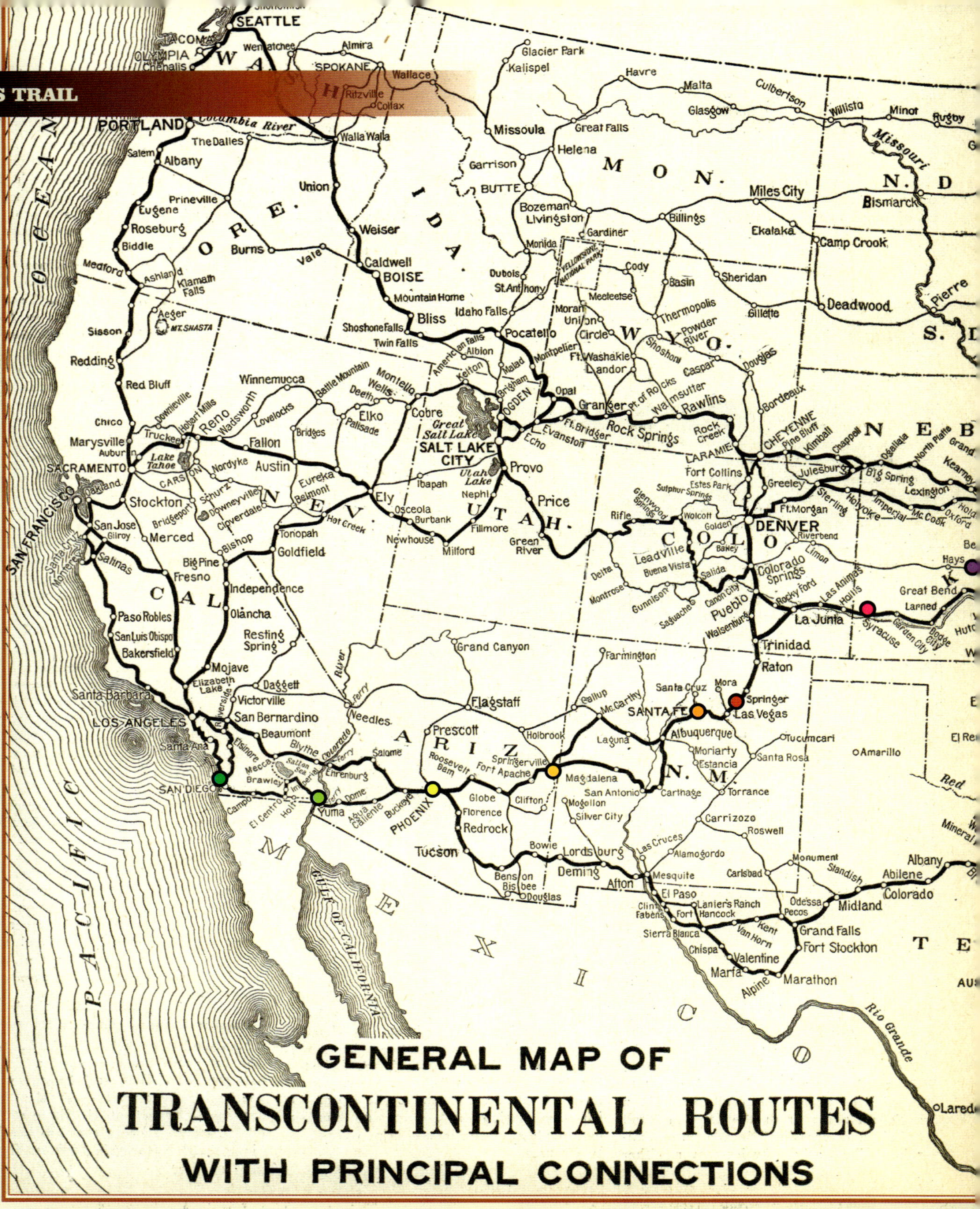


START

| MAY 3, 1914: | MAY 3, 1914: | MAY 4, 1914: | MAY 5, 1914: | MAY 6, 1914: | MAY 7, 1914: | MAY 8, 1914: |
|---|---|---|---|---|---|---|
| SAN DIEGO | YUMA, AZ | PHOENIX, AZ | SPRINGERVILLE, AZ | SANTA FE, NM | WATROUS, NM | SYRACUSE, KS |

MAY 9, 1914: ELLSWORTH, KS

MAY 10, 1914: LEXINGTON, MO

MAY 11, 1914: GREENVILLE, IL

MAY 12, 1914: COLUMBUS, OH

MAY 13, 1914: GREENSBURG, PA

END MAY 14, 1914: NEW YORK CITY

# 2012:

**After riding on the National Road (US Highway 40) for four days, it was great to take off from Greensburg on another historic American highway—the Lincoln Highway—designated U.S. Highway 30. This photo shows the road as we were leaving the Greensburg area and heading east into the countryside.**

**Joe and I had Gettysburg on our list of planned stops that day, but I did not realize until we saw signs for it, that the entrance to the Flight 93 National Memorial was also right on US 30. It is located in an area that was little known before the 9/11 attacks, but on September 11, 2001, the world learned about Shanksville, Pennsylvania. It was where United Airlines flight 93 went down in an open field there. Just as rain began to fall, we turned in to go check out the National Park.**

The morning of July 24, 2012, Joe and I were virtually right where Baker was on Day 11 in 1914...Greensburg, Pennsylvania. We took off on the KTMs, heading east on US 30, the historic Lincoln Highway. The weather had continued to be warm and humid, as it had been ever since we had flown back to Ohio from California a week earlier.

As I am sure it was for Baker, we were starting to feel the excitement of completing our ride, although business and other circumstances required that this leg of our mapping rides would only go as far as Philadelphia this time. Our final "sprint" to Manhattan was another couple of months off.

As we rode that morning I saw some road signs along Highway 30 for the Flight 93 National Memorial, where United Airlines flight 93 had gone down on September 11, 2001. The crash site was in a field in Shanksville that we would be passing. It wasn't on my planner for the day, but since Joe and I were connected by radio, we talked and both agreed that it would be worth the time to go check it out. We thought it could possibly be a suggested stop for our Centennial riders in 2014.

Just as we got to the turnoff to the park, the weather made a rapid change, and in a matter of minutes we were totally surrounded by clouds and the thunder we

**As Joe and I proceeded on the entrance road to the Flight 93 National Memorial the weather began to get very wild. The entrance parkway is void of any trees, so Joe and I were pretty exposed and took note of the loud thunder, high winds and lightning striking the ground as we rode in. We had no other options and continued at a safe pace for the five-mile ride to the Park site. When we arrived we spotted a Visitor Center where we quickly parked the bikes and took shelter.**

heard sounded very close. There were not many trees there at the entrance and as we started riding into the park we saw lightning, and soon after heard its thunder. The rain was picking up and it was getting very windy. I've ridden in thunder and lightning a few times in my life and whenever it seems to happen I never can remember what all the "do's and don'ts" are. Are we more likely to get hit by lightning riding, or should we park and wait it out (while standing on wet ground)? All I knew at the time was that without any trees, Joe and I were the tallest objects and maybe we'd be like lightning rods, but we didn't have any options.

We just kept going and followed the signs to the Visitor's Center where we hoped there might be some structures to get under. It was about a five-mile ride, but when we got there we saw the main building that was mainly restrooms, but there was some shelter and we quickly got off the bikes and under the cover.

The weather was really wild for a few minutes and the rain was dumping down in buckets. But as quickly as it arrived, it passed by, and Joe and I were able to take a few minutes to look at the display boards, right across from where Flight 93 had crashed on that tragic day.

We soon were back on the bikes, while keeping an eye on what direction the storm was heading, compared to where we needed to go. No way did we want to possibly catch up with it, but luckily U.S.30 went in a different direction.

The next stop that was on our ride plan was the Gettysburg National Park and Museum, virtually right on the Lincoln Highway. I'm kind of a Civil War buff, as is Joe, and we had long looked forward to going to see it in person. It was a few hours ride from Shanksville, but when we got there we made our way through the town and over to the museum. We parked and took the tour of the museum, which included some great film and audio-visual programs.

**The wild weather actually only lasted a few minutes and it quickly moved past. We spent a little time there checking out the displays at the Visitor Center, and also giving the storm some time to get beyond the park exit that we needed to take.**

The minutes raced by quickly, and sooner than we wanted to we knew we needed to get back on the road. We mounted up, but before we exited the park we rode into the battlefield area and took some photos. We could have spent a week there and not seen everything, but were grateful we had the time there that we did. We knew we'd be coming back and it became a planned stop on the 2014 Centennial Ride.

Back on U.S. 30 we headed east towards Philadelphia. Once we got past York, (home of the Harley-Davidson factory), the towns start stacking up one after the other and traffic slowed considerably. Late in the day we made it to the west side of the Philadelphia metro area and found a hotel in Malvern, the

**US Highway 30 goes right through the town of Gettysburg, making the Gettysburg National Military Park a must-stop. Both Joe and I call ourselves "Civil War Buffs," so we headed straight for the Visitor Center where watched a short film and checked out as many displays as we could cram into our brief stop.**

**The view of "The Valley of Death" looking west from an area in the high ground called Little Round Top. As many as 51,000 soldiers on both sides lost their lives at Gettysburg in the three day battle in 1863. There were approximately as many soldiers killed, injured or reported missing there as the entire Vietnam War.**

**After touring the Visitor Center, Joe and I rode around in the battlefield area, stopping to check out many of the monuments that were erected to honor famous Generals, armies and more from both the North and South.**

**The cannons are silent now.**

next town over from Paoli, where Baker had made his dinner stop in 1914. Our part of the journey would end here, as I needed to fly home again to take care of business matters.

A friend there in Malvern, John Lawless, had arranged that Joe and I could park the KTMs at the Simeone Foundation Automotive Museum, right near the Philadelphia International Airport. So the next day Joe and I would ride there to the museum and park the bikes and our riding gear, then they had someone take us to the airport to catch our flight. The final leg from Malvern to New York City would have to wait just a little longer.

I had been invited to come back in September to be a Grand Marshal of a very upscale auto and motorcycle event called the Radnor Hunt Concours there in Malvern. John Lawless was involved with the event and kindly offered to assist with any final details of my Cannon Ball Project that needed to be done. So it worked out that when I came back in September, he and I, and his brother Michael Lawless would take a ride to map that final link to Manhattan. In the five weeks in between, John and Michael, and Ron McGill, a former pro roadracer from the area, had transferred the bikes and gear from the Simeone museum to Ron's garage.

The day after the concours, we all gathered at Ron's house to take off on our ride. Ron had commitments that day that prevented him from going with us, but John, Michael and I were on our way. Joe didn't make that trip with me, so I let John use the white KTM 990, and Michael had his own bike.

This day truly was exciting for me, as I knew I would finally fulfill the coast-to-coast route that Baker had ridden. Ironically, where we took off from Malvern that morning, I had to be within just a mile or two of where Baker had met up with George Maslen and his crew in Paoli in 1914.

We got onto U.S. 30 east and the traffic was really bad. The key problem is the route is essentially a couple hundred years old, so some of the intersections go through historic areas that were built so close together there is no way to widen them for left-turn lanes. John knew I wanted to map the true road, but after a while he let me know that there was an alternate road that parallels Route 30 and traffic flows well on it. So he led me onto Montgomery Road and the pace immediately picked up.

We next came to Route 1 which went due north, and we were Manhattan bound! We rode for about two hours heading north on what was the historic old road Baker took, just that its now three- and four-lanes wide in each direction. We eventually passed the Newark airport and followed the signs from there for the Holland Tunnel. In Baker's day there was no tunnel there. He crossed over on the Weehawken Ferry boat. But we went through the tunnel and followed the signs to Battery Park. I had studied Manhattan a bit and knew that I wanted to end our ride in sight of the water, and also the best symbol I could think of to signify an ocean-to-ocean ride...the Statue of Liberty.

It was kind of comical when we got down there to Battery Park, as I was hoping we could park our bikes in a place so we could take photos with the Statue of Liberty in the background. Well...it was a nice thought, but there were tourists and taxis and buses, and police cars everywhere.

Luckily John spotted a parking area down the street along a building on the waterfront that read in huge letters: "Homeland Security" and "National Guard." Well, it seemed that they probably didn't want any motorcycles riding around, but we really didn't see any "Keep Out" signs. So we parked the bikes and hatched a little plan to get the "Money Shot" of the whole ride, the whole project for that matter, with the Statue of Liberty in the background.

Alongside, we noticed the next building was a restaurant, but we couldn't see any parking. So we had Michael take my camera and when he was ready to shoot, John and I rode the KTMs over between the Homeland Security building and the restaurant and suddenly we had the clear view to the Statue of Liberty and Michael took the all-important photo. Mission accomplished!

**There is no better place to end an "Ocean to Ocean" motorcycle ride than across from the Statue of Liberty. This hurried photo of myself (left) and John Lawless was taken by John's brother Michael on the walkway alongside the Homeland Security office at Battery Park on Manhattan.**

**Many people helped me during my multi-year project when the need arose. Such was the case with the Lawless brothers, John (middle) and Michael (right) who were the perfect guides for my final leg of the mapping ride. They live near Philadelphia and are familiar with nearby New York City.**

Our next thoughts were, "We're not authorized to be parked here, and we better go before National Guard commandos or Homeland Security agents drop down on us loaded with AK47s." Then we looked around and realized we weren't doing anything that was drawing any attention. Our bikes were already in actual parking spots so we decided to walk next door and have a soda before we hit the road back to Philly.

So John, Michael and I celebrated with soft drinks at the patio bar of the Battery Gardens restaurant and basked in the moment. It seemed pretty unreal, thinking of all the other mapping rides I had done the last few years and with the exception of a few little sections to tie together out west, this part of the project was now complete.

Gazing out at the New York harbor, I pondered the fact that I had not only "found" Cannon Ball's trail, but had also ridden it.

# CHAPTER 15

# NEXT UP: PLANNING THE CANNON BALL CENTENNIAL RIDE

As I sat at the Harbor View bar of the Battery Gardens Restaurant gazing at the Statue of Liberty and enjoying soft drinks with brothers John and Michael Lawless, I began to think about not only what was now behind me, but what was still ahead. As previously mentioned, it had been the plan from the start of the project that we would celebrate Baker's 1914 ride with a Centennial ride 100 years to the day that he had. Now it was time to put that together.

The three of us headed south back to Ron McGill's house in Malvern. The next day John got me to the airport and I flew home. The two KTMs and riding gear were shipped back using the Federal Companies, a century-old specialized vehicle transportation company that I have used many times in the past.

The idea was this: Now that we knew the route…we had "*found*" Cannon Ball's Trail, next we wanted to honor Erwin G. Baker with a celebration ride. It would be on his route and begin exactly 100 years to the day that he had ridden it.

I wasn't sure then exactly how many people would be going. Maybe just Joe and I could do it? But soon I started getting requests from people who heard about the project and wanted to go. I also wasn't sure what it would cost to make it an actual group ride? There were a million questions in my head then, most without answers.

**Here I am giving a Power Point presentation about the Cannon Ball Centennial Ride at a monthly meeting of the San Diego Adventure Riders club. I was looking for volunteers to serve as guides on Day 1 for the ride over to Yuma. This was the part of the whole route to New York that I worried most that our Cannon Ball riders could get off course in the desert and perhaps stuck out there in 100+ degree heat. SDAR came through with plenty of skilled riders to keep everyone on track.**

As I began to think of it as an event, I figured I'd start at the top and lock in my sponsors. In all the mapping and pre-running I had great support from companies providing products for us. This included the two motorcycles from KTM North America. When they loaned me the two Adventure 990s, there were no commitments made at the time that they could or would sponsor me any farther than the mapping work. We had some talks about financial sponsorship, which went back and forth for about a month. But in early July I learned they did not have any financial support to offer.

So now I had a problem. To properly support a group of riders going coast-to-coast, partially on dirt roads, we needed a support truck and trailer, plus I'd have to feed and house the people driving it, and numerous other expenses. Obviously we had come a long way with KTM, but my options were either to pay it all out of my own pocket, or find another company to sponsor us. I felt we had a great story to tell and that I could provide some company a good sponsorship value, so we said thank you to KTM, returned the two bikes, and continued the sponsorship search.

Luckily, I was attending the annual MotoGP races at the Indianapolis Motor Speedway that August and I was able to arrange a meeting with Bob Starr, General Manager of Communications at Yamaha Motor Corp. USA. So with exotic MotoGP race bikes howling in the background, I explained to Bob what we were doing and what my needs were for some corporate help. I had one advantage there as I was a former Yamaha rider back in my racing days and Bob was eager to hear my plans.

After only a few minutes into my "pitch" he jumped in and said, "We want to do this. How much do you need?" So I gave him a couple of prices, as I had done with KTM, that could include different things at

Chapter 4—starting on page 41—tells how Joe and I got off course on a mapping ride in 2012 and ran into some other problems that almost led to us spending the night out in the desert between Yuma and Phoenix. As a postscript to that story and the lady from the Arizona Historical Society who had told me that "you could drive a motor home down that road," well...she was right. After we got the Yamahas, we still had that one section of Arizona to get right, and to bookmark on our Garmin GPS files. That was a fun road on the adventure bikes, and I would not have hesitated to drive a motor home down it either.

different levels. So Bob left Indianapolis after the races with the information he needed and said he would need a few days to come back with what they could do. And within a week or so, I got the green light and Yamaha became the Presenting Sponsor of the Cannon Ball Centennial Ride.

In the months to follow, the pace really picked up. Calls and emails were coming in from people who wanted to go with us. I soon had entry forms with all the necessary "legal-eeze," and an entry fee ($750). Initially I was thinking a group of 20 riders would be about right. Before it was over, that number crept up to about 25.

Luckily for me, my sister, Nancy Emde-Steward and her husband Chris Steward wanted to get involved. They have been running Trail Boss Tours, a motorcycle adventure travel company for many years and they came on board with their expertise with working with big groups, hotel planning and reservations and other logistics. Nancy was busy right away getting arrangements with the hotels that Joe and I had picked out in our pre-runs, and getting our entered riders booked with their rooms.

While all that was happening I traveled to Yamaha Motor Corp. USA and took possession of two 2013 Yamaha Super Tenere adventure bikes for the ride. So it was off to Boyko Racing again in Costa Mesa. After setting up the two KTMs for the mapping rides, I knew they would do a great job outfitting the Yamahas, and they did.

Our other prime supporters of the KTMs were still with us to outfit the Yamahas. That included Butler Maps, Continental Tires, DP Brakes, Moose Racing, Motion Pro, Parts Unlimited, Saddlemen Seats & Luggage and Touratech.

Once we had the bikes all outfitted, in mid-February (2014) Joe and I did a break-in ride over to Arizona to check out the new bikes, and we also rode the one section we had not ridden yet from Agua Caliente to Buckeye. (That was the part Joe and I missed when we got stuck out in the hills). Old family friend and racing legend Ralph White ands his brother Tom came along with us, as did my sister Nancy to drive the support truck and trailer. Everything went great on this test ride, and all of the rest of the plans came together as well.

We had the kind offer from one of our Centennial riders, Randy Aron, to use the parking lot at his Cycle Visions motorcycle retail store in the Old Town district of San Diego on May 2nd. This is where the riders came to sign in and unload their bikes. That night we had a festive Mexican dinner and welcome party at the Old Town Tequila Factory restaurant for all of the riders and their families and our crew.

Then the next day, May 3rd, at 9:00 a.m., which was exactly 100 years to the minute since Erwin G. Baker left, we departed from San Diego and headed east. The "Cannon Ball Centennial Ride, Presented by Yamaha" had begun.

When Joe and I let it be known that we still had that one section of Arizona to get bookmarked on GPS before the Centennial ride, two old friends who had signed up for the ride said they wanted to go along. Ralph White (left) is a legendary motorcycle racer with a Daytona 200 victory, among many others, to his credit. He was inducted into the AMA Motorcycle Hall of Fame in 2001. He and his brother Tom (middle) talk with Joe at a stop we made that day.

In addition to Joe Colombero—who was not on this ride—the key members of my team that put together the details and logistics of the Centennial ride were my son-in-law Ryan Rose (left), sister Nancy Emde-Steward and her husband Chris Steward. This photo was taken when the four of us made a pre-ride trip to Brawley to work out a couple of skill-level options for riders to get through the desert sections on the first day of the Cannon Ball Centennial ride.

The Motorcycle Industry Council was celebrating its Centennial in 2014, so they partnered with us with Media support, provided a set of these decals for the all bikes, and covered the costs to have Gary McKechnie and a videographer come along on the ride to produce a daily blog of the ride. It can still be seen online at *http://www.motorcycles.org/cannonball.aspx.*

After all of the pre-runs were done, we took the two Yamaha Super Teneres back to Boyko Racing in Costa Mesa for a final service and to install the bodywork back on my bike after getting a new "Molly-inspired" paint job by Boris Landoff of California Cycle & Watercraft, reminiscent of the original 1970s design by the late-great Roland "Molly" Sanders. Proprietor Ted Boyko is on my right and his assistant Casey Driggers on my left. The bikes they prepped for us all ran flawlessly for the whole ride.

(Lower left): This is our trailer we used to transport the rider's gear bags, with room on-board when needed to rescue a broken down machine. Graphics by Jim Conquest of Imagine It Graphics. (Below): One of the people who signed up to go on the Cannon Ball Centennial Ride was Steve Read, who works at the Toyota U.S. headquarters in Torrance, CA. He was able to arrange for us the loan of a Tundra pickup truck to use as our lead support vehicle. We also used my personal Chevy Silverado as the sweep vehicle.

Before the start of the Cannon Ball Centennial Ride, *Orange County Register* writer Susan Carpenter wrote this story about me and my Cannon Ball project.

ORANGE COUNTY REGISTER

FRIDAY, MARCH 21, 2014

# WHEELS

RETIRED RACER AND MOTORCYCLE HISTORIAN DON EMDE AIMS TO RETRACE THE 1914 CROSS-COUNTRY RIDE BY ERWIN GEORGE BAKER.

Don Emde, 62, former Daytona 200 race winner, reconstructed the path he believes Erwin George "Cannon Ball" Baker took during an 11-day cross-country ride on an Indian motorcycle. Emde plans to ride the path in May.

## LIKE A 'CANNON BALL'

BY SUSAN CARPENTER
STAFF WRITER

A century ago, Erwin George "Cannon Ball" Baker set out on a journey that would make history. Traveling alone, with nothing but a camera, a map, a few tools and his wits, the 32-year-old racer threw a leg over an Indian motorcycle and trekked from San Diego to New York.

Despite running out of gas, hitting a dog and other impediments common to an era that lacked paved roads and, for the most part, gas stations, he made the 3,379-mile trip in a mere 11 ½ days.

"It was such a big accomplishment in its time. Baker was very well known for these cross-country records," said Don Emde, a retired racer, Motorcycle Hall of Famer and Aliso Viejo magazine publisher who will re-create the 100-year-old trek in an event he's calling Finding Cannon Ball's Trail.

"The reason we're trying to do this on the same days is to try to help people put it in perspective – to show what it was like then and what's going on now to see the differences."
DON EMDE

Emde, 63, plans to leave from the exact same location on the exact same date as Cannon Ball Baker did in 1914 and to arrive on the exact same date and in the same city as his inspiration. He intends to depart San Diego on May 3 and, if all goes well, to arrive in New York City on May 14.

"The reason we're trying to do

SEE CANNON • PAGE 2

A contemporary promotional booklet showcases Baker's 1914 "Cannon Ball" ride from San Diego to New York on an Indian bike.

Cars 2 | Friday, March 21, 2014 WHEELS Register

## CANNON: Same path, but different bike

FROM PAGE 1

this on the same days is to try to help people put it in perspective – to show what it was like then and what's going on now to see the differences," said Emde, who owns an original 1913 Indian motorcycle but will leave it parked in his office during the trip. In Finding Cannon Ball's Trail, he will mount a Yamaha Super Ténéré dual sport that can traverse the ride's first 250 miles on dirt and the remaining 3,000-plus on pavement.

Emde had been hearing about Cannon Ball Baker for years, he said, but he hadn't read an in-depth description of the ride until 20 years ago, when he happened upon a booklet titled "Coast to Coast" that chronicled the journey. The ride was just one of 143 records Baker set riding motorcycles and driving cars in the early 20th century, mostly as promotional gimmicks for the manufacturer that made the vehicle he used to break the record, including Indian.

The "Coast to Coast" booklet is one of thousands of historic items Emde keeps in an office that's a motorcycle museum as much as it's a publishing headquarters. Its conference room is anchored with a replica of the Indian 648 Scout his dad raced to victory in the 1948 Daytona 200. An enormous photo of his grandfather's Indian looms over the copy machine en route to Emde's collector's room.

It's there that he keeps the vintage Harley-Davidson racing sweaters, Champion spark plug match books and an original artwork of legendary stuntman Bud Ekins drawn by the equally legendary Von Dutch. Bound volumes of Motorcycle Illustrated magazine dating back to 1912 and other titles from motorcycling's earliest days, such as The Horseless Age from 1902 and The Motorcycle from 1895, yield only to a line of seemingly endless filing cabinets stuffed with archival racing photos, maps and race programs.

"Cannon Ball is now a generic term for coast to coast. It's the fastest way from L.A. to New York," said Emde, adding that the term Cannon Ball was first used to describe what the route looked like on a map – a cannon ball shooting across the sky. "The term has just stayed out there, so when I saw something that had to do with Cannon Ball Baker, the historian in me had to come back and say, 'How does this relate to the original guy?'

"That's where my project of retracing what he did came from," added Emde, who isn't just a historian but a maker of history himself.

In 1972, he won the most famous motorcycle race in the U.S., the Daytona 200, on board a Yamaha 350 two stroke – a feat that is impressive in and of itself but even more so because his father, Floyd Emde, had won the same race 24 years before, in 1948. To date, they remain the only father and son to have won the Daytona 200.

Other racers from Emde's heyday, including fellow Daytona 200 winner Ralph White and Keith Mashburn, whose enduring claim to fame was riding through a fence in the big-screen bike classic "On Any Sunday," are among the 25 riders who will accompany Emde on the trip.

Emde has spent the last three years choreographing the route, using Baker's journal as the starting point for research that took him to local libraries across the country so he could more accurately interpret the exact course with maps from 1914. Traveling out of San Diego a century ago, there was only one route for cars and motorcycles, and it went through the Cottonwood Mountains into Ocotillo and up toward Brawley – on dirt.

"Then he got on the railroad track and rode it down to Phoenix," Emde said. "We can't do that. So we found a road that pretty much goes right alongside the tracks, and that'll be the route we take. A lot of (the route planning) was comparing his riding to period maps and going there and checking it out to figure out how to connect all the dots."

In 2012, Emde tested the route in pieces. On May 3, he'll set out for real.

"It will be an adventure," Emde said, "but maybe in a different way than Cannon Ball Baker did it 100 years ago."

PHOTOS: CINDY YAMANAKA, STAFF PHOTOGRAPHER

Don Emde is no stranger to motorcycles. With his 1972 Daytona 200 win, he followed in his father's footsteps – Floyd Emde won in 1948.

Don Emde's Aliso Viejo office is filled with motorcycle memorabilia, such as this 1913 Indian.

Don Emde, 62, will ride this Yamaha 2013 Super Ténéré adventure bike on his ride from San Diego to New York City in May. He'll follow the path of Erwin George "Cannon Ball" Baker.

## CANNON BALL LOG BOOKS

Before he took off on his ride, Baker approached the F.A.M. (Federation of American Motorcyclists) to officially recognize his record if he achieved it. They agreed, but on the condition that his location be tracked all along the way. There were some places where he was able to send a telegram to the F.A.M. office in New York, but often he would not be able to rely on that, so it was agreed that Baker should keep a logbook with him that he could get stamped and signed by Postmasters at the towns where he stopped on his ride. To give our riders on the Cannon Ball Centennial Ride the same experience, we made up log books for them to get stamped each day by our acting Postmaster Nancy Emde-Steward.

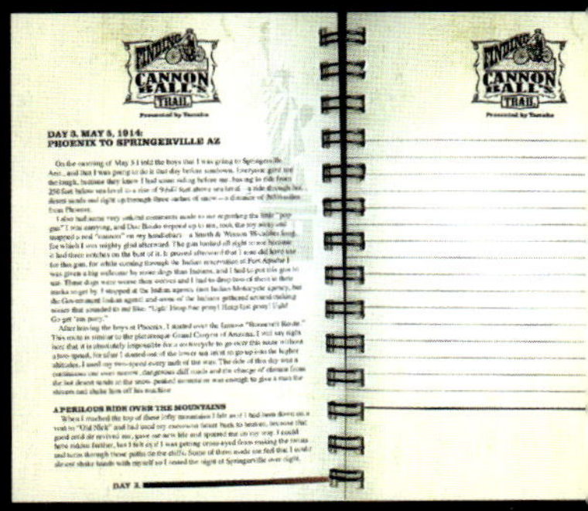

For each day of our ride in 2014, we included Baker's journal entry for what he experienced that same day in 1914, plus space to enter their own experiences in 2014.

This page from the 1914 Indian booklet show some examples of postmaster stamps and signatures from Baker's log book.

FINDING CANNON BALL'S TRAIL™

CENTENNIAL RIDE

MAY 3-14 2014

**Presented by Yamaha**

# PART II:

**MAY 2, 2014**

# CHECK-IN DAY / WELCOME RECEPTION & DINNER • SAN DIEGO

It worked out great that one of the riders signed up to do the Centennial ride had a place in San Diego that we could use for our rider check-in. Randy Aron owns Cycle Visions, a motorcycle retail store in the Old Town district of San Diego. It happened conveniently to be located just up the street from our host hotel, the Best Western Hacienda Old Town Hotel.

**Randy Aron's Cycle Visions store worked out great for an arrival station for riders to get checked in, meet other riders, and make any final adjustments to their bikes.**

**After three years of research, planning, promoting, organizing, and one mapping ride across the country, on May 2nd it all started to get real. The riders began showing up late morning and everything went as planned.**

**It was fun to see the many different bikes pull into the parking lot, all with the same goal to ride Cannon Ball's Trail to New York City.**

**My Yamaha Cannon Ball Super Tenere sits ready to ride alongside the Toyota Tundra that we borrowed from the good folks at Toyota Motor Sales. The rack on the ground is a motorcycle carrier that was lent to us by *Joe Hauler.com* so that both of our support trucks had the capability to pickup a broken down motorcycle if necessary.**

Once everyone got checked in, they had the rest of the day open to talk with old friends and meet new ones. From left are Cannon Ball riders Catherine Long, Ralph White, Bob Shurley and Glen Dickerson with Paul Collins who came down just to see the kickoff of the ride.

We had current and retired Firemen on the ride. My son-in-law Ryan Rose with his dad Roland were eager to hit the road. Ryan served as our EMT on the ride.

I was happy to meet noted motorcycle author and speaker Gary McKechnie (right) upon his arrival. In the middle is Ty Van Hooydonk from the Motorcycle Industry Council. To celebrate its 100th anniversary the same year as the Cannon Ball ride, the MIC commissioned McKechnie to go on the ride and produce a series of daily video blogs that were featured online at *Motorcycles.org.*

Gerald Tims is a motorcycle dealer from Oklahoma. He and another dealer, Dan Maxey, both rode out to San Diego, did our whole Cannon Ball Centennial Ride to New York, and rode home.

Rob Watt (left) from Butler Maps was not only one of our Centennial riders, but he was a great asset in the previous research and mapping rides that Joe and I took. Rob helped us convert our Garmin files into printable maps that we created for the Log Books. On the right is Court Butler, one of the principles at Butler Maps.

From left: California locals Bryon Farnsworth and Roger Riddell were two of many riders who came and rode with the main group just for the first day. With them are full-entry riders Pete Pfeifer and Perry King.

## MAY 2, 2014

Everyone attending the official kickoff dinner at the Best Western Hacienda Old Town were welcomed by a festive Mexican Mariachi band.

After the check-in day at Cycle Visions, the Cannon Ball riders and their guests enjoyed a great Mexican dinner prepared by the Old Town Tequila Factory restaurant which adjoins the Best Western Hacienda Old Town.

***Tomorrow we ride!***

**MAY 3, 2014**

# SAN DIEGO TO YUMA

## THE CANNON BALL CENTENNIAL RIDE BEGINS

I had many concerns in my head that morning about what lay ahead in the coming days. A lot could go wrong, but I knew I just had to take things now as they came up. The first important step was that I wanted the ride to take off exactly at 9:00 a.m., just as Erwin G. Baker had done on this date a century ago.

**May 3rd started at Sunroad Resort Marina on Shelter Island near downtown San Diego. The Toyota Tundra with trailer attached sits ready to go with the Cannon Ball riders lined up behind. There were also somewhere around 50 other riders who took off with us and rode just for the first day, then turned around and rode back home.**

**With downtown San Diego in the background, the full group of Cannon Ball riders posed with me and my Super Tenere.**

**Bob Starr (below-left) from Yamaha Motor Corp., USA rode down to be one of our "day riders" to follow us out of town. Bob was my key contact at Yamaha to get the needed sponsorship support we needed to pull off the ride as we did.**

**Robert Pandya (left) from Indian Motorcycle easily had the biggest motorcycle on the ride. He rode a highly modified Indian Chief that he personally prepared to handle the full Cannon Ball route (dirt and road). To his left is photographer Barry Hathaway, who rode with us to capture images for *Cycle World* magazine and many are seen here in this book.**

**The plan was that the ride would start <u>exactly</u> at 9:00 a.m. (Pacific Time), which was 100 years from that Erwin G. Baker left San Diego to begin his historic journey in 1914. Riders are seen here getting to go just prior to our "<u>on-time-to-the-minute</u>" departure.**

## MAY 3, 2014

# ON THE ROAD

The first part of the route on Day 1 was all-paved as riders made their way out of downtown San Diego. Some of the riders are seen here on Interstate 8 going through the historic old Devil's Canyon mentioned early in the book. What was once a narrow sandy trail is now a divided four-lane freeway.

A couple of riding hours east of San Diego, the group took its first break as we made a turn onto Old Highway 80 heading towards the desert.

Robert Pandya's Indian was the first bike to need our assistance. His front tire had apparently not been mounted properly and began to lose air just a few miles after the ride began. Our Toyota pulling the large trailer was already ahead of Robert. But our Chevy truck was running sweep and got the Chief loaded onto the Joe Hauler carrier. At our first stop we got it loaded into the trailer and off to a motorcycle shop in El Centro for repairs. Repairs were made and Robert was back with the group at our lunch stop in Brawley ready to tackle the first of the dirt sections we would ride that afternoon.

Our special guest on the ride, moto-journalist Gary McKechnie signals "A-OK" as the group arrives at the lunch stop in Brawley.

One of our Cannon Ball riders was none-other than champion racer Keith Mashburn, a long-time friend and fellow competitor from the 1960s and '70s. He is one of the racers featured in the epic motorcycle film *On Any Sunday*.

## MAY 3, 2014

# "ADVENTURE" ON TED KIPF ROAD

Our host in San Diego, Randy Aron from Cycle Visions on Ted Kipf Road. He had said he had never ridden in the dirt before and was riding a Harley road bike to boot, so we were a little worried about him, but he rode great with no troubles at all. *Barry Hathaway photo.*

Experienced adventure riders like "Mucho" Bill Wheeler took to our off-road section starting at Ted Kipf Road like ducks to water. They know momentum is key to keeping those big bikes going in a straight line. *Barry Hathaway photo.*

Robert Pandya's 750+ pound machine was a challenge in the deeper sand sections we had to ride through. He remounted and carried on. *Barry Hathaway photo.*

One of our "Day Riders" who only rode the first day also experienced the deep sand issues. *Barry Hathaway photo.*

**MAY 3, 2014**

## ADVENTURE IN THE DESERT

Randy Aron (left) shakes hands with Barry Hathaway after they had ridden together down Ted Kipf Road.

Pandya again churns through the sand as a fallen comrade takes a look to make sure he really is seeing an Indian Chief road bike pass him by. *Barry Hathaway photo.*

Some of our Cannon Ballers take a break where Ted Kipf Road comes back out to meet the paved road at Ogilby. From left: Bob Shurley, Keith Mashburn, day rider Charlie Hon, Gerald Tims, Perry Noel, Dan Maxey and Ron Niemeyer.

Pete Pfeifer was not only one of our Cannon Ball riders, but throughout our projects he was our "go to" person for feedback and information about riding in Arizona. He has ridden and explored Arizona most of his life and worked with the National Forest Service and Bureau of Land Management developing projects for motorized recreation. He has also served on the Arizona State Park's Off Highway Vehicle Advisory Group.

**MAY 3, 2014**

## YUMA RECEPTION

**Cannon Ball rider and Hollywood actor Perry King got a first hand look from the inside of one of the cells.**

**After arriving and cleaning up at our hotel in Yuma, Arizona, the Cannon Ball group was shuttled over to the historic Yuma Prison Museum for a dinner and reception hosted by the City of Yuma. It took in its first seven inmates on July 1, 1876 and handled 3,069 prisoners during its 33 years of operation. For a time in its later years, the facility also served as the local High School.**

**Tina Clark is the curator of the Yuma Crossing National Heritage Area, which includes the Yuma Prison Museum. She was the first person we met in Yuma about the project and after we told her about our project she immediately confirmed that the town would host us when we came through in 2014. She was true to her word and they put on a great reception and dinner for the Cannon Ball Centennial riders.**

**A relaxed Joe Colombero soaks up the experience at the reception. He was with me two years prior when we first visited Yuma. Since that time, he and I did one "mapping ride" across the country to figure Baker's route out, always keeping in mind that we'd be back to these places on the centennial.**

DOUGLAS J. NICHOLLS
MAYOR

CITY OF
YUMA
ARIZONA

**PROCLAMATION**
*"Cannonball Centennial Ride Day"*
*May 3, 2014*

*WHEREAS* Erwin "Cannon Ball" Baker departed San Diego, California on May 3, 1914; and

*WHEREAS* challenged to complete his 3,000 mile cross-country ride in twenty days, he amazed the nation when he reached New York City in just over eleven days; and

*WHEREAS* Baker's stamina, tenacity, and determination led to his nickname "Cannon Ball" which has since become the standard by which all other cross-country rides are named; and

*WHEREAS* to pay tribute to Baker's heroic efforts, motorcycle racer and author Don Emde teamed with motojournalist, Joe Colombero, to retrace the approximate route ridden by Baker; and

*WHEREAS* with support from the Motorcycle Industry Council, Yamaha, Butler Motorcycle Maps, Cycle Visions, Saddlemen, continental, Motion Pro, Moose Racing, Trail Bon, DPBrakes, Boyko Racing and Touratech the Cannon Ball Centennial Ride left San Diego on May 3, 2014 - 100 years to the minute of Baker's 1914 departure; and

*WHEREAS* just like 100 years ago, the first stop is in Yuma, Arizona, and riders will be celebrating their arrival in Yuma with a dinner at the Yuma Territorial Prison State Historic Park; and

*WHEREAS* recognizing that today's motorcyclists ride with the same independent spirit as generations of riders before them, the 2014 Cannon Ball Centennial Ride was created and completed in order to inspire future generations to re-discover the pleasures of safe motorcycling and the spectacular diversity of America; and

*NOW THEREFORE* ***I, Douglas J. Nicholls, Mayor of the City of Yuma,*** Arizona, do hereby proclaim May 3, 2014 as

"Cannonball Centennial Ride Day".

***IN WITNESS WHEREOF,*** I have hereunto set my hand and the Official Seal of the City of Yuma, Arizona, this 30th day of April 2014.

DOUGLAS J. NICHOLLS
Mayor
City of Yuma

**At the Yuma Welcome Reception I was presented with the first of numerous mayoral proclamations naming it "Cannon Ball Centennial Ride Day" in that city.**

MAY 4, 2014

# YUMA TO MESA: ANOTHER DAY IN THE DIRT

We're riding Cannon Ball's Trail! It's been widened a bit through the years, but this dirt road is the same one that Baker took from Yuma to Phoenix in 1914.

Knowing we rode the most difficult dirt sections of the whole ride the previous day, the group looked forward very much to riding the Agua Caliente Scenic route over to the Phoenix/Mesa area on Day 2. I had some reservations about my riders, since this was where Joe and I had our most serious problems during our pre-running. And Baker did as well in 1914.

Mucho Bill was always ready to ride.

As the group gets ready to depart the hotel in Yuma on Day 2, Chris Carter shouts out how he thinks things are going so far.

It was often necessary to hold some impromptu rider's meetings, especially in the areas where dirt roads were involved. With 100+ degree temps, we didn't want anyone getting lost in the desert. This meeting was at Dateland, AZ and the group was heading towards Agua Caliente where Joe Colombero and I got off track during our mapping ride in 2012 and I wanted to share with everyone things we learned then.

Keith Mashburn (left) and Tim Snodgrass discuss the route.

Dan Maxey, owner of Maxey's Honda-Yamaha-Polaris in Oklahoma City, navigates the dirt section on his Yamaha Super Tenere.

Steve Read is an experienced off-road rider from Aliso Viejo, CA.

Traveling photographer Barry Hathaway from Cycle World Magazine was one of the Yamaha Super Tenere riders on the ride.

Suzuki-mounted Gerald Tims is another motorcycle dealer from Oklahoma who was on the ride. Gerald owns Performance Cycle in Bethany, OK.

A personal friend that came on the ride was former racing great Ralph White. An AMA Hall of Famer, Ralph won the 1963 Daytona 200, 1965 Springfield Mile and many other National races in his career.

Denny Laidig, owner of Holeshot KTM Powersports of Akron, OH rode this KTM Adventure 1190 on the ride.

Day 2 and the Cannon Ball riders were up early and on the road from Yuma heading up Highway 95 a few miles to the turnoff for the historic Butterfield Express Stage Road.

Ralph White's brother Tom was on the ride on a beautiful BMW adventure bike.

We gathered up all of the riders up at the Butterfield Express Stage Road turnoff. The pavement turned to dirt in about a quarter mile leading us east to a gas stop at Dateland.

Another BMW rider, Ron Niemeyer, takes a break on the trail. He is from the San Diego area.

Parts Unlimited sales rep Mike Garrett (in orange Moose jersey) was one of many riders who rode with us to Mesa, AZ then rode back home. Here he is seen with Randy Aron and Chris Carter taking a break.

BMW rider Rob Watt from Butler Maps was not only one of our Cannon Ball riders, but we worked with him since the beginning of the project to create our route maps for the log books.

MAY 5, 2014

# MESA TO SOCORRO RIDING THE APACHE TRAIL

The first time Joe and I went through the Apache Trail we knew that it would be the best part of the Cannon Ball Trail. On Day 3 of our Centennial ride, the mostly unpaved 60-mile road—officially designated as Arizona Highway 88—delivered as we knew it would. It's the least-changed section of road on the whole transcontinental route since Baker rode it in 1914.

**Erwin Baker wrote in 1914 how similar the views along the Apache Trail were to the Grand Canyon and after riding it all of the Cannon Ball riders agreed. Here I am leading the group down the road, which has virtually remained just as he rode it a century ago. *Barry Hathaway photo.***

**The first few miles of AZ88 are paved up to this boat marina, which is down river from the Roosevelt Dam. It then becomes a dirt road.**

**Just as Baker rode it. AZ88 is only about one car wide in most places, but it's open for traffic in both directions.**

There is a lookout along the way that shows the road ahead. Baker saw it on May 5, 1914—we saw it on the same day...exactly 100 years later. *Barry Hathaway photo.*

What a great road on an adventure bike! I had many comments later from our riders who mentioned how great it felt to be truly on "Cannon Ball's Trail." *Kinney Jones photo.*

Barry Hathaway (left) and Robert Pandya cruising along on the Apache Trail. *Kinney Jones photo.*

The route continues north along a river heading toward the Roosevelt Dam.

Taking a break at the Roosevelt Dam. There are details on page 48 about how the dam and road got built way back in 1911, just three years before Baker came through. *Kinney Jones photo.*

North of Globe, Arizona, our dirt riding was now done and we enjoyed even more beautiful views that day along the highway. We rode all the way to Datil, New Mexico where we enjoyed our long-planned steak dinner at the Eagle Guest Ranch Cafe that Joe and I discovered in 2012 (see page 56). Then on to our hotel at Socorro, NM.

MAY 6, 2014

# SOCORRO TO TRINIDAD

Prior to our departure the morning of May 6th, the day started with a mayor's proclamation presentation at our hotel in Socorro. Then we headed north towards Santa Fe. Following lunch, the riders continued on to Watrous, the town where Baker had stopped for the night in 1914 when he got stuck at a water crossing. The postal staff there obliged the riders' requests to have their log books stamped, then we forged on to the famed Raton Pass and down the hill to Trinidad.

**Socorro city councilman Gordy Hicks (jacket with yellow sleeves) presented our group with the mayor's proclamation before we departed on our ride to Santa Fe. Gordy then hopped on his Harley and rode with us for a while.**

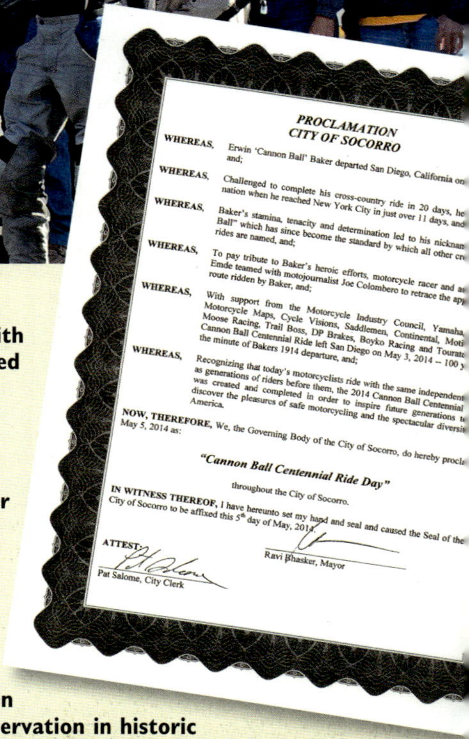

*PROCLAMATION*
*CITY OF SOCORRO*

**WHEREAS,** Erwin 'Cannon Ball' Baker departed San Diego, California on and;

**WHEREAS,** Challenged to complete his cross-country ride in 20 days, he nation when he reached New York City in just over 11 days, and

**WHEREAS,** Baker's stamina, tenacity and determination led to his nicknam Ball" which has since become the standard by which all other cr rides are named, and;

**WHEREAS,** To pay tribute to Baker's heroic efforts, motorcycle racer and a Emde teamed with motojournalist Joe Colombero to retrace the ap route ridden by Baker, and;

**WHEREAS,** With support from the Motorcycle Industry Council, Yamaha, Motorcycle Maps, Cycle Visions, Saddlemen, Continental, Moti Moose Racing, Trail Boss, DP Brakes, Boyko Racing and Tourate Cannon Ball Centennial Ride left San Diego on May 3, 2014 – 100 y the minute of Bakers 1914 departure, and;

**WHEREAS,** Recognizing that today's motorcyclists ride with the same independent as generations of riders before them, the 2014 Cannon Ball Centennial was created and completed in order to inspire future generations t discover the pleasures of safe motorcycling and the spectacular diversi America.

**NOW, THEREFORE,** We, the Governing Body of the City of Socorro, do hereby procla May 5, 2014 as:

***"Cannon Ball Centennial Ride Day"***

throughout the City of Socorro.

**IN WITNESS THEREOF,** I have hereunto set my hand and seal and caused the Seal of the City of Socorro to be affixed this 5th day of May, 2014.

**ATTEST:**

Pat Salome, City Clerk

Ravi Bhasker, Mayor

**On May 6th I received the second mayoral proclamation of the ride. The Socorro mayor Ravi Bhasker declared May 6th as "Cannon Ball Centennial Ride Day," in honor of our arrival there exactly 100 years to the day after Baker had.**

**Off we go from from the Best Western hotel in Socorro with a lunch reservation in historic Chimayo, north of Santa Fe and on the road we believe Baker could have taken in 1914.**

**Cannon Ball rider Bill Cooper snapped this photo of El Camino Real as it enters Santa Fe. The road dates back 1,500 years as the key trade route that extended north from Mexico City. *Bill Cooper photo.***

As pointed out back on page 62 when Joe Colombero and I were there, not much remains of the town of Watrous, including the original Post Office that is in ruins now. There is, however, a current Post Office and the Cannon Ball riders stopped there to get their log books stamped, just as Baker had done in 1914.

Sandra, the Watrous Postmaster, welcomed the Cannon Ball riders and stamped their log books.

The riders head out of Watrous for the afternoon ride to Trinidad where we stopped for the night.

Racing legends Ralph White (left) and Keith Mashburn on nearly identical Yamaha Super Tenere adventure bikes arrive at the Holiday Inn hotel in Trinidad, Colorado.

Perry Noel from Kentucky rode a single-cylinder Kawasaki KLR650 on the full Cannon Ball Centennial Ride.

# TRINIDAD TO DODGE CITY

High winds made the ride to Dodge City a rough one for Joe and me back in 2012, so learning from that experience we were up and rolling early the morning of May 7th. Nothing real noteworthy about the ride from Trinidad to Dodge City, but the Cannon Ball group was anxious to get to the historic "old west town."

**Cruising along the highway on the Yamaha Super Tenere. It had performed well on the sandy roads of California, the twisty mountain roads of Arizona and from there on it was a great touring machine. *Barry Hathaway photo.***

**Photographer Barry Hathaway stopped along the Santa Fe Trail to checkout this crumbling old adobe home. *Barry Hathaway photo.***

**Two of our "Big Twin" riders Randy Aron (left) and Robert Pandya cruising along on the Santa Fe Trail as the ride approaches Dodge City. *Barry Hathaway photo.***

We received a nice welcome at the historic Dodge House hotel. It's a modern hotel now, but its history dates back to 1873 when old gunslingers Wyatt Earp, Bat Masterson and Doc Holliday stayed there.

After checking into our hotel in Dodge City, local historian Jim Johnson welcomed us and gave us a guided tour of the original plot of land nearby where the inaugural 300-mile race was held in Dodge City on the 4th of July in 1914 (Read more on pages 70-71).

Steve Read arrives for check-in at the Dodge House.

(Below) It's all quiet there now, but a century ago this field hosted the biggest names and brands in the motorcycle sport for the 300-mile 4th of July classic that ran there for many years. From left: Chris Carter, myself and Ryan Rose check it out on our modern bikes.

Oklahoma motorcyclist Dan Maxey was probably the closest of the Cannon Ball riders to being home when we stopped in Dodge City.

The Cannon Ball Centennial Ride picked up a new participant in Dodge City, Yermo Lamers. He was riding back home to the Baltimore area that day when he met some of our riders at a gas station. When he heard about our ride, he asked if he could go along with us and we worked out the details.

Jack Broomall (front) and Ron Niemeyer in the Dodge House parking lot.

DODGE CITY DAILY GLOBE

E-verify; deferment addressed

Halfway there 100 years later

Jim Johnson arranged to have a reporter from the *Dodge City Daily Globe* come over to the hotel to get my story.

Saddlemen CEO Tom Seymour was one of our "working" sponsors that we did a lot of product trials with throughout the project on seats, saddlebags and other luggage items. When it came time for the ride, Tom came along with us.

Back at the hotel, Jim Johnson presented me with a proclamation from the mayor of Dodge City recognizing our arrival there one hundred years ago to the day that Baker had.

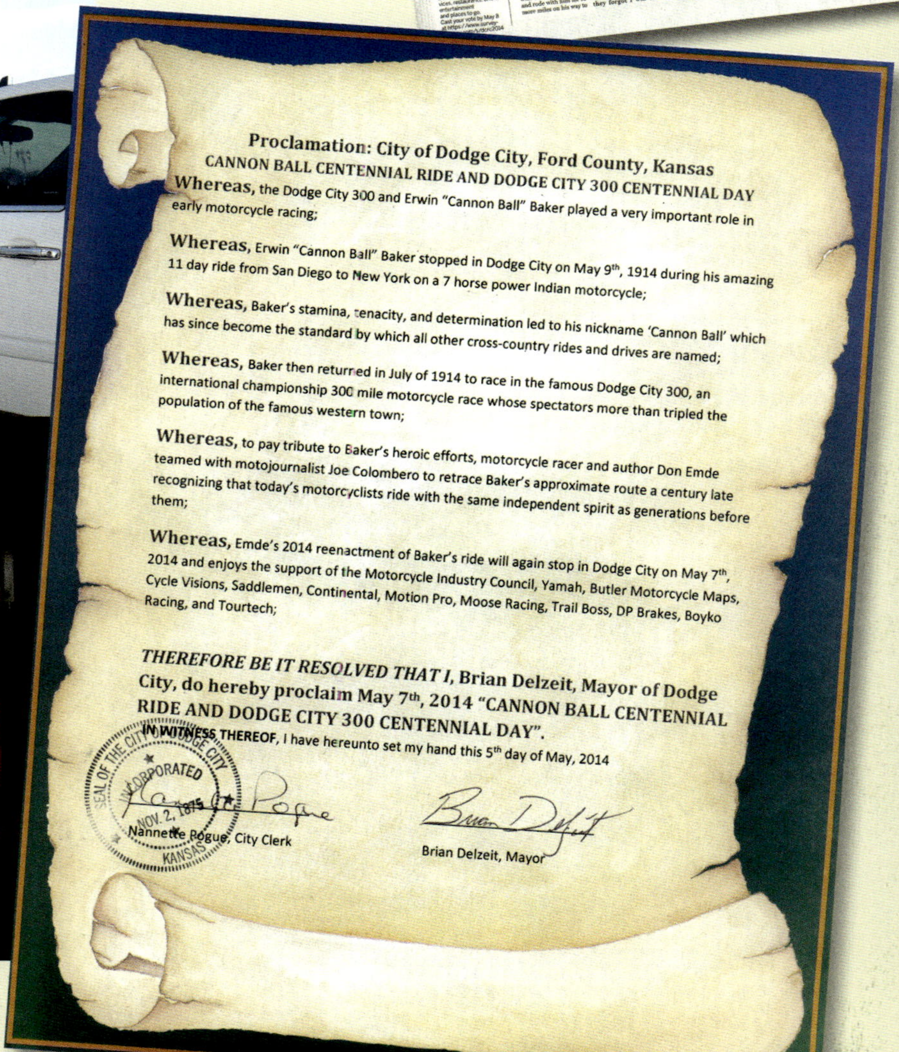

Proclamation: City of Dodge City, Ford County, Kansas
CANNON BALL CENTENNIAL RIDE AND DODGE CITY 300 CENTENNIAL DAY

**Whereas,** the Dodge City 300 and Erwin "Cannon Ball" Baker played a very important role in early motorcycle racing;

**Whereas,** Erwin "Cannon Ball" Baker stopped in Dodge City on May 9th, 1914 during his amazing 11 day ride from San Diego to New York on a 7 horse power Indian motorcycle;

**Whereas,** Baker's stamina, tenacity, and determination led to his nickname 'Cannon Ball' which has since become the standard by which all other cross-country rides and drives are named;

**Whereas,** Baker then returned in July of 1914 to race in the famous Dodge City 300, an international championship 300 mile motorcycle race whose spectators more than tripled the population of the famous western town;

**Whereas,** to pay tribute to Baker's heroic efforts, motorcycle racer and author Don Emde teamed with motojournalist Joe Colombero to retrace Baker's approximate route a century late recognizing that today's motorcyclists ride with the same independent spirit as generations before them;

**Whereas,** Emde's 2014 reenactment of Baker's ride will again stop in Dodge City on May 7th, 2014 and enjoys the support of the Motorcycle Industry Council, Yamah, Butler Motorcycle Maps, Cycle Visions, Saddlemen, Continental, Motion Pro, Moose Racing, Trail Boss, DP Brakes, Boyko Racing, and Tourtech;

***THEREFORE BE IT RESOLVED THAT I,*** **Brian Delzeit, Mayor of Dodge City, do hereby proclaim May 7th, 2014 "CANNON BALL CENTENNIAL RIDE AND DODGE CITY 300 CENTENNIAL DAY".**

**IN WITNESS THEREOF,** I have hereunto set my hand this 5th day of May, 2014

Nannette Pogue, City Clerk

Brian Delzeit, Mayor

# DODGE CITY TO KANSAS CITY

Kansas is tornado country. On May 8th Mother Nature showed us what it's like to have one bearing down on you. After hearing warnings the night before that "weather" was moving into the Dodge City area that morning, we again had the Cannon Ball riders up and rolling early for Kansas City. We had a planned group dinner that night arranged for us by old friends at Famous Dave's BBQ near our hotel in the Kansas Speedway complex area. We even had a dinner sponsor thanks to the nice people at Barnett Tool & Engineering.

The weather was definitely what you would call "Iffy" as we rode north from Dodge City towards Great Bend, Ellsworth and on to Kansas City. *Barry Hathaway photo.*

Ryan and Roland Rose were ready to go for our early departure from the Dodge House.

The wind has me in a slight "Kansas Lean" that morning as I lead the group out of Dodge City. The weatherman on TV said the chances of a tornado hitting was possible south of Great Bend, so we had a couple of hours of "drama." Luckily it never got any worse than this for us. *Barry Hathaway photo.*

(Left) After a stressful ride with wind and tornado warnings, the Cannon Ball riders got to unwind that night at Famous Dave's BBQ. Steve Read (black shirt) and Randy Aron (yellow shirt) get ready for a great dinner and fun evening.

(Right) Former racing star Keith Mashburn checks out the menu for our "gala" dinner at Famous Dave's.

The bikes are parked for the night and our hotel is next door to the restaurant, so Tom White ordered a tall one.

Cannon Ball riders Perry Noel (middle) and Denny Laidig (right). The unidentified person on the left is one of the locals who joined us that night.

Fun times at Famous Dave's. The left side of the table (Dan Maxey, Tom Seymour, Chris Carter and Gerald Tims) being entertained by Mucho Bill Wheeler.

From left: Barry Hathaway, Gary McKechnie, Ron Niemeyer, Catherine Long, unidentified, Glen Dickerson and Ken Freund.

From left: Roland Rose, Ryan Rose, Chris Steward, my sister Nancy Emde-Steward and yours truly.

From left: Keith Mashburn, Bob Shurley, Jack Broomall, Tim Snodgrass, Ralph White, Yermo Lamers and Bill Cooper.

After dinner our hosts from Kansas City had organized a little program with some "Wizard of Oz" themed gifts for us. Julie Davidson Biersmith points out to the group that Joe Colombero was the recipient of a "You ARE in Kansas" collector spoon.

Tom Seymour shows off the handy witch's broomstick he received.

Next it was my turn. Our hosts Patti Prestige-Frost (seated) and Julie Davidson Biersmith watch as I learned what Wizard of Oz gift they had for me. What else? Turned out to be a replica pair of Dorothy's ruby red slippers.

My sister Nancy and her husband Chris check out the ruby red slippers.

**MAY 9, 2014**

# KANSAS CITY TO GREENVILLE

As we did every morning, we held a quick rider's meeting in front of our hotel to get everyone pointed in the right direction. Soon after we were off to St. Louis where Donelson Cycles awaited our arrival for a planned lunch stop.

The group departs from our hotel at the Kansas City Speedway complex. That was a significant and exciting day for the group. Not only were we at the midpoint of our cross-country ride, but we had a lunch stop on the schedule at one of the oldest dealers in the St. Louis area, Donelson Cycles. The plan called for a two-hour stop there where Carl and Kathy Donelson and daughter Kim had lunch ordered for our whole group, and we would also get a chance to tour Carl's amazing vintage motorcycle collection.

As things like this can often go, we could have spent a full day looking at the old bikes and memorabilia, but we needed to get back on our bikes and head over the Mississippi River to get to Greenville, IL. There, a police car and fire truck were waiting to give us an escort to City Hall and a welcome from the mayor who officially proclaimed May 9th as Cannon Ball Centennial Ride Day in Greenville.

Steve Read wipes the bugs off his headlights before we hit the road.

Bob Shurley cleans up his Triumph adventure bike with some of Ultimate Xtreme Clean provided for the riders by Star Brite.

Tom White gets ready for another great day of riding.

After a successful off-road racing career that included a Gold Medal in the historic International Six Days Enduro, Chris Carter founded Motion Pro in 1984. The company continues to this day as an industry leader in tools and related service products for motorcycles. His company was one of our sponsors and also outfitted our two Yamahas with a full set of tools for our tool bags.

My Yamaha Super Tenere now carried the ruby slippers I was given at the previous night's dinner.

By mid-day, the Cannon Ball group had ridden across the state of Missouri to Donelson Cycles, Inc in St. Ann, (St. Louis area). Keith Mashburn (left) and Tim Snodgrass pull into the parking lot.

(From left): Kim Keen and her parents Carl and Kathy Donelson welcomed me and my Cannon Ball riders to their store for a lunch stop to tie in with their Open House. Thanks to them for their hospitality.

They even had a Welcome banner made for the group.

Top motorcycle industry companies such as Parts Unlimited, Dunlop Tires, Continental Tires and others supported our mid-day stop for an Open House there that weekend.

The Service Department was ready and waiting for any of our riders whose bikes needed attention, while others were having lunch in Carl's famous museum.

Donelson's back parking lot was filled up with Cannon Ball riders and their bikes, and a number of local riders who came by to check everything out.

The proprietor—and a long time family friend—Carl Donelson had tables brought in so we could enjoy lunch amongst the old motorcycles. Enjoying the meal with me are Ryan Rose, Roland Rose and Chris Steward.

Carl's museum at his store holds an amazing collection of historic motorcycle racing machinery and memorabilia. The #3 racer is a genuine factory-sponsored Triumph dirt tracker raced by 1970 AMA Grand National Champion Gene Romero. Race outfits of many former racing champions are also on display.

After lunch we rode over the mighty Mississippi River and east to Greenville, Illinois. *Barry Hathaway photo.*

The story about the stop that Joe and I had made in Greenville, Illinois in 2012 can be found on pages 80-81. John Goldsmith with the Greenville Chamber of Commerce told us then that the town would do something special when we came through in 2014. As we rode into town, we got some early indications of what he was talking about.

The city of Greenville was the most supportive of them all when it came to their efforts to welcome us and be a part of the history of Cannon Ball's 1914 stop there. This is the T-shirt they had made for each of us, and they used the same artwork to make a postal stamp for our logbooks.

Upon our arrival in Greenville we were met by a fire truck and police car that escorted us thru town to the city center.

My Greenville contact all the way through the project was John Goldsmith, who introduced me to the citizens of the town prior to meeting the mayor.

Mayor Alan Gaffner presented me with a key to the city and a proclamation naming the day "Cannon Ball Centennial Ride Day" in Greenville.

CANNON BALL CENTENNIAL RIDE DAY

May 9, 2014

PROCLAMATION

BY THE CITY OF GREENVILLE, ILLINOIS

*WHEREAS,* Erwin 'Cannon Ball' Baker departed San Diego, California on May 3, 1914; and

*WHEREAS,* challenged to complete his cross-country motorcycle ride in 20 days, he amazed the nation when he reached New York City in just over 11 days; and

*WHEREAS,* Baker's stamina, tenacity, and determination led to his nickname 'Cannon Ball' which has since become the standard by which all other cross-country rides are named; and

*WHEREAS,* to pay tribute to Baker's heroic efforts, motorcycle racer and author, Don Emde, teamed with motojournalist, Joe Colombero, to retrace the approximate route ridden by Baker; and

*WHEREAS,* with support from the Motorcycle Industry Council, Yamaha, Butler Motorcycle Maps, Cycle Visions, Saddlemen, Continental, Motion Pro, Moose Racing, Trail Boss, DP Brakes, Boyko Racing, and Touratech, the Cannon Ball Centennial Ride left San Diego on May 3, 2014 -- 100 years to the minute of Baker's 1914 departure; and

*WHEREAS,* recognizing that today's motorcyclists ride with the same independent spirit as generations of riders before them, the 2014 Cannon Ball Centennial Ride was created and completed in order to inspire future generations to rediscover the pleasures of safe motorcycling and the spectacular diversity of America; and

*WHEREAS,* Cannon Ball Baker remained in Greenville overnight on his cross country journey;

I, Alan Gaffner, Mayor of the City of Greenville, do hereby urge all residents of the community to welcome, congratulate, and honor those who commemorate this historic journey and do hereby proclaim, Friday, May 9, 2014 as "Cannon Ball Baker Centennial Ride Day." The attributes of adventure, exploration, and endurance evident in today's riders are reminiscent of the characteristics exhibited by Cannon Ball Baker 100 years ago.

*IN WITNESS WHEREOF,* I have hereunto set my hand and caused the Seal of the City of Greenville to be affixed at the Greenville City Hall in the City of Greenville, Illinois, this 9th day of May, the Year of Two thousand fourteen.

Alan Gaffner

Alan Gaffner, Mayor
City of Greenville
Bond County, Illinois

At the door, Roland Rose (left) and Gerald Tims show off their logbooks with the official Greenville Cannon Ball postal stamp. As noted on page 78, E.G. Baker came through that same doorway in 1914 to get his logbook stamped.

Cannon Ball rider Pete Pfeifer from Tucson, AZ gets a photo of his logbook getting stamped.

Our only female rider on the Cannon Ball Centennial Ride was Catherine Long, seen here getting her logbook stamped inside the Greenville post office.

Moto-journalist Ken Freund had someone get a shot of himself with the lady stamping the books.

**MAY 10, 2014**

# GREENVILLE TO INDIANAPOLIS

May 10th was one of the big days of the ride, since we would be arriving at Erwin G. Baker's hometown of Indianapolis. He was born, lived and died there. The day was also my sister Nancy's birthday. So even though it is a relatively short ride from Greenfield compared to some of our ride days, we had it planned that we would get into Indianapolis around mid-day and give the riders their first real break from riding since we had left San Diego. And to top it off, we had a banquet room booked for dinner at St. Elmo's, one of the top—and most historic—steak houses in Indianapolis.

**Between Greenville and Indianapolis, there is a road that branches off the National Road (US 40) that was part of the original route through that area. Located near Terre Haute, the road crosses through circa-1800s Jackson Truss Covered Bridge. Enjoying the moment are (from left): Ken Freund, Randy Aron, Robert Pandya, Yermo Lamers and Tom Seymour. More about that bridge on page 85.** ***Barry Hathaway photo.***

**(Left) Bill Cooper arrives at our hotel in Indianapolis, the Downtown Marriott Indianapolis. He has worked in the motorcycle industry since 1975 and enjoys riding street, dirt and dual purpose motorcycles as a hobby.**

**(Right) Motorcycle dealer Denny Laidig from Holeshot KTM, Akron, Ohio.**

**Erwin Baker lived in the Indianapolis area most of his life, so we had a special celebration dinner in his honor at one of Indy's most historic restaurants, St. Elmo's. Dating back to 1902, it's likely that Baker could have dined there himself.**

**I felt very humbled to be in Baker's hometown on our ride, since we really were celebrating his great accomplishment of a century ago. We all raised a glass in his honor.**

In addition to our celebration in Indy to honor Erwin Baker, May 10th was also Nancy Emde-Steward's birthday. Her husband Chris Steward is on her right.

The group got one of their rare opportunities to relax and enjoy leisurely dinner conversation with their fellow Cannon Ball riders.

(Right) St. Elmo's is a world-class steak house, but it's also famous for its spicy shrimp cocktails. As journalist Ken Freund watches, Ron Niemeyer from San Diego couldn't hide his first reaction to one.

(Left) Bill Wheeler aka "Mucho Bill" enjoys the dinner with Motion Pro's Chris Carter and Gerald Tims, owner of Performance Cycle of Bethany, OK.

While I was up in the credit office arranging a loan to pay for dinner (just kidding) the rest of the group gathered for a photo.

# MAY 11, 2014 INDIANAPOLIS TO COLUMBUS

Step 1 for the day was getting the Cannon Ball group out of our special garage parking area arranged at the Marriott Indianapolis Downtown hotel. With rain just beginning to fall, we were ready to head out for a couple of special stops in the Indianapolis area, followed by a good ride over to Columbus.

(Below) Dan Maxey from Maxey's in Oklahoma (left) and author/speaker Gary McKechnie lead this part of the group as we depart downtown Indianapolis.

Following our great celebration dinner the previous night at St. Elmo's, the Cannon Ball riders were up early and ready to ride... rain or shine. We had a lot on our agenda for May 11th beginning with a ride to the Crown Hill Cemetery to pay our respects to the man the ride and project was all about, Erwin G. Baker. Then we rode over to the Indianapolis Motor Speedway for a tour of the museum before heading east to Columbus, Ohio.

Our sweep rider Ryan Rose (left) is a Fireman with the Long Beach Fire Dept in Southern California. He was in radio communication with me at the front at all times during the ride. That's his dad, Roland on the red Harley. He's a retired Fireman from the same LBFD that his son Ryan works for now.

**Barry Hathaway (nearest to the camera) and Bill Cooper.**

A wet start to the day.

Our first stop was the Crown Hill Cemetery on the north side of Indianapolis to visit Cannon Ball Baker's final resting place. The group lined up along the path in front of the Baker family gravesite.

We think Cannon Ball would have been very happy to have us stop by.

Michelle Pemberton from *The Indianapolis Star* came out to get photos and a video interview for stories on the Cannon Ball Centennial ride.

Our next stop was a visit to the Indianapolis Motor Speedway and museum.

Except for one nephew, Erwin Baker did not have any family heirs when he passed away, so some of his artifacts ended up in the Indianapolis Motor Speedway collection. On display at the museum is this one-of-a-kind motorcycle with a four-stroke rotary valve design that he had created. He unfortunately was never able to cash in on his invention by selling the concept to a manufacturer or investor.

Donald Davidson, one of the world's premier motorsports historians and statisticians, welcomed the Cannon Ball group in the parking lot and gave a brief talk on the history of Indianapolis Motor Speedway. We then went inside for a tour of the museum.

As told in Chapter 2, before he did his cross-country ride in 1914 (or had his famous nickname), Erwin Baker did some track racing. On display at the museum was a restored 1909 Indian that is one of Baker's old race bikes. With permission from Donald Davidson, I was allowed to saddle up on it for the group photo. *Barry Hathaway photo.*

(Above) You literally could spend a week at the Indy museum absorbing the histories and details of the many cars and motorcycles on display there. Their collection is larger than what can be displayed at one time, so the exhibits are rotated often.

Now that's a trophy! Tom Seymour reads the story about the Wheeler-Schebler Trophy.

As the group enjoyed a tour of the museum, Chris Carter from Motion Pro chatted with Donald Davidson about motor racing history.

(Left) Mostly racecars are on display at the Indy museum, but there are a few motorcycles, including this historic Harley-powered streamliner that Cal Rayborn set the world motorcycle land speed record on at Bonneville in 1970. His 265 mph run is seen in the original *On Any Sunday film.*

After a busy morning in Indianapolis, it was time for the group to get back on the National Road (U.S. 40) and head east to Dayton, Ohio and then on to Columbus as Baker had done in 1914.

As the white marker has shown travelers for hundreds of years, its 29 miles from this spot on the National Road to Columbus, Ohio.

## MAY 12, 2014 PICKERINGTON TO GREENSBURG

After making it the previous night to our hotel in Pickerington, Ohio, our first order of business on May 12th was to make a stop for the Cannon Ball riders to get a tour of the Motorcycle Hall of Fame Museum at the AMA headquarters campus. We would also return Cannon Ball Baker's Hall of Fame medal that I had borrowed at the beginning of the project. From there it was back on the National Road heading to Greensburg, PA., with a planned stop along the way at K&C Cycle in Hebron, Ohio. Co-owner Christy Klamfoth's father is Hall of Fame racer, Dick Klamfoth, a three-time winner of the Daytona 200.

**Cannon Ball Baker's Hall of Fame medal. Having it with us for our mapping work and the Cannon Ball Centennial Ride always made us feel like he was riding with us.**

**Ryan Rose with Cannon Ball's Motorcycle Hall of Fame medal before we left the hotel that morning to return it to the AMA.**

**Steve Read fires up his Suzuki V-Strom for the short ride over to the AMA headquarters and Motorcycle Hall of Fame Museum. He works at the TRD Division at the Toyota Motor Sales headquarters in Torrance, CA.**

**Ken Freund is a moto-journalist from California who has been all around the world riding and writing about motorcycles.**

The Cannon Ball Centennial Ride arrives at the AMA headquarters in Pickerington.

Jack Broomall is a lifelong motorcycle rider from Malvern, PA. He is a member of the Iron Butt Association, the Bonneville 200 MPH Club and veteran of seven bike trips across the USA.

Tom Seymour (left) and Keith Mashburn.

Rob Dingman, President of the American Motorcyclist Association, was there to greet us upon our arrival and to receive Cannon Ball Baker's Motorcycle Hall of Fame medal that I had borrowed three years earlier.

**(Above), AMA's Rob Dingman and the Cannon Ball group pose for a photo near the museum entrance.**

**(Left) Inside the museum, 2001 Motorcycle Hall of Fame inductee Ralph White checks out his plaque on the wall.**

**At the museum Nancy Emde-Steward enjoys a look at the actual Yamaha race bike from my 1972 Daytona 200 race victory. Nancy, the travel coordinator for the ride, was at Daytona when I won the race. *Barry Hathaway photo.***

**Not far from the Columbus metro area, the group made a stop at a Yamaha dealer, K&C Cycle, owned by racing legend Dick Klamfoth's daughter Christy Klamfoth and Al Charles.**

**Our stop at K&C provided a rare opportunity for a photo of three Daytona 200 race winners: Myself (1972) on the left with Ralph White (1963) and three-time winner Dick Klamfoth (1949, '51 and '52).**

## MAY 13, 2014

# GREENSBURG TO MALVERN

**Tim Snodgrass, Keith Mashburn, Ryan Rose and Roland Rose head out from the Courtyard Marriott Greensburg.**

It was getting more and more exciting the closer we got to New York, yet each day's ride held some special significance as well. The Cannon Ball riders would get their first experience on the historic Lincoln Highway on May 13th, with some planned stops for some that included the Flight 93 National Memorial Park and/or the Gettysburg National Military Park.

**A few hours ride east from Greensburg took us to the town of Gettysburg, where one of the most famous Civil War battles was fought. The large Gettysburg National Military Park features many statues that honor many battles, heroes, and Army regiments from both sides who gave so much in July of 1863.**

**We had great weather and great roads on May 13th as we rode east on the Lincoln Highway (aka U.S. Route 30).**

**From the high ground at Little Round Top is a view of much of the Gettysburg battlefield. On the left, along the road is Devil's Den, a rocky sharpshooter's location made famous from Civil War photos published by Matthew Brady.**

L-R: Ken Freund, Tom White, Ryan Rose, myself, Ralph White and Roland Rose enjoying a break in the Gettysburg National Military Park at the historic battle area known as Little Round Top.

It was great to have a reserved parking section reserved for our group right in front of the hotel.

The Cannon Ball riders appreciated the extra efforts that the staff at the Courtyard Marriott Malvern made to make us feel welcome when we arrived there.

After a full day in the saddle, even small touches like bottles of water are greatly appreciated.

(Above) After ten days on the road (and some off-road), my Super Tenere was still running great.

The Courtyard Marriott Malvern even had a "Spirit of Cannon Ball" character dressed up in a period outfit to greet us when we arrived. He is seen here with Bill Cooper, Pete Pfeifer, Steve Read and Bob Shurley.

# MAY 14, 2014 MALVERN TO NEW YORK CITY

## THE FINAL DASH TO NEW YORK

So the final day's ride was at hand. It was May 14th, exactly 100 years to the day since Erwin G. Baker had made it to New York City and we would soon match his achievement. The Cannon Ball Centennial Ride group was to a man—and one women—anxious to get going and conclude our riding adventure, with one added twist to how Baker did it. We were actually a few insignificant hours ahead of his 1914 pace and rather than end during the night like he did, our ride would conclude mid-day on Manhattan. So feeling that New York City would not serve as a very convenient location to disband the group after our nearly two-week event, we planned to make Manhattan a lunch stop that day, and then carry on to the town of Newburg, NY, and end our actual riding there at the Motorcyclepedia Museum.

**By mid-day the Manhattan skyline was visible to the group. Robert Pandya and Randy Aron head for the finish line. *Barry Hathaway photo.***

**One unplanned activity that almost everyone took part in at breakfast the morning of the ride was passing around our logbooks to all the Cannon Ball riders so everyone could all sign them. Here Gary McKechnie gets Bob Shurley's autograph.**

**(Right) Any kind of travel on Manhattan can be tricky, so I had my iPad map out to show Tom Seymour and the other riders how we would get down to our lunch stop at Battery Gardens.**

**Catherine Long passes her logbook to Yermo Lamers for a signature.**

Jack Broomall (left) and Perry Noel get a last cup of coffee before our morning ride began.

Ron Niemeyer (left) and Pete Pfeifer were ready to go.

Denny Laidig

(Right) For Keith Mashburn, our ride to New York City must have brought back some great memories from his racing days. In 1971 motorcycle racing came to the historical Madison Square Garden on Manhattan. Then a Yamaha factory rider, Keith set the fastest qualifying time on the tiny indoor cement track, besting the efforts of 129 other riders. He then went on to make it into the Main event and scored an impressive 3rd place finish.

Of all the hotels we had stayed at on our transcontinental ride, none made a better effort to connect with our group and be a part of the Cannon Ball theme than the Courtyard Marriott Malvern. On my way out of the parking lot I stopped to thank the staff for their efforts.

It took us a few hours to make our way up Route 1, the alternate for Interstate 95, which basically dates back to the old road Baker would have taken. Not far after passing the Newark airport we picked up the route to Manhattan via the Holland Tunnel.

Once on Manhattan, we had technically completed Cannon Ball's Trail and his itinerary, but we had lunch reservations at Battery Gardens—which would also give us the setting for the main photo of the whole ride—a group shot with the Statue of Liberty in the background.

Some of our group had gotten separated en route to New York City and arrived at slightly different times. Here, the main group makes it to Battery Gardens, which is at the southern tip of Manhattan. Everything seemed to be under control until we arrived at a parking garage that we had contacted in advance and made a reservation for 30 motorcycles and our sweep truck. Well, to make a long story short, they didn't hold the reservation and, as Jerry Seinfeld says, "It's not the taking of the reservation, it's the holding of the reservation that counts." We found out what he meant and soon the scramble was on to park all of our bikes and the truck. ***Glen Dickerson photo.***

If there was anything symbolic for me to see to think of as the finish line, it was the view of the Statue of Liberty. Seeing it took me back to the morning of May 3rd when we left San Diego and had last seen ocean water. We had truly, literally done a coast-to-coast ride.

Being connected with communications radios, when my son-in-law Ryan Rose heard that we had been turned away from the parking garage, he spotted the National Maritime Center, home to the U.S. Coast Guard and Department of Homeland Security offices. Being an active fireman, he said over the radio, "Hey, let me go see if I can pull any weight here." It sounded great to me and sure enough, in a few minutes, I heard in my earphones, "Don, bring the guys over here, we've got a place to park." As we rode up to the locked gate, it swung open and we rode into the facility where they had a large parking lot, plenty for the remainder of the group that had stayed with me. It was obvious this wouldn't happen for just anyone, but with Ryan's current LBFD fireman's ID and a quick story about how this group had ridden all the way across the country to get our picture taken with Lady Liberty, they knew we were legitimate and offered the parking space. We were, and still are, very thankful for their generous allowance of the use of their facility.

Motorcycle riding aficionados Glen Dickerson and Catherine Long had ridden from their home in New Mexico to California to catch the start of our ride, then they both rode their own bikes on the full ride, and after making it to Manhattan, headed back with a few extra side trips included in their return route. Unfortunately Catherine would hit a dog somewhere along the way and the accident brought their long trip to a halt. She did suffer injuries, but has thankfully fully recovered.

A quick photo with our new best friend from the United States Coast Guard, then off to join the rest of the group for lunch and the full group photo.

# 2014 CANNON BALL CENTENNIAL RIDE
## SAN DIEGO TO NEW YORK CITY
## MAY 3-14, 2014

Riders and staff (L-R): Bill Wheeler, Tom White, Chris Carter, Bill Cooper, Ron Niemeyer, Jack Broomall, Pete Pfeifer, Denny Laidig (front), Glen Dickerson (rear), Catherine Long, Gary McKechnie, Robert Pandya, Ralph White, Ryan Rose, Bob Shurley, Roland Rose, Don Emde, Steve Read, Nancy Emde-Steward, Perry Noel, Ken Freund, Dan Maxey, Gerald Tims, Randy Aron, Barry Hathaway, Tom Seymour. *Photo by Joe Colombero.* Missing: Chris Steward, Keith Mashburn, Yermo Lamers, Tim Snodgrass.

FINDING CANNON BALL'S TRAIL™

CENTENNIAL
MAY 3-14 RIDE 2014

Presented by Yamaha

# MAY 15, 2014 NEWBURGH, NEW YORK

Our arrival on Manhattan the day before officially concluded our re-run of Baker's 1914 transcontinental ride and we celebrated with a group lunch and photo at Battery Gardens with Lady Liberty and the New York harbor in full view. We all soaked up the feeling of completing our mission, but lower Manhattan is so busy there really wasn't a good place to properly disband our group. So following the activities at Battery Gardens, the Cannon Ball Group made one last ride up to Newburgh, New York for a closing reception and lunch on May 15th at the Motorcyclepedia Museum.

**The Motorcyclepedia Museum was just a short ride from our hotel in Newburgh.**

**Catherine Long had already ridden from New Mexico to San Diego for the start of the Cannon Ball Centennial Ride, then rode the whole ride with us. Always eager to ride, she was one of the first to arrive at the museum for the tour, lunch and closing ceremonies.**

**Museum owner and founder Ted Doering (left) was there to greet us as we arrived. Ken Freund and Randy Aron were with me as Ted explained a few things about his amazing museum.**

**I guess if you spent a week in this room, you could learn about all the historic machines on display.**

**Every year of production of the original Indian Motocycle Company are represented in Ted's collection.**

(Left) A close-up of the powerplant of a rare 8-valve Indian boardtrack racer.

(Right) The Cannon Ball riders got a tour of the Dodge City 300-mile racetrack when we were in Kansas. The Motorcyclepedia Museum has one of the actual Harley-Davidson factory racebikes that raced there back in the teens.

(Left) My sister, Nancy Emde-Steward was our official "Postmaster" on the ride. She shows the whole set of stamps we made up for her to stamp the rider's logbooks on the ride. That desk, by the way, belonged to Steve McQueen and was acquired by Ted at an auction in 1984.

(Right) Busted! When Nancy wasn't looking, some of the guys put their own postal stamps in their logbooks. From left: Ralph White, Dan Maxey, Denny Laidig, Jack Broomall, Glen Dickerson and Tom White.

The group showed its appreciation to Ryan Rose, Nancy Emde-Steward and Chris Steward for all of their hard work and help along the way.

Following our "Farewell" activities at the museum, it was time for everyone to depart for home. Some rode their bikes, while some flew and had their bikes shipped from the museum. Our Cannon Ball trailer was used to haul our bikes back.

Since we were then at the "finish line" of the ride, Catherine Long presented me with a checkered flag that she had picked up along the way and had all of the riders and crew sign it. That was a great gift which I will keep in my collection. Thanks Catherine.

Thanks to Ted Doering and the staff at the Motorcyclepedia Museum for your great hospitality and help with our final day of the ride. It could not have ended better.

For more information about the Motorcyclepedia Museum, log onto:
*http://www.motorcyclepediamuseum.org*

FINDING CANNON BALL'S TRAIL™

CENTENNIAL RIDE

MAY 3-14 2014

**Presented by Yamaha**

## EPILOGUE
## BIBLIOGRAPHY
## ACKNOWLEDGEMENTS
## RIDER'S LIST

## EPILOGUE: Cannon Ball Baker

Following his 1914 transcontinental record ride, Erwin G. Baker was forever more known as "Cannon Ball" Baker, a nickname that he even trademarked. He was very much in demand, not only by the Indian Motocycle Company, but other motorcycle makers and even some automobile manufacturers.

One of his accomplishments made not long after he set the San Diego to New York record was to compete in the 1914 "Race to Phoenix." As he prepared to leave the morning of May 3rd Baker told the press that he would come back to San Diego in November for the San Diego to Phoenix race...and would win it. It turned out he did win the "Race to Phoenix" on November 8th, but with a slightly different twist. For the first time there were two endurance races held simultaneously with each ending the same day in Phoenix. So Baker took a pass on the 1914 San Diego to Phoenix race (won by fellow Indian rider Lorenzo Boido), instead opting for a new event that started in El Paso, Texas and ran west to Phoenix. Erwin paced himself for the first two days with Harley-Davidson rider Al Rhodes from Tucson, Arizona, then blasted ahead into the distance. Despite one bad crash where a wood splinter was driven five inches into his forearm, he continued on and won, finishing one hour and 38 minutes ahead of the Harley rider. He averaged 34 miles an hour over the 537-mile mountain and desert course.

**Cannon Ball Baker in 1915**

He set many different types of speed records in the years to come, including breaking the "Three Flags Record" at the end of August, 1915. He rode from Vancouver, BC, Canada to Tijuana, Mexico in 3 days, 9 hours and 15 minutes.

The automobile manufacturers came calling too. He would set over 100 major records on four wheels in his career, as well as racing in the 1922 Indianapolis 500 where he finished 11th following some lengthy time in the pits to repair mechanical problems.

With the roads much improved, in September 1922, Baker again tackled the coast-to coast motorcycle record, this time on a 4-cylinder Ace. He covered 3,332 miles in 6 days, 22 hours, 52 minutes.

As previously mentioned, Elenora gave birth to a son, Sherman W. Baker, on September 24, 1914. Sadly, Sherman died from complications of an infected tooth in 1929 at age 15. Both Erwin and Elenora were understandably devastated to lose their only child. According to Russ Catlin's 1975 *Automobile Quarterly* story on Baker, both went into "deep mourning." He reported that following Sherman's death Baker became inactive for the first time in his life. Luckily he had many friends who encouraged him to eventually resume his pursuit of speed records.

He did so in 1933 when Neracar convinced him to try an economy ride on one of their scooter-style motorcycles. He would set a record, riding 3,364 miles from New York to Los Angeles in 7 days, 5 hours and 28 minutes. He used only 45 gallons of gasoline and 45 pints of oil and the story headline was, "How I crossed America on a Neracar for less than $20."

In his lifetime, Baker made 126 transcontinental runs on motorcycles or in a car. His friend and journalist Russ Catlin wrote that when he passed away in 1960, Cannon Ball had logged over five and one-half million miles of motor travel on two continents and set records in seven foreign countries.

After he quit the record-run business, Cannon Ball was on the lecture circuit for some years, as he had many fans eager to hear him recount his many adventures. He also spent much time in his shop at home working on many inventions and technical improvements for motorcycles and cars. One of his inventions, a rotary valve engine design—shown on page 143—is on display in a motorcycle at the Indianapolis Motor Speedway museum.

Then, not long after the end of World War II, he was contacted by people from a new organization called the National Association for Stock Car Auto Racing. After hearing their plans, Baker accepted the offer to become NASCAR's first commissioner for racing.

Baker lost his dear wife Elenora in 1950. He lived on for another decade, dying on May 10, 1960 from a massive heart attack that ended the life of one of the greatest pioneers in the world of motorsports. He was America's first true motorcycle Adventure rider.

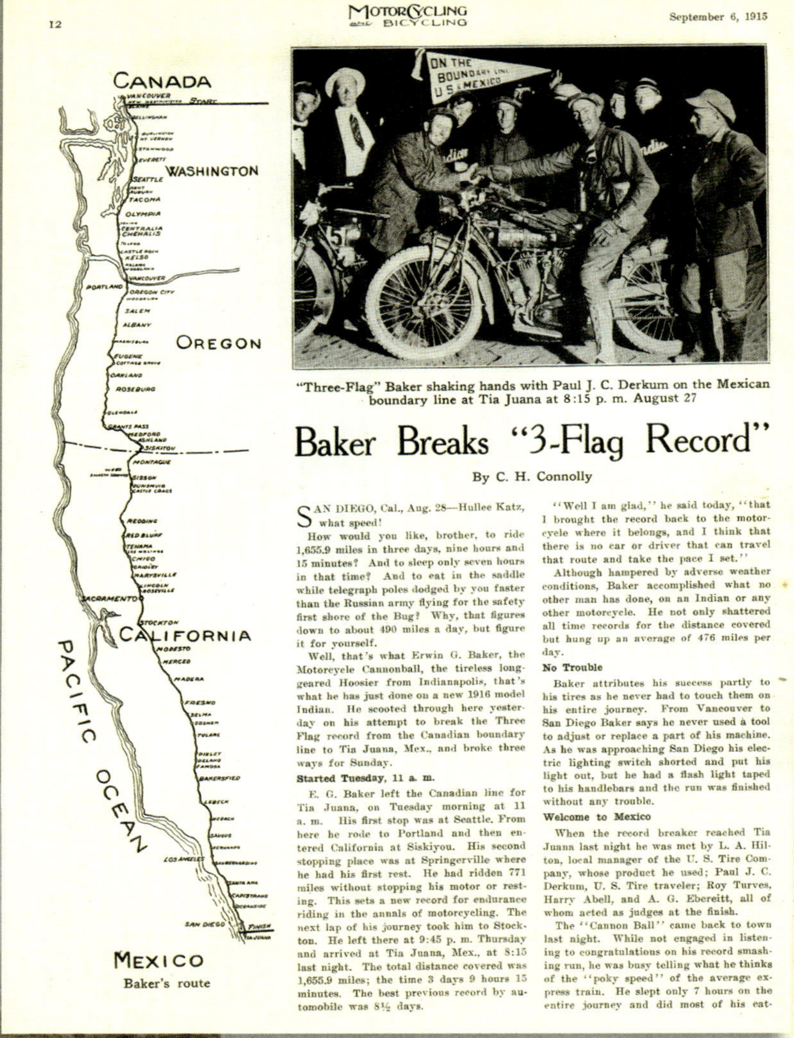
12 MOTORCYCLING AND BICYCLING September 6, 1915



"Three-Flag" Baker shaking hands with Paul J. C. Derkum on the Mexican boundary line at Tia Juana at 8:15 p. m. August 27

# Baker Breaks "3-Flag Record"

By C. H. Connolly

SAN DIEGO, Cal., Aug. 28—Hullee Katz, what speed!

How would you like, brother, to ride 1,655.9 miles in three days, nine hours and 15 minutes? And to sleep only seven hours in that time? And to eat in the saddle while telegraph poles dodged by you faster than the Russian army flying for the safety first shore of the Bug? Why, that figures down to about 490 miles a day, but figure it for yourself.

Well, that's what Erwin G. Baker, the Motorcycle Cannonball, the tireless long-geared Hoosier from Indianapolis, that's what he has just done on a new 1916 model Indian. He scooted through here yesterday on his attempt to break the Three Flag record from the Canadian boundary line to Tia Juana, Mex., and broke three ways for Sunday.

**Started Tuesday, 11 a. m.**

E. G. Baker left the Canadian line for Tia Juana, on Tuesday morning at 11 a. m. His first stop was at Seattle. From here he rode to Portland and then entered California at Siskiyou. His second stopping place was at Springerville where he had his first rest. He had ridden 771 miles without stopping his motor or resting. This sets a new record for endurance riding in the annals of motorcycling. The next lap of his journey took him to Stockton. He left there at 9:45 p. m. Thursday and arrived at Tia Juana, Mex., at 8:15 last night. The total distance covered was 1,655.9 miles; the time 3 days 9 hours 15 minutes. The best previous record by automobile was 8½ days.

"Well I am glad," he said today, "that I brought the record back to the motorcycle where it belongs, and I think that there is no car or driver that can travel that route and take the pace I set."

Although hampered by adverse weather conditions, Baker accomplished what no other man has done, on an Indian or any other motorcycle. He not only shattered all time records for the distance covered but hung up an average of 476 miles per day.

**No Trouble**

Baker attributes his success partly to his tires as he never had to touch them on his entire journey. From Vancouver to San Diego Baker says he never used a tool to adjust or replace a part of his machine. As he was approaching San Diego his electric lighting switch shorted and put his light out, but he had a flash light taped to his handlebars and the run was finished without any trouble.

**Welcome to Mexico**

When the record breaker reached Tia Juana last night he was met by L. A. Hilton, local manager of the U. S. Tire Company, whose product he used; Paul J. C. Derkum, U. S. Tire traveler; Roy Turves, Harry Abell, and A. G. Ebereitt, all of whom acted as judges at the finish.

The "Cannon Ball" came back to town last night. While not engaged in listening to congratulations on his record smashing run, he was busy telling what he thinks of the "poky speed" of the average express train. He slept only 7 hours on the entire journey and did most of his eat-

**The story in *Motorcycling and Bicycling* magazine shows the route Baker used to set a new "Three Flag" record.**

**Cannon Ball Baker poses at the U.S./Mexican border after breaking the existing "Three Flag" record in 1915. He accomplished the 1,655.9 mile ride from Vancouver, British Columbia to Tijuana, Mexico in 3 days, 9 hours, 15 minutes.**

**After being the big newsmaker in 1914 going west to east, Baker changed it up in 1915 and got the press coverage riding from north to south. The weary-looking Cannon Ball is greeted in Los Angeles on his way to San Diego and the finish of the ride at Tijuana.**

**Always eager for some angle, or type of record to set, Baker drove this 1918 ReVere 16,234 miles to make a stop in the state capitals of all 48 states in the USA at the time. *Image: Indianapolis Motor Speedway Archive.***

**On his way to some new record in 1919.**

**(Left) In 1922 Baker landed a ride in a racecar for the Indy 500. With no previous experience in that type or level of auto racing, he qualified 16th fastest for the race. He suffered some ignition problems in the early laps and was in the pits for an extended stop. When his crew got the problems sorted out, Baker began moving back up through the field and he finished 11th. *Image: Indianapolis Motor Speedway Archive.***

**(Right) In 1922, despite staying very busy with automotive work, Baker became interested in resetting the cross-country motorcycle record. His record from 1914 had been lowered in 1917 to seven days, 16 hours, 16 minutes by a 4-cylinder Henderson rider from California named Alan Bedell. The roads were much improved since Baker had first set the transcontinental record six years earlier and motorcycles were capable of higher speeds. So in the fall 1922, Baker signed on to ride a 4-cylinder Ace motorcycle from Los Angeles to New York. What made his attempt unique from his usual style of record attempts was that Californian Wells Bennett had the record in mind as well. He departed from Los Angeles on a 4-cylinder Henderson 28 hours after Baker had departed. So Baker had the added incentive to go as fast as he could to lay down a time that would not only break the existing record, but also hold up against whatever time Bennett could achieve. When Baker arrived at his New York destination, his time was clocked in as 6 days, 22 hours and 52 minutes, approximately 21 hours less than the record held by Bedell—the man who had broken Baker's 1914 record. The less-experienced "transcontinentalist" Bennett put up a game fight to Philadelphia, but numerous crashes and other delays put him more than two hours behind and with no hope of beating Baker, Wells Bennett ended his ride there.**

12 MotorCycling and Bicycling October 4, 1922

# Baker Shatters Transcontinental Record

**By H. Vincent Smith**

NEW YORK, Sept. 28.—The ol' war-horse, on a stock Ace motorcycle, rolled his seemingly brand new Traxion treaded front wheel off the Amboy-Tottenville ferry at 12:52 a. m. this morning. Having left Los Angeles at 11 p. m. Wednesday night, September 20, Pacific coast time, which was really 2 a. m. Thursday, New York time, he succeeded in lowering the trancontinental record for motorcycles to 6 days, 22 hours and 52 minutes.

What a figure he presented, as Rudolph Stern of the New York Stern Bros. "tribe" and the writer met him outside of Metuchen, N. J., late last night. First, a distant murmur was audible, gradually increasing to a low, deep moan, then two long beams of light appeared. The moan became a roar and the big, hulking figure humped over the bars, slipped through the night, his tail-light soon becoming a mere speck.

**Big Crowd Waiting**

Arriving at the ferry, he was immediately engulfed in the waiting crowd. He was in unusually fine shape after the gruelling test and but for his week's growth of "alfalfa" and the circle of face exposed to and covered with grime, one would merely have thought he finished a most commonplace ride. The wind had, in some unaccountable manner, worked past his goggles and left his eyes in a heavy and somewhat blood-shot condition. Otherwise, both he and the machine were ready for more. In fact, he claims the machine is five miles an hour faster than when he started, which speaks volumes for the way the Ace stood up.

At Needles, Ariz., the thermometer registered 118 degrees, and in what seemed to him an incredibly short time, he had risen into the mountains and had become so cold that he had to go into the station at Flagstaff to warm up his numbed fingers and body. He remarked that three weeks ago, while covering that territory, preparatory to his record-breaking dash, he had seen snow on the peaks surrounding Flagstaff. At Seligman, Ariz., he encountered the only rain on his trip, and strange enough at this spot he had his first and last puncture. While he was satisfying the "inner man" willing hands patched his tube. It never even came out of the casing.

**Missouri Mud!**

Nothing further of special interest occurred till he reached Missouri, where the entire distance across the state (300 miles) was nothing but mud! It had rained for five days prior to his arrival. He was sure that fully 250 miles of the distance was negotiated in "second," the rest being divided between low and high. It took him 18 hours to get over this particular stretch,

Baker at the finish at Tottenville ferry

which is averaging little better than 17 m.p.h. At one of the towns along here, where he was scheduled to take on gas and oil and get a bite to eat, no one appeared, and being late at night he wasted many precious minutes hunting over town for an open tanking station.

From St. Louis, his ride was practically over as far as bad roads and extreme conditions were concerned. At Terre Haute, Ind., he first got wind of Wells Bennett's attempt to further lower the record. Bennett had started 28 hours after the old warhorse, and on the morning of Baker's arrival in New York Bennett was reported "somewhere in Missouri mud."

**Wifey Greets Him at Philly**

At Philadelphia, Baker was greeted by his wife, who was probably the first to congratulate him. Being some 21 hours ahead of Bedell's record, he eased along over the 80 miles into the city's limits at Tottenville, L. I., in two hours and some odd minutes. This was his fourth attempt this summer for this record. He expressed himself as being darn glad he had made it and it was all over. Chief Engineer Henderson of the Ace factory was there to welcome him and managed to get his man away from the admiring crowd immediately after the finish and recrossing the ferry to Perth Amboy put him to bed at the hotel. Besides his ride he had been "shot" by three cameras, thrice, while waiting for the ferry to complete the run.

Baker used Traxion Treads, front and rear, original tires and tubes still on at the finish and California air in the front, Arizona air in the rear. His Splitdorf electrical equipment gave absolutely no trouble and furnished all the illumination desired. A special accessory, which was examined with much interest, was a huge spongy rubber pad, screwed on top of his saddle, about an inch thick and perforated with many holes. A trial on this seat revealed a luxurious softness and Baker could not praise it enough. He only had one blister on his right hand, but his large hands were so calloused that it was even a surprise he had that. He was too sleepy to remember exactly what mileage had been on his speedometer at the start, so that the actual distance was not obtained. However, it was between 3,300 and 3,400 miles.

**CROTONA PROTEST OVERRULED**

THE COMMITTEE of three, members of the Competition Committee, Stanley Kellogg, Carl Bush and E. B. Holton, gave their decision on the Crotona Motorcycle Club endurance run protest and appeal, held May 13 and 14, last week. Considerable delay was attached to this decision for various reasons and the majority of the committee voted to sustain the referee's decision.

**Another unusual record set by Cannon Ball Baker came in 1923 when he drove an Oldsmobile from New York to Los Angeles locked in high gear. It took him twelve days to make the trip. *Image: Indianapolis Motor Speedway Archive.***

**Cannon Ball on a road trip in 1920. *Photo courtesy of Dale Walksler / Wheels of Time Museum.***

**(Above) One trip across the country didn't always offer the satisfaction that Baker was looking for. In 1928 he drove this Franklin from Los Angeles to New York, then turned right around and drove back to Los Angeles. His combined mileage was 6,692.8 miles which he achieved in 6 days, 13 hours and 23 minutes. *Image: Indianapolis Motor Speedway Archive.***

**Ever a friend of Indian motorcycles and riders, Cannon Ball Baker was on the scene at Daytona Beach, FL when my parents, Floyd and Florence Emde, celebrated Floyd's victory of the 1948 Daytona 200 moments after the race.**

**(Above) Cannon Ball (left) makes an appearance in the pits at the 1949 Indy 500 to visit with old motorcycle buddies Floyd Clymer and Joe Petrali (sitting on the Indian motorcycle), who was being interviewed by a journalist. *Photo courtesy of Dale Walksler / Wheels of Time Museum.***

Following the completion of the Cannon Ball Centennial Ride in May, 2014, I was invited to participate in the 2014-2015 International Motorcycle Show series. I gave multiple 30-minute Power Point presentations about the whole Cannon Ball project at all 11 shows.

**(Left) In addition to my time on the stage giving the presentations, the IMS staff provided a space for the bike and display board in the show halls.**

**Being introduced at one of the many presentations that I made at the IMS shows. My talks were each 30-minutes long supported by Power Point slides running on the monitors.**

**It varied by show location, but the crowd size and numbers of questions asked were generally good.**

**I was really honored to have a poster made by Yamaha to celebrate the Centennial ride. My friends Bob Starr (center) and Derrick Brooks invited me to Yamaha's USA headquarters to pick up a framed print. Thanks to everyone at Yamaha for your support.**

# BIBLIOGRAPHY


## MAGAZINES:

Magazine issues from Don Emde's personal library: 1909 – 1914 used for reference:

*Motorcycle Illustrated*, *The Bicycle World and Motorcycle Review*, *Motorcycling* and *Pacific Motorcyclist*.

*Automobile Quarterly* Vol 18, No 1. First quarter 1975 issue. "The Inimitable Mister Baker," by Russ Catlin.

*The Automobile*, December 21, 1905

*Motorcycle Illustrated Magazine*. May 28, 1914. "Baker's Own Story of His Record-Breaking Trans-Continental Trip."

*The Motorcyclist Magazine*. February 1944. "Transcontinental Record Makers of the Early Days of Motorcycling," by J.J. O'Connor.

*Motorcycle Collector Magazine* (Don Emde Publications), July 1993

*Road Rider Magazine*, August 1979. Insert: Reprint of "Across America On A Motor Bicycle," Originally written by George Wyman in June, 1903.

*Motorcyclist Magazine Online*, Dec 13, 2011 "Erwin Baker Gets Cross-Country Motorcycle Record."

*Traces Magazine*, Winter 2003. "The King of Speed. Erwin 'Cannon Ball' Baker," by Ray Featherstone.

*The Journal of San Diego History*. July 1955. "Mountain Springs," by B.B. Moore

## BOOKS:

Pacific Coast Blue Book Publishing Co. May 1913

American Racer 1900 – 1940, *by Steve Wright*

The American Motorcycle 1869 – 1914, *by Steve Wright*

California Over The Santa Fe Trail, *by C. A. Higgins*. 1914.

First Mail West, Stagecoach Lines on the Santa Fe Trail, *by Morris F. Taylor* 1971

Horatio's Drive, *by Dayton Duncan and Ken Burns* 2003 (Also a PBS film documentary)

Records and Maps of the Old Santa Fe Trail, *by Kenyon Riddle* 1963.

The Santa Fe Trail Yesterday and Today, *by William E. Hill* 2009.

The Motorcycle Industry in New York State, *by Geoffrey N. Stein*.

Guide to Arizona's Backroads & 4-Wheel Drive Trails, *by Charles A. Wells*. 2001

Backcountry Adventures: Arizona, *by Peter Massey and Jeanne Wilson*. 2001

The Old National Road. A Chapter of American Expansion, *by Archer Butler Hulbert*. 1901

The Big Roads. The Untold Story of the Engineers, Visionaries, and Trailblazers Who Created the American Superhighways, *by Earl Swift*. 2011

Thomas B. Searight's The Old Pike. An Illustrated Narrative on the National Road. 1971

## ONLINE SOURCES:

Crown Hill Funeral Home, Cemetery & Heritage Foundation. Online search: Erwin George "Cannon Ball" Baker.

"Building the Apache Trail" - Excerpt from *Arizona Centennial: A Century of Cooperation*. U.S. Dept. of the Interior. www.usbr.gov/lc/phoenix/AZ100/1900/apache_workers.html.

# ACKNOWLEDGEMENTS

Many people and organizations made significant contributions to the Cannon Ball Project and/or the production of his book. I owe them all special thanks for their assistance and support.

My family, as always, were behind me right from the first ideas around 2010 all the way through to the publication of the book. My wife, **Tracy Emde**, applied her editing skills, as well as being my sounding board for just about every decision along the way. Our kids, **Jen Rose** (proof reading) and **Jeff Emde** (webmaster) pitched in to cover some important functions and when it came time for the Centennial ride, my sister **Nancy Emde-Steward**, **Chris Steward**, and my son-in-law **Ryan Rose** were there to hit the road with me. They did, without hesitation, whatever needed to be done. Beyond family, many friends and associates applied their expertise as needed. That list begins with my good friend **Joe Colombero**, who was with me all the way from picking up our loaner KTMs in 2011 to driving the truck and taking pictures on the Centennial ride in 2014. We work with some very talented people in our publishing business and thank **Nancy Wegrowski** for all of her long hours and outstanding work producing this book, and also designing the amazing leather-bound Cannon Ball logbooks for the ride. **Morgan Williams** of Morgan Williams Design designed the "Finding Cannon Ball's Trail" logo and **Jim Conquest**, Imagine It Graphics, printed trailer graphics, decals, shirts and other materials. In addition to Joe Colombero's many photos in the book, we were fortunate to have two other great photographers contribute their expertise on the Centennial ride: **Kinney Jones** and **Barry Hathaway**. **Dick Lague** and the staff at Ignition3 created our website and the maps for the book were created by **Bill Tipton** of Compart Maps. And we thank **Sanjay Mehta**, BB&T Insurance Services of California, Inc. for working out our insurance needs for the Centennial ride.

Thanks to **Jon-Erik Burleson** and the staff at KTM North America for the use of two KTM Adventure 990s for our research and mapping rides, and **Bob Starr** and everyone at Yamaha Motor Corp. USA for jumping in as our Presenting Sponsor of the Centennial ride and providing the two Yamaha Super Tenere Adventure bikes. **Ted Boyko** and **Casey Driggers** from Boyko Racing did the service and installation work on both sets of motorcycles. Other than one glitch that wasn't their fault, they kept everything running well the whole three years. And speaking of vehicles, we appreciated one of our Centennial riders, **Steve Read**, going to bat for us at Toyota Motor Sales headquarters to arrange the use of a Toyota Tundra for use as one of our sweep vehicles on the Centennial ride. When we hit the road in 2012 to start gathering the data on our Garmin GPS, we were in contact with **Rob Watt** at Butler Maps. He helped us all the way and eventually spliced all the data together to make one master file of our route from San Diego to New York City. We were then able to download a file for everyone on the Centennial ride, and also printed daily maps for their logbooks. Rob and **Court Butler** also came out and rode the first few days of the Centennial ride. We appreciate all of their support along the way.

We had some great industry support and appreciated all the product and financial sponsorship we received. **Tom Seymour** and his Saddlemen company supported us in every way they could. We actually tested some of their new adventure products that were coming to market and appreciated all of the seats, saddlebags and other luggage they provided along the way. Thanks to **Kimmo Lassila** at Touratech USA who sent us any adventure product we asked for when we were outfitting both the KTMs and the Yamahas. **Chris Carter**, owner of Motion Pro, was a great partner in the project, supplying full sets of tools for our fanny packs, a set of tools for our sweep truck, as well as some replacement tools when our truck was broken into. He also provided some financial assistance and came along on the ride. Those Motion Pro guys are great supporters of the sport. Other great product and/or financial support of the project and ride came from **Parts Unlimited**, **Continental Tires**, **DP Brakes**, **Moose Racing** (Expedition outfits and other gear), **Cardo Systems** (helmet radios), **Alpinestars** (boots) **Icon Helmets**, **AFX Helmets**, **Star Brite Inc**. (fuel treatment and coolant), **National Cycle** (windscreens), **Akrapovic** (KTM exhaust), **Warn** (spot lights), **100% Goggles**, **PCI Race Radios** (communications equipment) and also thanks to Joe Desrosiers at **Joe Hauler.com** for the use of a Joe Hauler Bike Carrier for our sweep truck.

There were a number of people and organizations with valuable local knowledge that were helpful in my research, as well as some who arranged the use of historic photography or materials for the book or other assistance when we were in their areas. Thanks to **Chris Travers** and the staff at San Diego History Center; **Tina Clark**, Curator of Yuma Crossing National Heritage Area, Yuma, AZ; **Pete Pfeifer** (Arizona); **Glen Dickerson** (New Mexico); **Roger Pattison** (New Mexico); **Ernie Henderson** (Missouri); **Malcolm Wood** (Missouri); **Susan Sutton** and the staff at the Indiana Historical Society; **Mark Mederski** (Ohio); **Aaron O'Donovan** and the staff at the Ohio Historical Society; **John Lawless**, **Michael Lawless**, **Ron McGill** and staff at **Simeone Foundation Automotive Museum**, Philadelphia, PA; **Mary Ellen Loscar**, **Michael Roth** and the staff at Indianapolis Motor Speedway Archives; and thanks to **Dale Walksler** from the Wheels of Time Museum for the use of some great Cannon Ball Baker photos.

As was pointed out in the book, we had many great publicity opportunities before, during and after the Cannon Ball Centennial Ride. Thanks to **Tim Buche**, **Ty Van Hooydonk** and **Brian Hardyman** at the Motorcycle Industry Council. They sponsored a ride entry for **Gary McKechnie**, who with Brian produced those great daily blogs from the road for Motorcycles.org. They were also successful in landing us many press contacts and arranged for the mayoral proclamations that were mentioned. There were many journalists that covered us, in particular **Susan Carpenter**, *Orange County Register*; **Barry Hathaway**, *Cycle World*, **Aaron Frank**, *Motorcyclist*, **James Holter**, *American Motorcyclist*, **Ken Freund**, *RoadRUNNER*; **John Gastaldo**, *San Diego Union-Tribune*; **Jerry Garrett**, *New York Times*; **Christopher Guinn**, *Dodge City Daily Globe*, **Joe Michaud**, *Motorcycle Consumer News* and **Scott Cox**, **Bobby Wooldridge** and the team at *Bike Week Radio Show*.

Along the way during the Centennial ride, we had so much great help and support. In San Diego, we thank **Randy Aron** for providing the parking lot at his Cycle Visions store to get everyone checked in, **Marty Kamery,** who organized the morning breakfast and kickoff at Sunroad Resort Marina, all of the day riders who came out and rode with us to Yuma or Mesa, and **Randy Lazar**, **Chris Crawford**, **Chris, Nelson**, **Arnie Fry**, **Todd Whiteside** and the San Diego Adventure Riders club for their assistance as guides through the desert. Thank you to **Mayor Douglas J. Nicholls** and the people of Yuma, AZ for the great reception that you hosted for us at the Yuma Prison Museum; **Mayor Ravi Bhasker**, **Gordy Hicks** and the people of Socorro, NM for the welcome gifts; Mayor **Brian Delzeit**, **Jim Johnson** and the people of Dodge City, Kansas for your reception and tour of the historic old race track; **Pattie Prestige Frost**, **Julie Davidson Biersmith** and other friends for arranging that great Kansas City BBQ experience; **Carl and Kathy Donelson** and **Kim Keen** and the staff at Donelson Cycles in St. Louis for the lunch stop and shop services, **Todd Sheedy** of Parts Unlimited for arranging the open house there, and **Jeff Reid** of Continental Tires for your assistance. To Mayor **Alan Gaffner**, **John Goldsmith** and the people of Greenville, IL, thanks for the amazing Police and Fire escort, mayor's welcome, key to the city, Cannon Ball graphics, shirts and dinner. Thanks to **Donald Davidson** for your warm welcome and tour of the Indianapolis Motor Speedway Museum; also **Rob Dingman**, **Katy Wood** and the staff of the Motorcycle Hall of Fame Museum for hosting a morning reception there, and **Christy Klamfoth**, **Al Charles**, **Dick and Bev Klamfoth** at K&C Cycle for the coffee stop as we rode east. And thanks to **Ted Doering** and the staff of the Motorcyclepedia Museum in Newburgh, NY who opened up just for our group to hold our Farewell lunch.

We had some friends who kicked in some helpful cash donations. Thanks to **Jim Giuffra**, **Mike and Colleen Taylor** (Barnett), **Denis LaBonge**, **Bill Gikling** and **Jerry Bartlett** for your generosity; **Jennifer Gibbs** at the motorcycle shipping company, Federal Company, who helped arrange return shipping for many of our rider's motorcycles from New York, and **Tracy Harris** and the staff at International Motorcycle Shows who invited me to tell my stories to the attendees of their 2014/2015 show series.

FINDING CANNON BALL'S TRAIL™

CENTENNIAL RIDE

MAY 3-14 2014

Presented by Yamaha

## RIDERS / CREW

Randy Aron
Jack Broomall
Court Butler*
Chris Carter
Bill Cooper
Glen Dickerson
Ken Freund
Barry Hathaway
Perry King*
Denny Laidig
Yermo Lamers**
Catherine Long
Keith Mashburn
Dan Maxey
Gary McKechnie
Ron Niemeyer
Perry Noel
Robert Pandya
Pete Pfeifer
Steve Read
Roland Rose
Tom Seymour
Bob Shurley
Tim Snodgrass
Gerald Tims
Rob Watt*
Bill Wheeler
Ralph White
Tom White

Cannon Ball Centennial Ride Crew:
Don Emde
Joe Colombero
Nancy Emde-Steward
Chris Steward
Ryan Rose

Brian Hardyman (MIC Video Blog Production)

*San Diego to Trinidad
**Dodge City to New York